God Sex

Sexuality, the Bible, and the 21st Century

By: Dr. Jillian Sweetman

Edited By: Amanda R. Gabrell
Gina Aliff
Paul W. Conant
Cover Illustration: Jerry Sabatini
Brittany Sharp

Published: 2013

This book contains material that may not be suitable for readers under 18 years of age; however, the reality of this book is that many of the issues addressed within involve young adults and children less than 18 years of age. Use discretion when reading and when recommending it to younger readers.

Table of Contents

Stories Archive i

Acknowledgments iii

Foreword v

Introduction 1

Our Journey 5

Part One: Sex, Today's Culture, and the Bible ... 9

Chapter 1: What is Sex? 11

Chapter 2: Maintaining Virginity 17

Chapter 3: Premarital Sex 25

Chapter 4: Abortion 35

Chapter 5: Polygamy 53

Chapter 6: Further Socio-Cultural Arguments 61

Chapter 7: Sex in the Bible 71

Part Two: Inappropriate Sexual Behavior 77

Chapter 8: Promiscuity 79

Chapter 9: Pornography 89

Chapter 10: Masturbation 99

Chapter 11: Adultery 109

Part Three: Sexual Misconduct 121

Chapter 12: Sexual Addiction 123

Chapter 13: Sexual Abuse 131

Chapter 14: Rape 141

Chapter 15: Pedophilia 149

Part Four: Same-Sex Attraction 157

Chapter 16: An Introduction to Same-Sex Attraction.......
....159

Chapter 17: Understanding Same-Sex Attraction.......163

Chapter 18: Social Pathways to Homosexuality..........177

Chapter 19: Cultural Effects of the Same-Sex Lifestyle....
....193

Chapter 20: The Church's Response to Same-Sex Attraction
....207

Chapter 21: Biblical Arguments For and Against Same-Sex Attraction...215

Chapter 22: Hope for the Hopeless 235

Part Five: Marital Sex 239

Chapter 23: The Marital Sexual Relationship..............241

Conclusion 265

Biography 269

Glossary 271

Abbreviations 275

Bibliography 277

End Notes 297

Stories Archive

God Sex contains personal stories submitted by brave men and women who have walked through some of the darkest depravities known to man. I have done very little to edit or alter these stories so that the true voice of the teller is captured.

The names of these people have been withheld to protect the integrity of the tellers.

Our Journey.......... 5

The Virgin.......... 21

Reclaiming My Virginity After Being Sexually Active.......... 23

A Story of Lost Virginity.......... 25

I Was Sixteen.......... 35

Multiple Abortions.......... 35

The Decision To Not Abort.......... 46

Adoption.......... 50

A Quest for Love.......... 79

Promiscuity.......... 79

Overcoming Pornography.......... 89

From a Porn Star.......... 92

Overcoming Masturbation.......... 99

Overcoming Pornography and Masturbation.......... 100

A Story of Adultery.......... 109

Story from an Adulterer.......... 110

Story of a Sex Addict 123

Sexual Abuse by a Family Member 131

Rape Victim 141

Date Rape 142

Overcoming Rape 142

Story of a Pedophile 149

Pedophile in the Church 153

Same-Sex Attraction from a Female Perspective 177

Same-Sex Attraction from a Male Perspective 178

Story of Marital Sex 241

Acknowledgments

It's been a lot of fun writing this book. I've had so many wonderful people who have helped me gather materials, inspired me with their stories, and brought many new insights through daily conversations. It was these people who helped turn *God Sex* from simply a book of research on human sexuality to an honest exploration of sex and its effects on real people's lives.

Within these pages you will find stories submitted by people whose names have been withheld. Apart from one or two articles that have been taken from the Internet, these stories have been entrusted to me to share, both from old friends and new. These stories are the reality that people face amongst statistics and theories. Real stories provide hope that lives can mend and still succeed, despite being broken. I know that these stories are true and not embellished. Today these people, from all around the world, live lives that are rich in relationships. They were willing to tell their stories so that others can live life better. I am very grateful to these storytellers.

Gina Aliff, my faithful personal assistant, has been a great help. This beautiful blonde—who is recently engaged—is studying psychology. We found ourselves swapping information and statistics because, funnily, at the time of these writings, she was completing courses regarding sexuality. Many colorful anecdotes have been contributed by her. Both her insight and her informative textbooks helped build many of the secular perspectives found in *God Sex*. These books revealed what is being taught today in universities and colleges—vital information that we should be aware of for our children. Apart from this, Gina spent countless hours helping in discussions regarding chapter order, footnotes, and really anything that related to *God Sex*.

Amanda Gabrell has spent countless hours editing and rewriting *God Sex* so that the pages make sense. She has been faithfully working with me in the preparation of my dissertation and eagerly took on the challenge of this new book on top of that, her job, and her participation as one of our youth leaders. She'd work late into the night, knowing how important this book was to me. Her sense of humor was remarkable! No matter the dilemma, she would determine a strategy to complete this project. She causes my words to make sense and sound so much better than I ever could on my own.

Brittany Sharp inspired me continually. She could hardly wait for this book to become a reality. She is our marketing and media guru in C3 Lawrenceville. She and Jerry Sabatini, from C3 Silver Lake in Los Angeles, were the creative brains for the cover art.

Special thanks to Paul Conant for coming in for final cleanup and formatting of the manuscript. We could not have finished *God Sex* on such a strong note without him.

Then of course, I have to thank my boys, Barn and Jake, and their gorgeous wives, Holly and Nic. They cannot swap out their mum. They have sat through many marital, relational, and sexual forums, and they have been willing to add their comments that have guided some of these writings. I could not have two greater sons and daughters-in-law.

Lastly, there is my best friend and husband, Dean. He believes in me as no other person does, and it is because of his belief that this book is here. It was his idea before it was mine. Throughout all our travels, living on and off planes, going from Atlanta to Los Angeles and beyond, he would cheer me on. It makes me wonder what else he has in mind for me to do.

I am blessed. All of these people including my wonderful C3 Churches enrich my life in so many ways. Many of my thoughts have been refined through pastoring our great churches. I hope that you learn as I have learned, as you read the following pages.

Foreword

I have wanted a book like this for a long time. I knew my wife could write about such a huge and confusing subject, after a little prodding.

After nearly thirty years of ministry and serving God's people, I have heard just about everything when it comes to the depravity of the human condition. In no other area have I seen the destructive force of sin at work more than sexuality. It has the power to both bind up and liberate. Bind up in the sense that Christians feel so guilty living outside God's clear boundaries and liberate in the sense of what it can be within a marriage.

Sex is a huge issue in our society, for the Christian churchgoer and the unchurched. The media, television, movies, and the Internet scream a message concerning sex. It's about time the church spoke out about real issues that can confront and heal people of sexual confusion. There is a very mixed message being presented. This book will provide many answers and clarity to some of the huge issues facing the church in the 21st century.

God Sex won't give you all the answers, but with a balanced biblical foundation, you will be equipped to cope personally and maybe help others who face debilitating shame because of guilt and misinformation.

–Dean Sweetman

Introduction

Sexual sins and confusion are not things that were invented in the 21st century. As much as each generation questions the moral codes of the next, historical research reveals that sexual issues have been around since the beginning of time. We live in a world filled with opinions regarding sex, sexuality, and sexual behavior. The conservative Christian stance is that sex was made for a monogamous marriage between a man and a woman—what society has deemed "heterosexual" relationships. Others believe that "both heterosexual behavior and homosexual behavior are normal aspects of human sexuality. Both have been documented in many different cultures and historical eras."[1] The constant fluctuation in the acceptance or non-acceptance of sexual standards can bring great confusion and even greater pain, and society may never settle on an answer that will suit all of humanity despite how hard it tries to do just that.

Sexual choices and freedom are highly promoted in this day and age—to the point that new and tempting ideas about sex and sexuality seem to come out all the time, and yet people are in agony due to these misconceptions. Sexual issues are tearing our churches apart today as never before,[2] and humanity as a whole suffers more and more each day because of these dilemmas. Years after abortions, women cry secretly, and yet, they have been told that it was a wise choice. Children experiment with sex because they claim it is their right. Their choice to have sex, though, leaves them disappointed. The issue of homosexuality threatens to fracture whole denominations, as the issue of slavery did a hundred and fifty years ago.[3]

People both young and old are constantly baffled and confused regarding sexuality.

> Homosexuality is an ever-increasing issue within American society. In recent years, several mainline denominations have abandoned traditional interpretations of Scripture and have embraced the Gay-Christian movement. Are people born

> gay, or is it a choice? Can homosexuality be changed? Questions abound, and many Christians are confused about what they should believe or how to respond.[4]

In the secular world, abortion is viewed as a woman's right. Addictions are being deemed diseases that take away the addict's choices—including the choice to change. Pornography is sometimes viewed as harmless and as something that can enhance a marriage. Some parents see premarital sex as a good thing and even encourage their children to have it. Society itself teaches that it is a good idea to live together outside of marriage. We have moved a long way from biblical teachings.

Recently I heard of a sixteen-year-old who was defending her sister's choice of lesbianism. Understandably she loves and reveres her older sister, yet, she is oblivious to any consequences regarding her sister's decision. Even though she is a regular attendee of her church's youth group, she views the Bible as though it was written for "those times" and is no longer relevant to today. If we, like this young woman, decide that the moral values of the Bible change with time and society, then where do we draw the line? Is the salvation of humanity brought about by Christ's death and resurrection now considered obsolete since it happened "back then" instead of now? The consequences of these ambiguous standards are disastrous.

After tumultuous teenage years filled with misery regarding right and wrong sex, my freedom in this matter came from Scripture. There is one Scripture that stands out in the Bible that has helped me comprehend the relevance of God's words to a frustrated world. The verse is found twice: first in Isaiah 40:8 and then again in 1 Peter 1:25. The verse reads, "The grass withers, the flower fades, But the Word of our God stands forever."[5] Isaiah spoke these words centuries before Peter; and the message is still relevant today. The message is that, while psychological theories and scientific notions come and go, "the Word of our God stands forever."[6]

Despite popular belief, the Song of Solomon is not the only book of the Bible that talks about sex. The Bible contains great revelations and stories regarding sexual issues; including the origin of sex, marital sex, group sex, seduction, sex as a form of worship, promiscuity, prostitution, rape, polygamy, homosexuality, bisexuality, incest, bestiality, and coitus interruptus. God is not silent about sex. In some ways, God presents "Fifty Shades of Grey" about the most controversial topic in the world, and yet, at the same time, He provides freedom and safety because He sets the guidelines for what is a huge part of our lives. The many translations of the Bible and the shifting in language over the centuries have served to mask the Bible's information concerning sexuality. That or perhaps we just don't read it enough to discover the shocking facts!

This book will uncover the Bible's truths about sex and sexuality. Within these pages is a collection of people's stories; an exploration of the secular and socially popular theories regarding sexual behavior; and the hope, healing, and truth found in Scriptures. My aim is to bring hope, not friction (excuse the pun) to those who read this book. I will write with a bias because I am a Christian, and I have found that those who do find contentment in life are those that have found freedom through an adherence to biblical principles and through worshipping God. I also intend to use this book to educate people, for if we do not understand that sexual issues do not define a person nor do we offer hope to those struggling with their sexuality, we will cause greater pain than ever. While you are reading, I hope you will keep an open mind and allow God's Word to illuminate a subject that can bring happiness, joy, and contentment to your life. Here we go!

Our Journey

From early life, we can find ourselves struggling with something. Something physical or mental or both; something we both love and hate, want to reject and yet embrace. From early years, we comprehend and attempt to find right and wrong and then apply that meaning to our lives. That something—in many cases (like mine), that sexual something—does not hold up against this meaning of right and wrong, thus, we instinctively can tell that it is wrong. So why do we struggle with it? Is this struggle a demonic spirit that can be easily prayed away? Is it a choice of our minds that we, ourselves, must take the steps to change? Can we win this fight on our own? Do we even want to?

I was an abused child in a fatherless home struggling with sexual fantasies that no one my age should have to face. Is this not so similar to so many of our lives? After all, abuse is a common factor in sexual issues. The struggle always begins in the mind, and it is the mind that tells the body to act. The desire is so strong. At such a young age, when the mind is filled with sexual thoughts and fantasies born from abuse, we act out without boundaries, and the addiction to sex begins.

Time passes all around us; we are not given the luxury of coping; we move forward with it and continue to struggle. Now, we are adolescents and our bodies are changing. These changes seem to give power to the struggle. We now crave and even embrace it. We've already been touched by and exposed from abuse; we then want to replicate those sexual feelings. It is almost a cycle: do we decide to stop only to trip up or do we purpose to indulge? We struggle with wondering, "Why am I this way? Does it make me an outcast?" Then we reason, "No! I am normal...just a little more colorful." The temptation of our addiction sings in our veins. It is so strong! We decide that we are going to have sex and enjoy it. We'll work out the consequences tomorrow.

This mental battle is a common struggle; one we all face in some form each and every day. Sex is great; it feels great! Opposite sex, same sex, any sex is good sex, and yet, how much longer can we avoid the issue? We know what we are doing is wrong, but we don't stop. We tell ourselves we can. Then why can't we? We wonder "Why me, God?" We get angry and bitter because it seems so unfair! The victim mentality drives us to find comfort, and it is only in our addiction that we find relief. It is our crutch. The identity of the victim is a mentality that strips us of responsibility, and we like it that way. However, this does not take the battle or responsibility away because it is ignored. We have made the choice. Will we ever choose to change?

We are young people raised in the new normal. Why change? Society reared us to embrace the chaos. Why can't we just evolve? Everyone else around us is doing exactly what we are doing and they are enjoying it! So why should we want out? Maybe we can cope with our addiction; let it rule our lives. We may find moments when it plateaus and we gain a sense of control, but these moments don't last.

When we continue to live and think like this, we get set in our ways. We believe that this is who we are; that we can never change; and that God could never redeem us. But God is a BIG GOD and His Word is true. His mercies are new every day,[7] *and His grace is sufficient to meet our every needs.*[8] *These verses are encouraging and mean that there is always a way out of our dilemma. He says that He does not allow anything into our lives that we cannot handle,*[9] *and that if we choose Him, He will guide us out of our struggle.*[10] *God gives us a gift of choice. It is a great gift, and, when we know this, our lives can become clear. Our struggle may not have been our choice, but how we handled it was. We chose every moment, every action, and every indulgence. How, then, do we turn our struggle into some form of strength and victory?*

God did not create us to be like this; to struggle every day with a sexual addiction. So what happened? We have taken the body that God created for us, and we used it for our own entertainment. We think, "This is my body! I can do whatever I want with it!" We allowed sex to become a "god" in our lives. Sex can begin as a small act and then escalate into an obsession that life revolves around. How then do we change?

To answer that, another question must be asked: Where is our mind? This sounds so simple, but, as we found out as children and walked out as adults, it is the mind that convinces the body to act. We find that we struggle with our thoughts and that they take us to places that are not good for us. When we've allowed ourselves to be ruled by our minds, it takes time to retrain our thought patterns, and yet, no matter the struggle, God promises to empower us.[11] *He says that we can renew our minds.*[12] *God knows us so well, as our Creator. Every day is a new day and a new chance to change.*

Each day, we have a choice to renew our minds. It is a new day with new beginnings and new chances to heal. Our minds change a little at a time and we find ourselves exercising some form of power in our lives. God's power helps us as every new day there are new temptations. Temptations are attractive. As we walk out our journey, we find ourselves in moments where we put ourselves in a place of weakness where we know temptation will meet us. We know the answer, yet, we still must make the choice. The mind may try to counter-argue: "Just one last time. I'll do it. It's fine. I'll start again tomorrow." If we fall in this moment, we can blame the circumstances, but it was still our choice. Good and bad opportunities will come. We can see these moments as tests, and like tests, we need to pass them; otherwise, the same test returns.

It is foolish to test ourselves by being in tempting situations. We have the power to not act on the thoughts as they creep into our minds. This, in turn, starts to weaken the power that sex has over us. It has ruled us for so long and ruined much of our lives. There are days when we struggle to follow the simplest guidelines of His Word. We can get frustrated and wonder why God doesn't choose between right and wrong for us, but who would want to serve and worship a God who is so controlling? Choice and responsibility are amazing gifts that empower us to live a fulfilled life!

We must be realistic in this new life. This journey to freedom is a very long one. There are no quick fixes. We will still be tempted. There will still be attraction. We see a naked body and then we have a choice. Where will we allow our minds to go? If we allow our minds to pursue this sexual path, then the body will follow; if we stop our minds from going there, our bodies will, again, follow. As we keep pursuing the path of renewing our minds, this process becomes more natural. It becomes a habit after a while, if we do it enough, and, eventually, it becomes a way of life.

There is a spiritual world that will keep on going even if we don't believe. In it, there's good and bad. God is fighting for us in this place. He knows that we can beat this sexual struggle. Nothing makes the enemy more unhappy than someone pulling himself together. The enemy fuels the battle in the mind, trying to tell us that we've not really changed or that other people will not believe that we are truly different. Doubt enters our minds but we have the power to defeat these lies through God's truths. His Word is a powerful tool in the renewing of our minds.

Another great asset is to find a true friend or leader that has some form of a spiritual compass. This means that we are guided in the right direction. We are not judged and placed on the naughty table. With this friend or leader, we can shine the light on our hidden world and find freedom there. Revealing the truth and not being afraid of exposing each area is the start of breaking the hold it has over our lives. This does not mean that in one session, we are going to reveal everything. Walking with someone over time and building trust mean that we can let the walls down. The journey takes time. There is a process of discovering ourselves. The mind and thought patterns need to be aligned. Strength comes in support; having that person by our side empowers us in our choices. We sometimes think that we can do this on our own. God knows the power of two or more.[13] *We need help, and this journey cannot be taken on our own. A structured daily routine will also add to our advantage. Having too much time leaves our minds open to wandering; therefore, having simple daily routines will keep us active and occupied.*

We should not fool ourselves into thinking that we don't need these basic tools in the battle against our sexual struggles. Living and breathing sex in so many different ways has taken up much time in our lives. We may have lived each day looking for that quickie. We may have paid to just get that feeling. We may even have had days where we complained that we were moody because we needed a good session. Our entire lives have revolved around this one act. Sex is addictive, and, like all addictions, it is not satisfying. It's amazing that one physical act can take us away from living our best life! It is our choice as to how much power it has. If we are honest with ourselves and renew our mind and see our thought patterns in a different way, we can let go of how one-track minded we have become. Then the healing begins.

Today: This story comes from someone that I admire immensely. Few would know what he has defeated when looking at him. In a profession fraught with dilemma, he continues to stand out for not just talent but integrity. He is greatly admired by many. –JS

Part One: Sex, Today's Culture, and the Bible

Society is steeped in sex. It is everywhere; on television, in books and music, and discussed constantly in schools around the world. Intermixed with this saturation are a thousand and one ideas of what sex is, what it is all about, why we should or should not be having it, ways to have it without having it, and with whom we should be having it.

This first part of *God Sex* is dedicated to the study of what society is saying about sex. These first few chapters will help better define what sex actually is, how society presents it, and what the Bible has to say on the matter. Nothing is sacred, so get ready, because we are about to dive deep and figure out the truth concerning the meaning of sex.

Chapter 1: What is Sex?

A discussion on sex and all it entails would not be complete without first defining sex. Most citizens of any first-world nation have had some sort of exposure to sex—whether it was through general sexual education provided by schools or the more likely scenario of viewing sex through media and entertainment. It is this overindulgence of knowledge that, ironically, requires a clear defining of sex to set the stage for the rest of the book. Simply saying that sex is the moment when a man inserts his penis into a woman's vagina and repeats said insertion until climax is reached is, sadly, inadequate. This black-and-white definition has birthed a slew of loopholes, as it were—ways to have sex without actually having sex.

The clarifying question must then be asked: When is sex... sex? With all these loopholes, it can become confusing to the younger generations growing up in an openly sexual society. Young minds are taught that acts such as oral sex or touching genitalia with the hands do not count as intercourse; however, these acts still count as sexual acts and thus should be included in the broadening definition of sex. This chapter is dedicated to helping readers understand what sex includes since there are so many new and inventive ways to experience sexual pleasure.

Sexual Desire

A great place to begin the defining of sex is with sexual desire. Sexual desire can sometimes be used as an excuse for engaging in sexual acts. This excuse is more of a misunderstanding of the mental and physical aspects of sexual desire than a valid reason for acting out sexually. As much as one can say that sex just happens, this is not true. We can control our thoughts, fantasies, and desires, and we can control whether we act upon these things or not. The wise person can fantasize about another but then choose to change the direction of his thoughts, knowing that the fantasy could damage his life.

Most researchers define sexual desire as the "wish, drive, or motivation to engage in sexual activities or the anticipation of sexual pleasure in the future."[14] Sexual desire, sometimes referred to as an active libido, is typically a conscious and deliberate act. It can be expressed as an extremely obvious act, or it can be much more subtle, such as a wink at another person. The expression of sexual desire differs amongst cultures.

Sexual desire is cognitive—involving thoughts, wishes, fantasies, or desires—as well as physical—genital arousal. It is also thought to be psychosexual, meaning that "every one of our senses gets involved."[15] Sexual desire is not necessarily the same thing as physiological or genital sexual arousal—though it can be a component. There can be an absence of sexual activity without a lack of desire. On the other hand, a person can engage in sexual behaviors and activities without feeling sexual desire. So many young people engage in said activities so that they can feel a part of a clique with whom they hang out; however, the sexual experience leaves them disappointed. An understanding of sexual desire and the fact that they do not need to give in to these acts just to "feel good" about themselves can help spare the younger generations the heartache that comes from premature sexual activity.

Foreplay

Another important aspect in understanding sex is foreplay. Foreplay is greatly debated today. Whether young or old, we hear that foreplay outside of marriage is fine. I've heard some Christians refer to it as Christian sex. It's a way of fulfilling each other without actually doing the deed—one of those loopholes mentioned earlier. In fact, many of the loopholes that can be listed under "having sex without having sex" can be found in the act of foreplay.

Foreplay is part of the bigger picture of sexual intercourse. It is the forerunner to sex and is meant to ready the body for intercourse. Foreplay is used to discover the likes and dislikes of each other. The problem, though, lies in the design of foreplay. It feels good. Each step we take in the foreplay process arouses us more and more to the point that we refuse to think of the consequences should we allow ourselves to go all the way. Our minds start justifying that it's all good because sexual experience is important. Why would anyone want to commit to another if the sex is not working? Even Christians fall prey to this temptation. Many say that, since God is forgiving and gracious, to be in love and to express oneself sexually through intercourse is not a problem. We begin to think that we could allow ourselves this supposedly minor slipup, and He would be okay with it; however, foreplay is like turning on a car engine. The engine is meant to power the car to its chosen location. The stimulation of genitalia means that the body wants more. The sexually stimulated body wants intercourse, but how far should we go until it is considered sex? Remember, the black-and-white definition does not seem to count anymore.

The decision that a little foreplay is alright usually results in a couple pushing the boundaries until, over time, the boundaries are gone altogether. Although they may say that they will never have intercourse, the result of foreplay often is intercourse. A couple becomes more comfortable with their behavior and, therefore, looks for the next form of sexual excitement. This couple spends less time with friends and more time alone where they can remain uninterrupted by others. The time spent exploring each other's bodies is time that could have been spent in exploring each other's dreams and plans, likes and dislikes, family history, and fears and talents.

Oral Sex

Oral sex is another type of foreplay that is often considered "not sex;" however, like foreplay, oral sex is a part of the sexual acts that "turn on" the engine and stir up the desires to reach their destination. Oral sex is the mimicking of the act of sex using the lips and tongue to stimulate the genitalia of the one receiving the pleasure. Oral sex almost always results in orgasm and, while this relieves sexual tension for an individual, it builds disappointment. The mystery of intimacy is stripped away, leaving nothing to which the couple can look forward. The secret areas of the body have already been explored, and all that is left in the aftermath of oral sex is shame for the person or persons involved.

Anal Sex

Anal sex is stimulation of the anus during sexual activity. It is increasingly practiced and accepted these days by both men and women, particularly amongst the younger generation. Placing the penis into a woman's rectum, known as anal intercourse, is commonly done since it avoids pregnancy. Men tend to hold a fascination for this type of sex and not because they are homosexual. While this type of sex is not forbidden in the Bible between husbands and wives, it is again a form of sex that detracts from the future mystery of marriage. Apart from this, as we will discuss further along in these writings, the bacteria found in the anus can interfere with the bacterial balance in the vagina, and a mixing of these bacteria can cause serious infection.[16]

Why Couples Default to Sex

Since we have established a basic understanding of what sex is and what it includes, we can take a look at the possible reasons as to why dating couples default to sexual activities instead of working to deepen their connection through commitment and self-restraint. The demands of popular culture have backlashed on the emerging generations and given them the false impression that sex is the only good thing they have in a relationship. In fact, "the failure of romantic love as a solution to human problems is so much a part of modern man's frustration" that "both the stereotypically male and female idolatries regarding romantic love are dead ends."[17] When there is no true romance to bring surprise, fun, and delight to a relationship, couples default to sex as the only joy left to them.

Perhaps one of the biggest reasons that sex is the easy alternative to relational growth is the frequent attempts of society to pretend that there are no differences between the genders. Rather than cherishing the things that differentiate male and female, we make them out to be problems. Because of this, guys and girls struggle in knowing what to do in a dating situation.

Girls have been taught that modesty is a thing of the past; that they need to be independent and free of the need for a man. Ironically, the deepest desire of a girl's heart is to be cared for and accepted by a man, but they are encouraged to not care. Girls are put on antidepressants and anti-anxiety drugs in an attempt to reduce their tendencies toward sensitivity and intensity. All that makes a girl unique and wholly feminine is stripped away, leaving behind a confusion that is damaging to a girl.

The identity of men as men is also misconstrued in the midst of current opinions. Most young men are clueless as to how to be around a woman. They are ignorant because they have not been taught how to treat a woman. Most young men are told that women do not desire chivalry. Boys are placed on any drug that will quiet them down. They are not given the chance to step out and be the knight in shining armor for his anxious princess who is eagerly waiting to be rescued.

Both sexes are confused regarding the true needs of the other sex. Both sexes are also probably embarrassed to express their heartfelt wants when it comes to chivalry. The reality is that God created men and women as two separate genders. Each gender has distinctive trains that are meant to bring fulfillment to the other. When we accept all of God's given differences of the other sex—emotional, sexual, physical, etc...— then the relationships become much more satisfying.

Rules of Dating

This may sound old fashioned, but when you begin a new relationship, have rules established at the get-go regarding physical and sexual touch. Holding hands but then keeping touch above the neck is a good guideline. These rules display respect for the other and for oneself. 1 Corinthians 6:19 explains that each of us is "a temple of the Holy Spirit."[18] We each need to respect that God has created us as this. Sex is the culmination of two people's love and commitment to each other; therefore, foreplay and intercourse are not things that need to be practiced in the growth of a dating relationship. Both acts belong in the sanctity of marriage.

Dating is meant to be a time of getting to know one another, exploring the differences of the other person, and determining if those differences make us stronger or weaker. A guy gets the chance to see the true side of a girl. She is going to have hang-ups; dating is the time in which a guy discovers if these hang-ups are something that endears her to him. Can he live with these and help her with them? At the same time, he is going to have energy and habits that are strictly male. She will determine in dating if these are qualities to which she can commit in life. An understanding of a healthy dating environment can help couples curb the need to engage in premature sexual behavior.

The definition of sex has expanded to include several other "not really intercourse"-style activities. These activities, however, remain part of the sexual process. These acts still arouse sexual desire and create a sense of physical connection that was designed to be shared solely in the intimate confines of marriage. When we understand what is and is not appropriate, we are one step closer to God's idea of sex.

Chapter 2: Maintaining Virginity

In the next few chapters, we are going to explore some of the more socially accepted sexual practices found amongst youth and adults alike and discover to what these practices can lead, but before we dive into the details, let's lay the foundation of sexual purity. Let's discuss the importance of maintaining virginity.

I once watched an episode of CSI where the victim was a college girl who had maintained her virginity and viewed it as sacred until her sorority sisters mocked her purity. She broke under their cruelty and agreed to give up her virginity to the boy of their choice. She was willing to sacrifice a most sacred gift on a whim just to fit in. This sense of peer pressure is not limited to the television screen. We live in an age where virginity and male honor are both supposed to mean nothing.[19] Many young people lie regarding their heartfelt standards or cave under the supposed social norm.

For teens and adolescents, there is huge pressure in some environments to be sexually active. Too many people view modesty as a sign of sexual repression. If you are found to be a virgin then you must have no sex drive, be pretending that you don't want to have sex, or have limited opportunities in which to express yourself sexually. Virgins are often ridiculed for their standards. High school girls put pressure on their girlfriends for not being sexually active. Needless to say, the pressure to fit in is enormous.

Not everyone wants to have intercourse. There are brave youth out there who stand against the social flow. These young people find their dilemma is in knowing how to say no. Interestingly, the "failure to sleep with someone is now an act of hostility, whereas it was once understood to be part of the natural process of searching for one's mate."[20] We as adults can laugh at the pressures that confront young people, but these pressures are very real. Young girls especially have difficulty telling boys "no" after the boys have professed supposed undying love for them. If the girls resist, the boys may resort to pressuring statements such as "If you loved me, you would." Young girls feel the pressure the most on their self-esteem. They want to be loved by a boy; it is seen as a mark of feminine maturity; however, many studies correlate early sexual intercourse with poor self-esteem, while waiting until we are older is a sign of great self-worth. If our young people can grow in a sense of self-esteem and purpose that rise above the pressures, they can succeed where so many have fallen. How does one then maintain sexual purity until marriage? Here are a few things to which we can commit that can help.

God

See God for who He is—the perfect and unlimited Father who has your best interests at heart. As a teen, I viewed God as a strict authoritarian waiting to beat me up every time I failed. This was an obstacle that caused me to not want to draw close to Him. My answer lay in reading the Bible and praying, not just as a duty but as a way to get to know God. When we want to get to know someone, we need to participate in the relationship. Great relationships always involve two people investing into each other.

When we spend time getting to know God, we begin to see that He is neither a grim school teacher nor Santa Claus. He is a loving and understanding God that wants to help us achieve our very best in this life. This best life is created when we commit to Him. Our commitment to worship and love God means that we will submit to Him and what He says. He desires that we respect the body in which He placed us. This respect manifests in our commitment to sexual purity until marriage. Jesus says in John 14:15, "If you love me, you will keep my commandments."[21] Loving God does not always involve feelings but sometimes means that we obey Him even when we don't want to obey.

Friends

Of course the journey of our mind regarding sex means that we hang out with those that approve of our journey. There is peace in a unified mindset. Great friends are there to challenge us to grow and change, so there will always be times of friction; however, we should recognize that this friction can be good. Friends who have known us longer than our new-found romantic interest can recognize when a relationship or an event is harmful to us. Friends can warn us when we are about to enter into something dangerous—such as a relationship that could compromise our standards. Great friends know our hopes and our dreams and will honestly speak their minds in defense of those things. Surround yourself with others that support your commitment to doing your relationships well. This limits the temptations and opportunities that could lead us to stepping out of bounds.

Mindset

The Bible instructs us to "set your mind on things above."[22] The mind and imagination are powerful tools when used according to God's boundaries. When left to their own devices, though, they cause devastation and heartbreak. Discipline of the mind is probably one of the greatest assets that God has provided. Mindset may mean that we place boundaries in our lives that are an enhancement. Changing our thoughts and mindset may involve altering our choice of reading materials, movies, music, or places we go. Sight, smells, touch, and hearing all feed our minds, so we need to get wise. What is affecting our minds?

I have seen people overcome addictions and bad habits and have seen marriages and families restored because they overcame the battle in their thoughts. Discipline of the mind requires work. We don't like to hear this part. We want a quick and easy fix. Discipline, when utilized, empowers us and gives us a self-confidence that is very rewarding.

Honesty

Being honest with ourselves is one of the primary tools for successful living. This level of honesty requires bringing those thoughts that can lead us into temptation to the forefront of our minds. We tend to shove these thoughts back and justify that nothing is wrong or that we can deal with them later. The more we ignore the signs, the quicker we can fall. Friends and leaders can warn us, but if we are not receptive to their words, we will deny the truth and proceed in our dishonesty. It is better to grab the thoughts at the start, confront them, and honestly work through them so that we do not have to face the consequences of acting upon said thoughts.

The Choice

When looking for love, don't settle for less than the best. When I say this, I am not referring to a list of physical attributes. I am talking about the spiritual aspect. The Bible says to not be yoked to a nonbeliever.[23] Looks, ideas, and emotions mature over time but the spiritual connection with another is of the utmost importance. Many of us have met someone who has assured us of their commitment to Christ. Often these words are spoken in an effort to get our interest; therefore, it is vital to watch habits such as commitment to church (hopefully one and not several), daily behavior, and types of friendships. These things speak volumes about a person. On another note, it is also important that, as a relationship develops, both are committed to the same type of church. I've seen too many couples get married and think that they will make this decision later. It often is not resolved, and one of the couple ends up going nowhere or they both attend separate churches. It's an unhappy scenario.

Principles and Safeguards

The Bible says not to follow our hearts but to guard our hearts.[24] The heart is prone to selfishness and sin. Guarding it is something that is pre-emptive. Think ahead and don't put yourself in a compromising situation. Don't have a lot of alone-time behind closed doors where the mind can wander on the Internet or TV. Stay social when you are single and when you are dating. Things can go wrong, and reactions that lead to regret tend to happen when you are by yourself or alone with your significant other for too long.

By waiting to give your virginity to the one you marry, you reserve a part of yourself for someone else, and you show the seriousness of this marriage pact. Wendy Shalit is a contributing editor of the Manhattan Institute's City Journal and has written for the Wall Street Journal.[25] In her book, *A Return to Modesty*, she writes the following regarding virginity:

> By reserving a part of you for someone else, you are insisting on your right to keep something sacred; you are welcoming the prospect of someone else making an enduring private claim to you, and you to him. But more significantly, not having sex before marriage is a way of insisting that the most interesting part of your life will take place *after* marriage, and if it's more interesting, maybe then it will last.[26]

Below are two inspiring stories. Each story contains some great advice from those who have walked through the sexual struggles and dilemmas we will be tackling in the pages of this book.

The Virgin

Growing up, my parents reiterated how important it was to "save myself" until marriage because it was the best gift I could give my husband. Although my parents didn't talk a lot about sex, they spoke a lot about waiting. They engrained into me that it's biblical and that it's wrong to have sex before marriage. I grew up accepting this—especially because I had always been one to follow the rules and submit to authority (authority here being my parents, but also God). I was firm in my stance towards sex before marriage and never questioned it nor questioned why I chose to stay celibate. Before, I chose it because my parents told me it was wrong and God also says it's wrong; I never wanted to let them down, so I refrained. That was a good response until I got older and realized I needed to make the decision for myself in order to remain celibate. It was only a few years ago that I made this cognizant decision for myself and not anyone else. I ultimately decided staying celibate was something I was able to do and could control myself to do—and this was because I wanted to align myself with God's intention and call for my life. I never felt as if I was missing out on something because "everyone is doing it" or "how can you know you want to be with him/her for the rest of your life if you don't test it out first?" I've been okay thus far and know that God is going to honor me because of my choice.

Staying celibate in my relationship up until marriage was interesting—because I was a virgin and he wasn't. I always wanted a guy who was going to honor me as I was honoring him by staying celibate, and I decided early on that it was going to be a "deal breaker" if he wasn't a virgin before we got married. Interestingly enough—it wasn't even an issue for me when we started dating. I never really thought about it at first, but, looking back on it, I realized that it was, in a sense, my maturity in my Christianity that allowed me to be okay with it (as ironic as that may sound). Jesus is the ultimate picture of grace, and God has called us to be in His Son's likeness—in other words, pick up grace and extend it towards others. If God has grace for all in all circumstances and all faults, why should I not extend the same grace that has already been given to me? In this way, God already forgave him and grace abounded towards him, so then I too was required to extend that same grace. After all, his walk with God is not my own.

That being said, we decided early on in our relationship to not have sex until we were married (we knew pretty much right away as we were dating that it was going to lead to marriage). It hasn't always been easy, I think especially for him, but we do joke that I have a chastity belt on because I am so firm with where we DON'T go physically! So much so, that we stopped "making out" a few years ago (at least on a regular basis) because we noticed in the beginning it could easily turn into something we didn't want it to. Therefore, we eliminated the possibility—which didn't kill us, or our relationship. In fact, I think it made us stronger because we decided together and, therefore, were able to both celebrate in our success. I know this isn't for everyone, but it worked for us! Also, it alleviated circumstances in which we would be tempted to do things we would later regret—e.g., don't be in a home together all alone. Why put yourself or the other person in that situation?

All in all, I think it comes down to choice—and knowing why you have made that choice. If there is no rationale and revelation behind the choice, there really is nothing keeping you from remaining with the decision you have made. When you make that choice, it is far easier to stick with it if you have a revelation behind it—as well as—making the conscious decision to protect the other's interest/well-being in the situation by not putting yourself in compromising situations.

Today: This gorgeous young lady continues to be actively involved in her church as a leader. She inspires many with the strength of her convictions. Recently married, she has no regrets regarding her standards. –JS

Reclaiming My Virginity After Being Sexually Active

Growing up, my parents always told me I needed to remain a virgin until my wedding night. They explained to me that it is the best gift you could ever give your wife. I really took this to heart and sincerely wanted to stay a virgin until my wedding night.

However, when I was 15, I met a girl who was 2 years older than me and really liked me. Our physical relationship progressed rapidly. I realize now, although I was saying I did not want to have sex, I was continually putting myself into situations where I would lead myself right to the brink. So it came as no surprise that once we started we didn't stop. We dated for about a year and then ended it, as the majority of young relationships do.

When I was 19 I started dating my fiancé. It was my first real relationship since the girl I gave my virginity to. We both pretty much knew each other's sexual past, and she held zero resentment or judgment toward me because I was not a virgin.

She is a virgin, however, and I found myself in a major complex. I am in love with this girl, and I felt almost unworthy because of my past; she didn't make me feel this way at all, it was my own guilt. I had to work through my own insecurities with God to let myself know it was okay. When we started dating, we would kiss and hold hands, cute stuff. Then, after a while, we started "making out;" we realized then that we had to discuss boundaries. We both wanted to refrain from having a sexual relationship till marriage. So we set ground rules:

> *Don't go somewhere we are totally alone.*
> *Don't make out. We found it led places.*
> *Keep accountable to other people.*

These were not easy for me to keep. I want to have sex with her. But I also want to do the right thing by God and her, to save sex until later. At times, I found myself frustrated both physically and mentally, but I know our relationship has been strengthened and refined because of this. I used sex as a way to avoid conflict and confrontation. This was not an option in my relationship now, so we have been forced to develop communication skills to deal with problems instead of relying on sex or use sex as a cage on a relationship.

I am proud that we have abstained from sex. I think, though, as I look back through the last four years of dating my wife to be, I still felt regret at times for my mistake. I know God has forgiven me, but I relate it to Paul's thorn in the flesh. I am forgiven, but every once and a while, I still feel a twinge of pain because of my lack of self-control.

Today: This young man is deeply involved in leadership in his church and encourages young men in their daily lives. He is unafraid to confront and call them out in areas where they could wreck their lives. –JS

Chapter 3: Premarital Sex

A Story of Lost Virginity

I grew up as the last one to do things. For example, while my friends were making out with guys in middle school, I did not want to do this. I was petrified. I would date, but, at the point at which the guy wanted more, I'd end the relationship. I knew that I wasn't ready for a full sexual relationship. While my parents thought I was weird and encouraged me to experience a sexual relationship, my friends were respectful of my decisions. I was one of those girls that, even if I physically craved sex, if I wasn't wholeheartedly into doing something, I would not do it.

By the age of about twenty-one, pressure was increasing. I was approaching my twenty-second birthday and didn't want to hit that birthday and still be a virgin. Around this time, I had numerous relationships and would do all but intercourse. I just did it, but it wasn't fun. I feared serious relationships because that meant that sexual intercourse was a must. I was known as the girl who would kiss a bunch of guys at parties. I was the big tease. Dancing was my thing as I could be sexual without having sex. It was my fix.

One night I went to my best friend's place and met a guy; because he was the best friend of my friend's brother, I assumed that he must be a really good guy. I was still very emotionally driven and convinced myself that he was the man of my dreams. We kissed a lot and exchanged phone numbers. Because he was the best friend of my friend's brother, I assumed a level of trust for this guy and credited him with being a better man than he really was. After telling me of a party, I went to his place. We never went to a party but spent the night drinking. My defenses were low and, after a lot of yes's and no's, we had intercourse. I remember thinking that I did not want to be the twenty-two-year-old virgin. He didn't pressure me, but, rather, I allowed this all to happen. It was a huge letdown as I remember pain, but no sexual pleasure. Most of all, there was no purpose to what we were doing while there was no connection of love. The next day, he went to work, and I went to Planned Parenthood. We'd had unprotected sex because, in the constant changing of my mind, we'd used up all of his condoms. I felt so alone and didn't tell my parents at this time due to shame. Even when my flat mate was proud of me, within myself I was disappointed. He never called me even though he said he would. He stood me up four times, and, to this day, I've never seen him again. Around this same time, though, I committed my life to Christ, and it was actually after church one Sunday that I felt God say to me that I didn't need this guy. Move on. To this day, five years later, I have kept to my commitment of no sex before marriage. I want the one with whom I build a sexual relationship to be my husband.

Today: I am so proud of this young lady. While living in a crazy world, she holds strongly to her convictions, leading many to Christ. She has a very successful career while being devoted to God. –JS

Premarital sex has become something of a social norm. The number of those involved in sexual activity that profess to be Christian is not that vastly different from the number found in the secular world. It is assumed a person will express himself physically in dating situations. It's difficult to place boundaries on male/female relationships where there is chemistry and attraction. The stroke of an arm or the rubbing of a leg sets off fireworks, and, as established in Chapter One, we can all too often use this sense of chemistry as an excuse to have sex. It was also established in Chapter One that we do not need to give in to these feelings and desires.

Most young people do not know nor understand the strength they have in saying, "No." This strength is not known to them because the message of society is "Have sex whenever and with whomever; there are no consequences!" There are consequences though, and more than just physical. Sex outside of God's boundaries is painful and destructive. It is disillusioning to those who dreamed of sex in its purity. This chapter focuses on how premarital sex is, in fact, the opposite of freeing, and how it can cause havoc in the body, soul, and spirit.

Parental Boundaries

The first place where the boundaries of sex should be established is in the home; however, some parents, in their quest to be relevant or simply because they do not want to lose their child, succumb to the same social pressures as their children—pressures that drive them to allow their teenage daughter to stay the night with her boyfriend or approve the couple's plans to move in together. The primary line of defense in the family is the parent, and yet parents are no longer protecting their children. They are doing the opposite. Most parents are encouraging their children in their independence. They want their children to have freedom of choice even when their children are too young to understand the power of their choices.

Adolescents, particularly young girls, are disappointed in the lack of boundaries enforced by their parents. Shalit writes of a young girl who was baffled that her parents allowed her to be alone so often with her boyfriend. No parental supervision made it difficult for this young girl to draw the line.[27] Young adults do not have a reference point for what is right and what is wrong if their parents do not teach it to them; they flow with whatever society says is okay at the time. This means that premarital sex is a good thing; even a rite of passage! The promise of "no consequences" is a lie, though, and the pain of giving oneself sexually outweighs the supposed sense of freedom.

The Myth of Compatibility

Young people are often led to believe that taking a relationship to the next level is living together. The concept of moving in with a boyfriend or girlfriend may seem like a good idea because it raises one issue that keeps coming up amongst people: compatibility. If two people do live together or have a sexual relationship, they—theoretically—will then find out if they are compatible. This reasoning assumes that a relationship is a stationary object. Two people may find that they have a high level of compatibility, similar interests, great chemistry, and a good sexual relationship. Their connection can be fuelled by this sense of compatibility for, say, a year, but then, one of them may change interests or find someone else more attractive. Suddenly, the compatibility ends! The couple breaks up, and the heartbreak felt by those who have lived in these types of relationships is often as devastating as those who go through divorce.

True compatibility means that a couple continues to make decisions that enhance the relationship in every way, including the sexual aspect. It is a choice that two people make. Relationships grow and change, and a sexual relationship develops and improves with practice and commitment over time. Long-term commitment means that a couple builds trust; from that trust, they discover each other's likes and dislikes. Society mocks the idea of commitment, claiming that it makes a relationship boring and monotonous. The comfort and trust that is built in a monogamous relationship actually enhances the experience instead of bogging it down. The relationship as a whole gets better and better with time because, as each person gets to know the other, there is an increase in caring and the desire to change for the betterment of the other. That is one of the truest manifestations of a real, loving relationship that can begin the process toward marital sex.

Approval of Contraception

Contraception, like moving in together, seems like a good idea at the time for those sexually active but not married. The advancements in this medication have helped girls regulate their period and, for example, decrease the risk of acute pelvic inflammatory disease; however, this safety net that contraception creates is counterproductive as it becomes another argument in the "have sex without consequences" debate. Obtaining contraception is a cold and clinical process where there is no celebration of a lifetime commitment or of the hopes for this relationship. It takes sex from being something to which a young girl can look forward to experiencing to another thing she can do if she feels like it.

Parents—who, again, are not acting as a line of defense for their children—will often support their daughters in the acquisition of contraceptives. Even if they do not, young girls are often protected by privacy laws that allow them to visit doctors and medical clinics to arrange for protection against pregnancy. It is regarded as the child's right. She is mature enough to make this decision regarding sex and children on her own. Behind all of this is often disappointment; not so much from parents but from the child. No one warned her that giving away her purity had consequences. Contraception made it easy; her parents encouraged her in her choice; and society said it would be okay. Now she is left feeling empty, alone, and without answers, all because the world around her lied.

The Consequences of Premarital Sex

There are other consequences that come as a result of premarital sex. These consequences are not ones that are often the first to come to mind. Premarital sex is far more than a concern about pregnancy and disease. The body and soul suffer in varying ways, as seen below.

Sex Cycle

Some justify premarital sex as natural. This supposedly natural act is accompanied by our emotions and thoughts. Our five- to thirty-minute sexual romp of enjoyment has greater ramifications than merely being a natural act. Sometimes we find that our guilt from this act leads to a repeat performance. The sexual deed is done, and it's like a drug. Sex does produce a high just as does a drug. Sex feels fantastic! We are wanted and desirable. In a way, it is a free emotional high. We feel good, someone finds us attractive sexually, and there is the satisfaction of the conquest of winning another. The high leads to a low, and so we repeat the action for the next high.

Loss of Control

Solomon writes on several occasions in the Song of Solomon "not to awaken love until the time is right."[28] The man of a thousand wives and concubines does speak wisely when he advises us to not awaken love before its time. Once sexual love is awakened, once an orgasm is experienced, it is difficult to shut this appetite down. So many in these situations claim that they can handle the sexual side of a relationship after fulfilling the sexual appetite, but they lie to self as well as others. Better to not awaken it at all. Leave it sleeping until marriage.

Loss of Simple Trust

Rob Bell is an internationally sought-after pastor, teacher, and speaker who has been named by *Time Magazine* as one of the most influential people in 2011.[29] He writes in his bestselling book, *Sex God,* that "we have to be very careful what we share. Because when you give it away, you no longer have it."[30] This applies to sex. Practicing the sexual act before marriage is not an enhancement but rather a deterrent. Many women confess in marriage that they wish that their husbands had been the only one. A marriage after sexual encounters with others only leads to sexual comparisons. It leads to a fear of comparisons for our partners regarding our sexual performance and appearance. Simple trust comes out of being one's first and only lover, thus trust takes longer to build for a couple who has had multiple sex partners before getting married.

Loss of Relationship

Often sex before the commitment of marriage stunts the growth of a relationship. Time spent exploring the physical instead of getting to know each other's character, personality, likes, and dislikes takes away the mystery in the relationship. Bell says that "racing ahead of the progression always costs something."[31] Many don't realize the link between the initial sexual connection of intercourse and the lasting love that comes after. That is the reason that sexual relationships are often harder to dissolve than nonsexual relationships. There has been little time expended in developing common goals or strengthening the relationship. Common bonds have not been formed. All too often, a relationship where sexual activity occurs early does not survive.

How Do I Stop?

What happens when we tire of these failed sexual relationships and decide to stop having sex until marriage? We know that, at some point down the road, we will have to face our urges again. Sexual attraction is a part of life. So what do we do? There is no easy answer; however, if we persevere and hold strong, we can live a life filled with new confidence and boldness. We will also be able to enter marriage knowing that we have submitted to God's plan for our life. We will never be physically a virgin again; that is a ridiculous notion in and of itself! There are always consequences to sin; to think otherwise is to live in false hope. God forgives, we forgive, but there are always consequences. Still, we can grow and move forward. Here are a few guidelines that can help us along in the journey from being sexually active to being celibate until marriage. A good portion of the following has already been discussed in the previous chapters, both through what I have written and the stories submitted. This repetition thus denotes its importance. Read it again and apply it.

Forgive Yourself

There is and always will be the issue of forgiveness. We all struggle with regret for past mistakes, and we all live with the memories of what we have done. The first step in moving on is to admit that we are fallible and make mistakes. God forgives us, and we must, therefore, forgive ourselves and others.[32] Our problem here is letting go of our pride and embarrassment over what we have done. We should not be in a resentful place nor can we afford to be a person that holds resentment. God encourages us to forgive, for it is in forgiveness that we are forgiven.[33]

We also have to choose to not dwell on our mistakes. Sexual sin is often difficult to forget because of the intimacy we held with others. It did not seem like a bad idea at the time, but when the relationship dissolves, we face the regret of giving ourselves over to something temporary. We have to choose to cast down our thoughts and imaginations.[34] If we keep on allowing ourselves to dwell on our mistakes then we are going to be depressed. Choose to move forward.

Honest Assessments

Paul writes that we should be honest in our evaluation of ourselves.[35] We need to be very honest with ourselves when dealing with our past and moving forward into a healthy future. We can think that we have it all under control, but there is no way to know if our personal accountability is working until it is too late. We may think that living alone will be okay or that we can still hang out with our old friends even though their standards do not match up to ours. We often make these decisions even though our friends and family see and know what will happen. We can too easily deny the truth and be less than honest with ourselves. In the end, the only ones who will suffer the consequences will be us.

We need to realize that sexual impurity is a wall that we have built between us and the Lord. We can be in church, serving our hearts out, and putting on a great front, but we don't really fool anyone. We definitely don't fool God; therefore, we need to work out our point of weakness and make changes in that area. We do worship a God of grace and mercy who loves us dearly. Living honestly is sometimes difficult, but in the long run, it is well worth it.

Accountability

We need to spend time with those who have similar standards. We cannot pretend that we have our lives under control. If we find ourselves pushing friends away with comments such as "You don't understand," "It's my life," or "It's not your place to tell me what to do," we are probably in a bad place mentally and are about to or have already made some bad decisions. Accountability to both God and others we trust protects us from moments like these. Thinking that all we need is God, prayer, and the Bible is a dangerous trap. God does speak through His Word, but He also speaks through others.

Accountability means that we will allow others access to our world. We submit to His correction and healing when we hear and take direction from those He has placed in our lives. We need to have a trusted friend or a few trusted friends to be the sounding board for our plans, goals, and future hopes. These friends can help us to build a list of essentials that will help with our day-to-day walk. This open communication will help us through single life to finding someone new who holds to our standards. To date anyone who does not respect our decisions is probably not the one for us, and our trusted friends will help us see the truth.

Society will not tell you what I have formerly written about. It does not want you to wait. However, if you submit to God's boundaries about sex, you can avoid these situations and many more. These first few chapters have delved into some topics that can easily be thought of as the least evil of the sexual dilemmas of society. What comes next is not so light-hearted and is the precursor to what is discussed in later sections of this book.

Chapter 4: Abortion

I Was Sixteen...

Why did I get an abortion? I was only sixteen. I couldn't even raise myself. Looking back, I do wonder what it would have been like to have my own child. I'll never know, now.

Today: This lady has come such a long way, walking away from a horrific upbringing, and is now happily married.

—JS

Multiple Abortions

The abortions? I terminated four pregnancies as a young woman, still in my teens. After each was immediate relief, but this was very temporary. Each abortion was more stressful than the last. As an adult and mother, they are children lost that I will never know, and, although embraces await in heaven, only a redeeming God can love with an understanding that is required for one such as me. Also are thoughts that if I meet these children in heaven, what would they think if they knew of what I'd done. It's my thorn in the flesh.

While some people openly slam abortion, how can I when I have done this very thing? I could not bring myself to take contraceptives in those years. As a young Christian woman, taking contraceptives seemed to be too great an evil. (I could or more honestly would not stop having sex, but, then again, I could sneak to a clinic and abort future life.) I was anti-abortion, but I often picture the lives that these young, snuffed-out lives could have had.

Over the years, I've wondered regarding the sexes, appearance, and personalities. Even as I write this piece, the thoughts bring an ache and tears to my eyes. I wonder what I would have named these children that would no longer be children but adults. Would I be proud of them as I am of my children on this earth today? Likely by now, they would have wives and their own children. Like any loss, the pain fades to a dull ache, and private tears are shed. There is no open grieving for those who have had an abortion. None can send flowers. One cannot come to an altar for prayer. Abortion is very different from one who has miscarried or lost a child. Abortion is a choice. Abortion carries shame. Ultimately, it's a selfish act.

I do believe that it is wrong. It takes life from an innocent one and gives them no choice. Few know my secret and few ever will. My parents knew but did not advise or intervene. I understand that I was so young but not such a child that I did not know the difference between right and wrong. Rather, I was one filled with fear and shame. I was afraid of judgment and afraid that I was not capable of raising a child. It was easier to get rid of the outcome of a secret sexual life.

I have grown and matured, but still I don't forget. I know, however, of God's forgiveness. I take great comfort in loving the many youth that come my way. I take great comfort in helping the brave solo mothers that have chosen to birth and raise their children. Most of all, I take great comfort in King David. He was a liar, adulterer, and a murderer, but God loved him and used him. Therefore, God can love and use me.

Today: This is one of my closest friends. She is an outstanding minister who encourages women to live their lives to the fullest. –JS

Abortion is a highly debated topic regarding sexual freedom and consequences. It is a hot-button issue with both sides making heated arguments for their stance. The truth about abortion is lost in the fighting, and women—young and old—suffer. Society teaches that abortion—like premarital sex—is okay. The church agonizes over how to best address abortion; do they come on strong with a moral stance or do they pull back so that they can comfort the women who choose to terminate? Only God knows the truth; only He sees the inner workings of the heart.[36] I hope that you will read this chapter with an open mind, for we all have gone astray and need God's grace every day, and this chapter specifically has a lot of things that we need to understand.[37]

An Introduction to Abortion

Abortion is "the termination of a pregnancy (an embryo or fetus) by various means before the end of its natural term."[38] There are "three basic positions on abortion, and they all center around the question of the human status of the unborn."[39] If one believes that the unborn is subhuman, then this person favors abortion on demand. If one believes that the unborn is fully human, then he is against abortion. Thirdly, there are those who argue that the unborn is a potential human; this party favors abortion in specified circumstances.[40] There are different types of abortion like "a spontaneous abortion" which "is an abortion that occurs naturally such as in the case of a still birth or miscarriage" or a "therapeutic abortion" that "may be performed to preserve the life of the mother."[41] Most abortions are performed as a surgery in specialized clinics.

Abortion Statistics

Abortion is "one of the most common surgical procedures performed on women in the United States."[42] In fact, "nearly half of all pregnancies" in the United States "are unintended; four out of ten of these are terminated by abortion."[43] Statistics regarding abortion are strongly related to ethnicity.[44] At the beginning of 2000, estimates indicate that several million female fetuses were aborted in the last two decades of the twentieth century due to the preference for a son.[45] This practice is not exclusive to Asia; aborting daughters for sons is also common amongst Americans and Canadians of Asian descent. One study revealed that the numbers of legal abortions were greatest in the Russian federation and the United States with more than a million abortions each in 2003.[46] In Cuba and the Russian Federation, more abortions than births occur annually.[47]

In some countries it has been estimated that, at current rates, a woman would have at least one abortion in her lifetime.[48]

> On average, women give three reasons for getting an abortion. Three quarters of women declare that having a baby would interfere with work, school, or other responsibilities. About three quarters of

> the women say that they cannot afford to have a child. Half mention that they do not want to be a single parent or are having problems with their partner. A mere twelve percent of women include a physical problem with their health. Only one per cent of these aborting women say that they were the survivors of rape.[49]

Age-specific abortion patterns portray that many women have abortions to limit family size.[50] Research also shows that abortion levels are closely connected to patterns of contraception use. Adolescent pregnancy rates have fallen in the USA in recent years due to the improvements in use of contraceptives.[51]

The statistics listed above are baffling, heart-breaking, and very real. All too often we can look at these stats and judge those who made it happen. This judgment is one of the reasons that women who have experienced abortions never step forward. These women keep the guilt and regret they feel buried deep inside so as to avoid the judgment of others.

Alone

In the event of an unplanned pregnancy, a woman will often find herself on her own—especially emotionally. She may tell a partner or boyfriend, but, while he may claim that he will support her no matter her decision, she most likely hears: "You are on your own." At an extremely vulnerable moment, she feels abandoned, and the decision she feels she has to make is often abortion.

A High Price to Pay

There is a stigma attached to abortion. Women do not often want anyone else to know what they are doing or have done. Because of this, women in these situations will pay upwards of $550 in cash in order to keep what they are about to do a secret.[52] The price of an abortion varies depending on how far the pregnancy has progressed. Statistics from the National Abortion Federation state the following:

> In general...women getting an abortion between six and ten weeks' gestation can expect to pay about $350 at an abortion clinic and $500 at a physician's office. Providing abortions later in pregnancy is somewhat more complicated, and is usually more expensive. For example, at 16 weeks gestation, abortion clinics generally charge around $650 and physicians' offices generally charge around $700. After the 20th week, the cost rises to above $1,000.[53]

Insurance companies do provide coverage for women getting abortions; however, "employed women with coverage by a company's self-insured plan may be reluctant to make a claim, given that the staff employee in the company's benefit office would be privy to the information."[54] In order to preserve their anonymity, women will avoid the hospitals; opting instead to have their abortion at a specialized health center, where about seventy percent of abortions are performed.[55]

An Unknown Truth

Women who often recount their sexual pasts do so with laughter or regret; however, abortion remains the one thing that is too difficult to discuss even years later. "Some organizations, such as Planned Parenthood, note that immediately after the abortion it is common for women to experience anger, regret, guilt, sadness, or depression; some feel relief."[56] State-sanctioned counselors note that psychological problems appear low for those women who have had abortions,[57] but this is due to the fact that these women have no desire to return to the doctor or clinic at which the abortion was performed;[58] therefore, the gathered data is inadequate.

One woman recounted her story to me of more than thirty years ago. She was only fifteen at the time of her abortion, actually legally too young to have this surgery. The assisting nurse was willing to record a legal age and lie about the young girl's weeks of gestation. At the time, this woman was close to sixteen weeks pregnant when the law forbade abortion after twelve weeks. She has memories of fear and shame while desperately wanting to get rid of the baby. At the same time, though, she was clueless regarding the procedure. She did not want to think of the effects of the procedure on the baby. She remembers that she deliberately averted her eyes from where the remains of the baby would have been after the procedure. She wanted to get in and out of the clinic as fast as she could. She never returned to that clinic for checkups or the supposed offered counseling.

The hurt felt in the aftermath of an abortion is probably one of the deepest hurts a woman can feel. It is in epidemic proportions, and yet, abortion remains the champion of women's rights. Why is that?

The Debate

The big debate surrounding abortion concerns the following question: At what point does a fetus become a person? With pregnancy, an egg and sperm have united to form a life. Without the egg, the sperm is not a person and vice versa. Their unity, though, contains all that is needed to make a person. Some say that a fetus is only a person when it can survive outside of the womb on its own. This is a difficult argument because, even after birth, a baby is dependent for life on another. Miscarriage or the unwanted death of a fetus causes loved ones to grieve. They grieve over the loss of what could have been, thus, in miscarriage and death, the fetus was viewed as life. So where does one draw the line?

The Beginning of Life

Some try to see the fetus as just a bunch of cells. People can easily conclude that their decision is not hurting anybody because there is no baby just yet. They still have time to rectify what they would assume is a mistake and thus choose to abort. Norman L. Geisler is a distinguished Professor of Apologetics.[59] He notes that unborn children have...

> their own sex from the moment of conception, and half are male, while the mother is female. Beginning about forty days after conception, they

> have their own individual brain waves which they keep until death. Within a few weeks of conception, they have their own blood type, which may differ from the mother's, and their own unique fingerprints. Finally, the embryo is only "nesting" in his or her mother's womb. Birth simply changes the method of receiving food and oxygen.[60]

Abortions are often performed beyond twenty weeks of gestation. Robert J. White, M.D., PhD., is a professor of neurosurgery for Case Western University.[61] He has testified that "an unborn baby at 20 weeks gestation is fully capable of experiencing pain.... Without question, [abortion] is a dreadfully painful experience for any infant subjected to such a surgical procedure."[62] There appear to be numerous methods in which an abortion can be performed. From conversations with women who have had an abortion, particularly those who are younger, they are often unaware of the effects of the procedure on the unborn child. The more information that one discovers concerning the unborn, the more human he/she becomes.

Rape

Not all pregnancies that are aborted are due to the coupling of consenting adults. One of the arguments used in favor of abortion is the argument of pregnancy due to rape. Should a rape victim carry the child fathered by her attacker? People's capacities and situations regarding these crises differ. Some women in this type of situation have aborted and some haven't. Some see abortion after rape as decreasing the pain while others see abortion after rape as doubling the pain. We need to take opportunities and allow God to work through our crises as well as our good days. God is a gracious God whose mercies abound every day.[63]

Concluding Thoughts

In concluding this discussion on the overall abortion debate, we can acknowledge that abortion is a complicated matter; however, abortion contradicts life in every way. The Bible teaches us, "And just as you want men to do to you, you also do to them likewise;"[64] "thou shalt not kill"[65] is one of the Ten Commandments. Legalizing abortion has not saved thousands of women's lives, and it has killed millions of babies. Before the legalization of abortion, there were not thousands of women dying from illegal abortions, but there were only forty-five maternal deaths from abortion according to the U.S Bureau of Vital Statistics. Regarding original statistics concerning the need for abortion, one of the first leaders of the abortion movement, Dr. Bernard N. Nathanson, admitted before he died that proponents of abortion lied about the statistics.[66]

The question fueling abortion is, "When is a fetus a life?" I would argue that this occurs at conception; others would argue differently. The abortion debate is probably unsolvable. Each side will argue for what feels beneficial to them. It has been this way for as long as humanity has been on planet earth.

Historical Abortion

Abortion is not a new practice unique only to this current era. "Both abortion and infanticide have been common practices since the earliest records of human history."[67] Historical abortion "methods included manipulation of the abdomen and uterus, herbal medications given by vaginal pessaries or by mouth, and a range of surgical techniques using tools specially designed for the purpose."[68] Greek and Roman cultures used abortion to hide extramarital affairs and as a way for women to preserve their figures. Abortion and infanticide were also used as rational and reasonable ways to prevent overpopulation.

The Greco-Roman culture was very hierarchical. Those who were called the elite were the politicians, athletes, and philosophers. After this class were the ordinary working people. Women were next, and at the bottom of the social classes were riffraff, slaves, children, and the disabled. Strength and athleticism were celebrated. Children were despised due to their dependence and immaturity.[69] This culture and others like it most likely believed that a fetus was of little value and easily disposable; a mindset that seems to have continued on and is now shared by those who debate abortion today.

Abortion in Biblical Cultures

The Jewish world, probably due to the influence of the Old Testament, carried a different attitude toward the fetus. It is written in Genesis 9:6 that "the deliberate destruction of any human life was an affront to the dignity of God."[70] Deuteronomy 18:10 condemns the pagan ritual of sacrificing children. While the New Testament does not refer to abortion, there is a term, "pharmakeia" that may refer to those who used herbal potions to poison or cause abortion. This term "is found in lists of evil practices which are incompatible with Christian truth."[71] One also needs to wonder how abortion aligns itself with the two great commandments referred to by Jesus: Love God and love our neighbors.[72] If we are to treat and love others as ourselves, then would we abort ourselves?

Solomon writes, "Children are a gift of the Lord. The fruit of the womb is a reward."[73] This verse does not specify details for a child—whether healthy, malformed, or a certain sex; however, it does specify and even emphasize that children are a reward. In the following verse, Solomon writes that, "Like arrows in the hand of a warrior, So are the children of one's youth."[74] Again, Solomon has emphasized the importance of children (though, it should be noted that he specified sons due to the importance of the son in the family; the son inherits the family name). Solomon calls children a prized possession and compares them to arrows. Arrows were valuable and necessary to a warrior; in the same way, children are valuable in life. The bow is useless without the arrow; mankind will perish without children.

Probably the Scripture with the greatest impact on the importance of life is Psalm 139:

> For you created my inmost being; you knit me together in my mother's womb. I praise you because I am fearfully and wonderfully made; your works are wonderful, I know that full well. My frame was not hidden from you when I was made

> in the secret place. When I was woven together in the depths of the earth, your eyes saw my unformed body. All the days ordained for me were written in your book before one of them came to be.[75]

This passage reflects the author speaking as one from a mother's womb. God sees and knows us before conception and during growth in a mother's womb. We are in His mind and imagination, even before the egg and sperm unite within the woman.

History shows that the questions that fuel the current abortion debate were very real and very present in the past. Humanity in every society has had to decide what defines a valuable life. Most ancient societies have determined that children and the deformed are easy to discard. We can assume that in our more advanced society the thought of discarding a life because it might be imperfect would be viewed as detestable. That is a sad lie, because, to this day, we are still trying to determine what is and is not a valuable life.

Defining Importance

John Wyatt was a Professor of Ethics and Perinatology at University College London.[76] He once described a scene in a National Health Service hospital. In one theatre, surgery was being performed by highly trained professionals to abort a child seen as disposable and inconvenient. Across the hall, in another theatre, highly trained professionals were doing everything possible to preserve the life of an unborn child seen as precious and uniquely valuable.

In another time and another place, Sarah Williams discovered that she was carrying a child that would not survive birth. She chose not to abort her child as her time of pregnancy would be all that she and her family would have with this child. Her decision to carry the baby to term and, therefore give birth, sparked the following accusation against her:

> ...to fail to abort in the case of proven fetal abnormality is morally wrong, because in doing so

> one is deliberately and willfully choosing to bring avoidable suffering into the world. It becomes an ethical imperative to abort in the case of suboptimal life.[77]

Another such controversy took place in Britain in 2011. Jacob McMahon became Britain's most premature surviving twin after he was born on February 22nd, only 23 weeks into his mother's pregnancy. "Doctors had advised Miss Fisher to abort Jacob after his twin sister, Emie, died when she was born at 21 weeks and six days due to an infection. But Jacob followed eight days later, twelve hours before doctors would have demanded a final decision from the family on whether to terminate the pregnancy."[78] Doctors had told the parents that baby Jacob wouldn't survive. The parents had 24 hours to decide whether the wife would take a tablet that could stop the baby's heart. Five months later, this baby was healthy enough to leave the hospital.

These stories all have a common theme; that there is a disagreement among humans as to what life should be valued. Jacob's story reveals the fallibility and limitations of man's knowledge. When we abort a fetus, we will never know what the life we chose to end could have achieved or what we, as parents to whom God specifically gave this gift of a child, could have experienced as part of this new life. We deny ourselves a type of future and are forced back into a place of imagination fueled by what could have been.

Society makes the decision to abort a deformed child sound like a mercy, and yet, extremely handicapped people express on many occasions gratefulness for their lives. We do not hear of organizations favoring abortion of the handicapped. In 2 Samuel, King David restored Mephibosheth to the palace. This young man was the last surviving member of King Saul's family, and he was a cripple. David did not allow this young man's deformity to act as an excuse to view him as anything less than a human being. David welcomed and honored him and made sure he was cared for until his natural parting.[79] Jesus, as portrayed in the Gospels, valued all humanity regardless of their age, sex, or state of health. He gathered children to Himself when the disciples tried to rebuke them.[80] He also healed the paralyzed,[81] the blind,[82] and the demon possessed.[83] Probably one of the best examples of the potential hidden inside what society would call an unnecessary life is Christopher Nolan. Christopher Nolan was born with cerebral palsy and could only move his head and eyes. He is famous for such writings as "Under the Eye of the Clock," "The Banyan Tree," and "Dam Burst of Dreams." Nolan died suddenly at age forty-three, but, of his life, the Irish president Mary McAleese wrote, "Christopher Nolan was a gifted writer who attained deserved success and acclaim throughout the world for his work, his achievements all the more remarkable given his daily battle with cerebral palsy."[84]

We should applaud those parents and relatives that raise handicapped individuals. It is a huge, lonely, and exhausting undertaking, and support is often very limited. Raising children with special needs can also be a massive financial cost. Apart from this, these children often can never function without lifelong support. These parents sacrifice much more than other parents and likely will never have the freedom that others experience. These are the things that parents of potentially deformed, unborn children need to consider when they decide whether or not to abort. Many of these parents though would still choose to carry through the pregnancy and have the child.

The following story concerns a woman who found herself with an unwanted pregnancy.

The Decision To Not Abort

At the age of 22 I found myself pregnant and not married. Yes, I made a call to an abortion clinic, but, as soon as they answered, I hung up the phone. God would know, and I would know; that was two too many. I had the option to marry but turned it down. Over the next few years, I sought God with all that was in me and had the support of a great church family. Through this, some deep internal healing took place. It was the hardest thing that I had ever done, but it was also the best. When my daughter turned three and a half, her father and I were married. God turned the ashes into something beautiful…a child, a marriage, a family.

Today: This woman has a wonderful family. She is a fantastic counselor to many women, particularly those

pregnant outside of marriage and those people raising children on their own. –JS

Misused Scriptures

The Breath of Life

There are those in the pro-abortion movement who have sought proof in Scripture to advance their cause. They have attempted to argue that "since breathing does not occur until birth...the unborn are not human until they are born."[85] Several Scriptures have been used as a way to back this argument. In Genesis 2:7, it is written that man became a living being after God breathed life into him. Job 34:14–15 also connects life with breath when it states, "If it were his intention and he withdrew his spirit and breath, all humanity would perish together and mankind would return to the dust."[86] Isaiah 57:16 "refers to the breath of man that I (God) have made."[87] These passages all seem "to make the beginning of breath the point of creation of a human being."[88]

The idea that breathing makes one human is, frankly, ridiculous. Animals breathe and they are not human. The verses about breath are not speaking of the commencement of human life but rather the commencement of observable life. "Breath" in Genesis 2:7, however, means life; life began when God breathed life into Adam and not simply because he began breathing. The people in the biblical era knew that there was life in the womb. In Luke 1:44, the baby leapt in Elizabeth's womb.[89] The formation of Adam is a unique case. He is the first human to be created, thus it is a misguided attempt to link the point of life's beginning with the moment he began to breathe.

Life and Death

Another passage that is misunderstood is Ecclesiastes 6:3–5:

> A man may have a hundred children and live many years; yet no matter how long he lives, if he cannot enjoy his prosperity and does not receive proper burial, I say that a stillborn child is better

> off than he. It comes without meaning, it departs in darkness, and in darkness its name is shrouded. Though it never saw the sun or knew anything, it has more rest than does that man.[90]

This is often interpreted to mean that the unborn are no more viable than the dead. This passage does not mean, though, that they are not human; otherwise, adults would no longer be human after their death either. "This passage is simply making the obvious point that people not in the world cannot enjoy its opportunities."[91]

Christians and Abortion

Abortion amongst Christians is a difficult topic. Interestingly, in Christian circles, the right to abortion is not what we may think. Evangelicals "tend to follow their educational group rather than their religion in their abortion attitudes."[92] Although they may resist liberal views on issues such as sexuality, sex roles, and civil liberties, their attitudes regarding abortion are the same as the general population.

Christian circles can all too often incorrectly handle abortion. Women who lose a child through a miscarriage or another form of natural death can receive ministry, prayer, and comfort without judgment. This is not the case for women seeking help after having an abortion. These women suffer alone. There are no flowers on the anniversary nor is there a grave to visit. There are no words or cards of condolence. A child dying through miscarriage or any other means is an accident; abortion is a choice. It is because of this that many women never reveal the secret of their abortion due to shame and fear of judgment. They face their pain alone.

God provided the Ten Commandments, not to be used as an excuse to judge or to increase evil. He gave them to us to help us identify evil and our need for His grace. As believers, we must take care with our thoughts. We pity the addict but judge the woman that aborts. We are not very judgmental of the believer that never puts money in the offering and, therefore, robs God, but we judge the woman that aborts. Here we see values that resemble those of many years ago where Greco-Roman culture clashed against that of early Christianity.

As a Christian, I believe that abortion destroys a life. I do know, though, of the tough choices women and men have made. I have talked with many that carry deep shame and pain due to past choices to abort. I have talked to moms with children whose very lives were threatened when having to carry through unplanned pregnancies. I remember visiting a family sitting beside their dead daughter who chose to birth her baby despite her poor health. Her family sat grieving with their other grandchild; the parents were left without a daughter, a child without a mother, and a husband without a wife. Yes, God carries us through every situation but, nevertheless, there are extreme cases where abortion seems the best option. Abortion for a pregnancy resultant out of sexual abuse or rape needs consideration. The carrying and birthing of this child that is the result of a horrific evil may be too much for an individual. Abortion may be a part of the victim eradicating this horrific event from her life. On the other hand, there are those women who see the birth of a child as the one good that comes out of an evil act.

God's thoughts and ways are not as ours. Each person is in a journey of growth. While some women will regret their choice to abort a fetus, some will never have this misgiving. God's forgiveness, grace, and love are never ending. He does not reject as does man. We must remember this as believers, and, although we choose life over death, I've found the benefit of carrying an open heart for those who have walked through abortion is a valuable asset. I have no proof of this, but perhaps Rahab, who may have been a prostitute, had abortions. She is the wonderful woman who hid the spies in the book of Joshua. Abortion was available in these times, and, if she was a prostitute, it is likely that she made use of this service. She is listed as a woman of faith in Hebrews 11.[93] She is in the lineage of Jesus Christ. Moses murdered an Egyptian soldier, and yet God used him to lead the Hebrews out of Egypt. Moses became a mighty leader. These occurrences were not accidents but were used by God. As people, we often are judgmental because an abortion takes the life and rights from another, the "another" being an innocent baby. God, though, views things from a higher perspective. He sees that each man has rejected Him at times, thus, while accepting that each pregnancy is a gift from the Lord, we must examine our own hearts and not be quick to judge others.

When a woman aborts a fetus, it is often for selfish reasons. She is desperate to rid herself of this new life and the overwhelming responsibilities that come with it. A woman is encouraged toward independence and self-sufficiency; it is, after all, her own body. Paul informs us, though, that we are to honor our bodies as temples of the Holy Spirit. We are commanded to love others after the command to love God. This then puts a different view on our right to an abortion. For most situations, to carry through an unplanned pregnancy brings growth that we would miss if we abort a child. Pregnancy is inconvenient and can be frightening, but vision means that we look to the future. Perhaps we embrace the new season of parenthood or perhaps we give the child to a family who is desperate to provide a loving home.

Alternative to Abortion

There are countless women who are unable to have children. Many married couples desperately desire to adopt a child. Like Hannah, they seek God with a deep yearning that only He can heal. These couples would be more than happy to take a child into their home and raise it. Adoption is an option. I could list more statistics, but I think the best evidence is this story:

Adoption

The dream started as far back as I can remember: Meet the man of my dreams and have babies. Finally at 28, I married the man of my dreams. Six months after we were married, we decided to start trying to get pregnant. After all, I was closing in on 30 and all of my friends' kids were starting elementary school, so I was feeling extremely left behind. After 6 months of trying with no luck, we visited the doctor for a series of tests and found out that both of us had fertility issues, and we would not be able to naturally conceive a child.

We started on fertility medications for a few months with no luck, then on to more medications, still with no luck. Turning 30 was hard; my life was not at all what I had dreamed. I had expected to be knee deep in diapers, baby food, and obnoxious toys by now. What was I doing wrong? Why wasn't God giving me the "desires of my heart"? My husband and I decided to take a break from baby-making madness (at least the part that wasn't fun), and, in that time, we moved back to Atlanta, Georgia (my home state). We decided to take a year finding jobs, getting settled before starting back on the fertility track. Six days after moving to Atlanta, we found our current church.

This church was the first church we visited but knew after one service there that it was home. We found jobs, got involved at the church, and were loving life. After a year had passed, we started the process again. We visited a fertility specialist and got the prices for treatments and then went home to think about it. We didn't have the money for multiple attempts at IVF, and the thought of scraping up $10-$15k for a one-and-only attempt and it not working just never felt right for me.

The next week at church I heard my pastor say, "You move; God moves." I had heard him say it before, but for some reason, that week it stuck, and on the way home from church my husband and I started talking about the ways we could "move." We decided to no longer attempt fertility treatments but to adopt. Once we made our decision, we told everyone! It just felt right. We knew that it might take a while, but we would be parents through adoption.

We started out with our County foster-to-adopt program. Eight weeks of classes, a home study, background check, drug tests, another home study, 25 pages of VERY personal questions later, we were approved to be foster parents, and now we just had to wait. Waiting is never easy but waiting for a call to say you are getting a baby is…well I don't know that there is an appropriate word to describe it for me. We were told in August that we would have a baby in our home by Christmas. For this southern girl that LOVES Christmas, I couldn't think of a better time to have a baby come into our lives…. How fun it would be to wake up Christmas morning and take hundreds of pictures of a baby opening gifts…or eating wrapping paper! Christmas came and went, but no baby.

After numerous phone calls, clerical errors, and lost paperwork, we were already at July and still no baby. I was mad! I was wondering why God had given me this heart to be a mom and not allowed any doors to open to be a mom. I just didn't understand. I told my husband that I didn't want to pursue anything else. It had been 5 years, my heart was broken, and I was done.

I received a phone call early September 2005 while on vacation. There was a 2-week-old baby boy, and the birth mother had chosen us; were we interested? Here is a fun fact…you can put a nursery together in just a few hours! We brought our baby boy home just a few days later. I loved him the moment I saw him, held him, and smelled his little head. He was ours…I was a mom! Any worries I had of bonding were gone in an instant. I couldn't imagine loving him more if he had my DNA. He was mine!

Everything I had imagined about being a mom was SO DIFFERENT…it was so much better in ways that could never be explained. Four-and-a-half years later, we were again blessed with another baby boy. We met with his birth mother at 20 weeks into her pregnancy and developed a wonderful relationship during doctor visits, lunches, calls, texts, and mani/pedis. We have an incredible open relationship with both of our boys' birth mothers. They chose life for their sons…our sons. I love them and my boys love them. They are being raised to know how loved they were from the moment they were made, and, because they were so loved, there were some really tough decisions that were made by their birth mothers on their behalf.

Looking back now on my dream to become a mom, it's funny how it changed shape a few times. I had to allow God to open my heart to something different than I imagined. I have never once felt like I received a consolation prize by adopting…it's actually just the opposite…. I think I hit the jackpot! If you've met my boys, you will agree…they are simply amazing!

Today: This lady is a fantastic leader and mother. She and her husband are full of fun and optimism despite their past battles to adopt. They are both part of a vibrant church where they serve in several ministries. –JS

Chapter 5: Polygamy

One would assume that polygamy is a thing of the past; however, polygamy is still practiced in both its purest and not-so-pure forms. Cultures and religions alike advocate polygamy, and as the world spins on toward more and more social ideas of sexual freedom, polygamy has come out of the proverbial shadows. If same-sex marriage is approved, the marriage debate could expand to include polygamy. Could one man have several wives or several husbands? What about a woman? Where does one draw the line? As such, this book would not be complete without touching on this subject.

An Introduction to Polygamy

Polygamy "means one party in a marriage having two or more spouses of the opposite sex."[94] Polygamy is usually applied when a man has multiple wives; polyandry is when a woman has multiple husbands. One of the most common questions I am asked in relationship and marriage seminars is the relevance and acceptability of polygamy. Some believe that because the Bible contains stories of polygamy, this is license for its use today. Polygamy, though, is still illegal in all fifty states of the USA.[95]

We already practice polygamy in some sense of the word. People practice sex with multiple partners at the same time, while others have experienced repeated failed relationships or marriages which can result in multiple children. No one can actually stop one from having two or more partners at the same time without a marriage license.

Some people believe that polygamy is a good idea due to the shortage of men. Women could experience "marriage" of sorts. One article noted,

> There aren't enough men: single, heterosexual, uninstitutionalized men available for the number

> of women looking these days. And [now that the war is over there are] even fewer. The only realistic solution to this problem is to redefine our expectations of marriage. We need to look at other cultures and the success of polygamous relationships.[96]

Another article surveyed reasons for polygamy in Dhofar. Due to the illegality of divorce, new wives were acquired to assuage a husband's unhappiness with his first wife, to produce a male heir that had not been achieved with other wives, to help him feel young again with a new and younger wife, or to show off his wealth.[97] Another article interviewed spouses and eldest children in polygamous relationships involving two wives. This article found that while some of these families functioned well and others did not, overall the wives were not happy.[98] While polygamy may be practical and good in theory, the reality of its practice has less than desirable results.

Polygamy Around the World

Polygamy has been accepted and practiced in different parts of the world. While we may look at it and regard it as ridiculous, there are sound reasons for its practice. We must, therefore, understand these reasons and the value that it has had for the various cultures. To merely state that it is wrong is not a solution. For some cultures, the production of children is valuable, and this production increases if there are more wives. Divorcees could find a home by becoming a second wife. The response to a childless marriage changes, not by divorcing the nonproductive wife but by taking on another. Polygamy was also useful as a protection for widows and handicapped women who otherwise had no husband. In some ways, it has been viewed as liberation for women.[99]

Polygamy in the Bible

People read of polygamous relationships in the Bible and think that it is acceptable. God provides examples of many things, but that does not make them acceptable. The Bible contains examples of both right and wrong behavior, showing that mankind is capable of both good and evil (which is a relief since we all make mistakes). God loves people in spite of these mistakes, and to this day, He does not condemn us because of our wrongs. We can learn from these biblical mistakes. Polygamy had lasting and devastating ramifications in the Bible.

King David

Probably the most obvious biblical example of a polygamist was King David. While David was "a man after God's own heart,"[100] he was also an adulterer, a liar, and a murderer. David had many wives which, at first glance, appeared harmless, yet, if one follows the life of David and his children, the results were disastrous. The rivalry between the wives for David's affection and their quest to have their child ascend the throne in David's place would have made life a daily battle. It led to jealousy between wives and his children. Rape, jealousy, and murder were some of the issues between the siblings.

David tried to buy favor with neighboring nations by taking kings' daughters as his wives.

> Many of David's marriages were politically motivated. For example, King Saul, David's predecessor, offered both of his daughters at separate times as wives for David. For centuries, this "bond of blood" concept—the idea that rulers feel bound to the kingdoms ruled by their wives' relatives—was often employed, and just as often violated.[101]

King David also had concubines who were not wives, but held the status of mistresses. Concubines were a part of many cultures in this era. What we see in these times is a blending of cultural practices and beliefs with God's ways.

King Solomon

King Solomon also had many wives and concubines; in fact, his numbered seven hundred wives and three hundred concubines. This situation particularly puzzles people as Solomon was considered a very wise man. Wisdom, though, is not perfection, and Solomon was a fallen man just as any other. Perhaps his greatest influence was his father; after all, we can repeat our parents' behaviors including their beliefs and mistakes. Deuteronomy 17:16–17 explicitly instructs a king to not "multiply wives."

> The king must not build up a large stable of horses for himself or send his people to Egypt to buy horses, for the Lord has told you, "you must never return to Egypt." The king must not take many wives for himself, because they will turn his heart away from the Lord. And he must not accumulate large amounts of wealth in silver and gold for himself.[102]

In the writings of Solomon, we see a man greatly affected by neighboring nations. History reveals that Solomon...

> was very aggressive in his foreign policy. In sealing treaties in ancient days, it was customary for a lesser king to give his daughter in marriage to the greater king (in this case, Solomon). Every time a new treaty was sealed, Solomon ended up with yet another wife. These wives were considered tokens of friendship and "sealed" the relationship between the two kings.[103]

Solomon was disobedient to God, being obsessed with power and wealth, which overshadowed his spiritual life. He fell into apostasy and worshipped many of the false gods of his wives. Solomon sinned and brought misery to himself and others. He engaged in polygamy, married pagans, and worshipped their gods; he collected huge numbers of horses and gathered vast wealth. His writings reveal his misery as much as his achievements.

Abraham

Abraham had one wife: Sarah. Deeply grieved by their childlessness, they divulged a plan to change this despite God's promise to them of a child. Abraham slept with Hagar, their servant girl,[104] with Sarah's permission. Hagar became pregnant with a child. While this was culturally acceptable at this time, it was not God's way nor did it enhance Abraham's and Sarah's marriage. Sarah became deeply jealous of Hagar and the child and mistreated Hagar.[105] Although God made a way for Hagar and Ishmael, the decision to have a child through Hagar has had lasting ramifications on this earth.

Hannah and Elkanah

Hannah and Elkanah are another couple who were childless. Elkanah had a second wife named Peninah who had children. While Hannah was Elkanah's most loved wife, Peninah's jealousy meant that she taunted Hannah in her vulnerability of childlessness.[106] Elkanah seemed clueless concerning Hannah's grief as he thought his love for her was worth more than any child. This story showed how, despite Hannah knowing that she was the favored wife, she was greatly hurt by Elkanah's choice to have a second wife, particularly since this other wife was achieving what seemed to be withheld from her—a child.

Jacob

Jacob also had two wives, and there was friction between these two.[107] He was tricked into his first marriage by his father-in-law.[108] Nevertheless, he married his second wife, Rachel, soon after having Leah, his first wife, forced upon him.[109] These two women were sisters, and yet, this sharing of a husband proved to be a miserable existence. These early stories reflect the same words that we hear today from wives that share one husband.

Polygamy and Today's Church

To me, polygamy only accentuates present relationship and

sexual problems. The surveys and examples in this chapter serve to show how polygamy can dull the concept of love and the desire to be wanted, needed, and find contentment; each are strong components in relationships. Polygamy sounds good in theory, but marriage is a promise of love and commitment between a man and a woman and does not work when placed in a realm of theory. We may try to make it an occurrence that can work. It is fraught with difficulty, though, as we share one relationship with others, rather than connecting with one with whom we can share our lives. The wives' dissatisfaction reflects this importance. For a woman, polygamy asks that she accept a part of a man rather than have one man fully for herself. She can never really relax or feel secure in his love since she is in a constant competition with the other wives. For a man, a few wives may sound exciting, but the burden on him in every way is huge.

As seen in the Bible, polygamy was not a practice based on love but was a practice of convenience. It was also a way for women to find security. While a woman's value in biblical times was taken from her ability to have children, particularly sons, the main source of security came from her man. Women did not necessarily have the privilege of education or the rights of men.

The difficulty for the church is determining how to handle polygamous families in the congregation. In its strict practice, it is still rare, but it will happen. While polygamy is not seen often in Christian churches, President "Obama's nominee for the EEOC, a lesbian law-school professor named Chai R. Feldblum, signed a 2006 manifesto endorsing polygamous households."[110] Society has never stopped pushing the church to change. It demands we understand homosexuality—which we are striving to do—and now, in the same way, we must understand polygamy. To merely deal with those in this situation with criticism and negativity is to be ignorant and repelling.

Simply dissolving a polygamous family in the name of "marriage is for one man and one woman" will do nothing save damage the people we are trying to help. There are multiple people involved in these situations. While the husband may be asked to keep only one wife and her children, the remaining wives...

> and their children are left unprovided for, and may
> be without a home or any place to go. Through

> the rigid policy of requiring all such wives to be put away, the Church, acting in the name of Christ's holy law, has been responsible for causing a very considerable amount of injustice and distress to women whose only fault was to accept and follow the customs of their own people.[111]

Change will be slow when dealing with these families. That each gets the care needed is essential. A child torn from what he knows as family and security is life-altering; to tear a wife from her only security is frightening; thus God's love and grace mean that we take each step in wisdom and care. As God loved and graced David, Solomon, and Jacob, He still today loves and graces us in our mistakes as we pursue Him.

Chapter 6: Further Socio-Cultural Arguments

Now that we have a general understanding of some of the bigger theories, ideas, and arguments that society and various other cultures have propagated regarding sex, we can take a look at some of the more subtle lies that have wormed their way into everyday life. People are desperate for answers regarding what is right and wrong, and these minor arguments help to smooth over the concerns we feel when we choose the paths that fuel our desired solutions instead of the paths that lead to God's ways. God's Word remains constant; theories, psychology, psychiatry, and therapies, while helpful on many levels, are only excellent until outdone by the next one. Each of the following ideas is a temporal one that can shape our minds unless countered.

Virginity/Promise/Purity Rings

Religion is a part of society and can have its own theories and ideas regarding sex. These concepts, though taught as something good and pleasing to God, can be equally as damaging as what has been discussed in the previous chapters. One such idea is that of virginity or purity rings. I remember hearing of these a few years back, and I cringed. A virginity ring is worn mainly by young women, though young men can wear something similar such as a silver band or a chain necklace. These things signify a promise to remain a virgin until marriage. I have a deep admiration for any girl or guy who keeps to their standards to stay pure until marriage; however, I don't believe that virginity is something that one displays in such a way. Virginity is a decision on which one stands.

Advertising your virginity by wearing a piece of jewelry can set you up as a target. There are those who do such things. Their mission is to steal another's virginity, and it's a game. Purity jewelry would better serve as a testament to remaining pure through a trying relationship; however, these pieces are mostly worn by those who have probably never faced sexual temptation. It's as if we are sending a child to war with no preparation or protection. If a girl or boy chooses to wear these items, let them do it out of a mature understanding of their decision. Those who do not understand their choice in this matter usually find their purity jewelry lost somewhere in the bottom of their drawer or worse, discarded after a weak moment.

Modesty

Fashion is another key point where the subtle message of sexual freedom is portrayed. Models and celebrities alike wear clothes that are immodest as if it were a badge of honor. Every year it seems that the outfits get worse and worse; full legs exposed, waistlines dipping to show the top curve of the buttocks, and necklines plunging to the point that we wonder why the person was wearing a shirt in the first place. This lack of modesty has gotten so bad that in 2013, network lawyers had to set a dress code for celebrities attending a popular award show frequently watched by families.

Young adults model their apparel after their favorite celebrities. Girls especially feel the pressure to impress. If their favorite actress/performer wears short skirts, they wear short skirts. Tight tops give the illusion of curves that have yet to be developed, and items such as wonder bras make still-forming busts the center of attention. Such items invite unwanted attention for girls who are too young to understand it. Girls find that they feel cheap and dirty at the extra attention. They fidget and try to adjust the length of the short skirt or tug up the neckline of the low-cut top in an attempt to hide the exposed skin. While these girls thought that these supposedly fashionable clothes would answer their deep-set questions of worth, the truth of the matter is that their clothing now gives the appearance of lessened worth and value.

Modesty is the counterpoint of this issue. If a girl dresses her body well, she receives the respect and reassurance she was seeking. She is given the proper amount of attention from a more positive standpoint when she covers "the girls" and wears skirts of a proper length. Men actually prefer women who do not flaunt all they've got. They want something left to the imagination, as it were. It is quite the reversal, but modesty is actually much sexier than exposure.

Romance in Novels

Romance in novels is probably the loudest advocate of the subtle lies about sex. Romance in books promises undying love without commitment, passionate connection without work, and never-ending sex without realistic limitations. Books like the *Fifty Shades of Grey* series set people up for sexual and relational failure from the get go. *Fifty Shades of Grey* is a book about Anastasia Steele, a young woman described as "unworldly." That all changed when she first encounters the "driven and dazzling young entrepreneur Christian Grey."[112] The book itself states that this meeting "sparked a sensual affair that changed both of their lives irrevocably."[113] The book is filled with sexual scenes that are arousing, erotic, and completely unrealistic.

Fictional stories like this one seem so harmless, and yet they are damaging without understanding relationships. Dramatic portrayals of overemotional and borderline violent relationships can warp our views of not just sex but of normal relationships as well. Lonely women and men read these books and think that that is how relationships work. It sets them up to fail because they cannot find a partner like the demi-god lovers they find in their books. None can compete, thus the hope of a real, loving relationship is squashed due to imagined expectations that cannot be reached no matter how hard we pray. God made men as men and women as women. Romance in novels skews the truth and causes only more heartache. We can read books that contain romance, action, drama, etc., but we must also be conscious of what we allow to creep into our concepts of reality.

Living Together

We touched upon this topic a little bit in Chapter Three while discussing compatibility. The idea of living together is perpetuated all throughout the media. Couples meet, go on one or two dates, have sex, and then, if the relationship is still going well, they decide to move in together. It seems like such a natural course, and yet, it is not uncommon today to hear of the lament between a boyfriend and girlfriend that are living together. They are frustrated that their relationship is virtually sexless. They have become two people sharing an apartment. It is my belief that the two have left nothing to which to look forward. There is no mystery to this relationship. There is no shyness in discovering each other's body and each other's likes and dislikes. There is no embarrassment and giggles with whoops moments. Compatibility has little to do with whether the sex is good or not.

Self-Esteem

Society implies that those who are having rampant sex are people with unshakably high self-esteem and unending confidence. Having low self-esteem is probably the single most over-used answer for many problems today. Low self-esteem is used to excuse poor work performance, ethics, and decisions. We do so many things—like having sex—just so we can feel good about ourselves, and when that good feeling wears off, we do it all again in a vain attempt to reclaim it. We want to feel like we are worth something, but, as the Bible teaches, we cannot live our lives by how we feel.[114]

Paul C. Vitz is a Professor Emeritus of Psychology at New York University.[115] He informs us that self-esteem is a chosen response to situations rather than being an inner problem.[116] "Try to acquire self-esteem and you will fail—but do good to others and accomplish something for yourself, and you will have all the self-esteem you need."[117] We live in a world where people visit counselors hoping to find the secret to unending self-love; however, the answer is never found in spending hours talking about ourselves. The Bible does not talk much about self-love. In fact, verses like Mark 12:31 note how the Bible assumes that we already like ourselves to some degree and, therefore, do not need to focus on that.[118] The Bible teaches us to focus on loving God and loving others, and it is in them that we find the illusive feelings of self-love.[119] My solution may seem harsh, but it was a remedy that I've had to apply to my own life. Sex will not make us feel worthy; sex with a lot of people will not bolster our self-esteem; however, if we align ourselves with God, He will guide us into a powerful sense of worth securely built on His love and acceptance.[120]

Isolation of the Opposition

The power of peer pressure is surprising. A young girl or boy can easily cave with the simple lie of "everyone is doing it." The conscious use of the word "everyone" immediately excludes the target from the group. Humans were not meant to be alone,[121] thus if we desire to shut another down, we isolate them. Society has taken this concept to a new level by empowering the word "they."

I've become increasingly aware over the years of the misuse of the word "they." "They" have found a cure or "they" have found proof of this, that, or the other. As I've researched information regarding addiction and sexuality, I have found that there is often little truth to the "they" statements. A classic example is that "they" had found proof that homosexuals were born gay; that the homosexual lifestyle was a biological and natural thing. I was told for years that this was an indisputable fact. I always wondered who the "they" were that were announcing these new findings. It was frustrating because I didn't want to seem to be anti-something when there was supposedly proof, but the mystery behind the "they" made it difficult not to wonder.

Interestingly, the following came to light regarding the facts solidified by "they":

> Although in 1998 the American Psychological Association (APA) made claims of biological contributors to homosexuality, in 2008 they updated their claims. In their newer document the APA (2008) admits that researchers have not found a biological basis for homosexuality: There is no consensus among scientists about the exact reasons that an individual develops a heterosexual, bisexual, gay, or lesbian orientation. Although much research has examined the possible genetic, hormonal, developmental, social, and cultural influences on sexual orientation, no findings have emerged that permit scientists to conclude that sexual orientation is determined by any particular factor or factors. Many think that nature and nurture both play complex roles; most people

> experience little or no sense of choice about their sexual orientation.[122]

Scientists have openly disputed their own findings, and yet, the power of "they" remains. Recently, I heard of a college professor stating the exact opposite of the above quote. He still held true to the claims of "they" and what "they" had found regarding sexuality. It matters little that arguments of the world have been disproven; people will still fight passionately for what "they" have said, for "they" is the same as "everyone," and if you are not with "they" or "everyone" then you are alone.

All the Women who are Independent...

The women's rights movement did many great things for women; it also did some significant damage. Women, liberated from the real oppressive stereotypes of life, are now pushed to go a step further. They are told to be independent and free of the need of a man to the point that it can be considered sexist for a father to give his daughter away in marriage. Girls are encouraged to be self-reliant and to stand up for themselves.

The call for freedom has actually backfired. Mary Pipher, an American clinical psychologist and feminist, notes, "Girls today are much more oppressed. They are coming of age in a more dangerous, sexualized and media-saturated culture."[123] She further says that among her patients, the only clients not struggling with issues such as self-mutilation and eating disorders are those who are not sexually active and often come from strict families with paternalistic fathers.[124] Pipher's studies show how there is a significant difference between independence and freedom. We may think that we are acquiring independence; however, are we free when our only commitment is to ourselves? We live in a world that involves others, and, in many obvious ways, we must depend on others for our survival. So what is so wrong with wanting to belong to someone? There is more freedom in committing than there will ever be in independence.

The Myth of Never Changing

The phrase, "You are who you are and that will never change" is probably one of the most depressing things I have ever heard. It locks us into a choiceless existence. The stereotype against change is seen rampantly throughout sitcoms. Such shows portray a group of people who live within their stereotype without changing throughout the course of the show's run on television. Some sitcoms run for ten years, and the characters never change. It is a subtle message, but it is there. If they cannot change, what hope do we have?

The above question is one that plagues a specific group of humans who have been under the microscope for decades. Like abortion, this group is surrounded with two very heated sides to an argument centered on change. Though humans were born with a free will, society is very certain that these specific people cannot change. This group is the homosexuals. Interestingly, the California State Government tried and failed to pass a new law in January 2013 that "bans non-scientific 'therapies' that have driven young people to depression and suicide"[125] and deny therapists the chance to counsel change for a homosexual under the age of eighteen. This law, had it passed, would have been a bizarre decision as it denies the one seeking counsel a choice. It is also odd since the law is based off a premise that change for the homosexual is not scientifically proven, yet homosexuality itself is still scientifically unproven. While we seem to have no problem in believing failed scientific theories, we like to emphatically deny the possibility of change for those things we wish to be true. Of homosexuality, NARTH reports:

> The myth that people cannot change is a myth for the following reasons:
>
> 1) It only takes one person having changed to nullify the myth that change is not possible.
> 2) There are thousands of people who claim various degrees of change in behavior, lifestyle, attractions, or all of the above.
> 3) Change is documented in the professional literature spanning at least the past one hundred years. A review of the literature demonstrating

> that change is possible is published in a peer-reviewed journal, *Journal of Human Sexuality*. This particular volume contains hundreds of references (NARTH, 2009).[126]

Change, like saying "no," is a lost power among humans. In Matthew, Jesus said that with God, nothing is impossible.[127] Whether it is changing our character or changing our orientation, God empowers us to decide our future and carve our paths.

The Dangers of Unproven "Truths"

Science, therapeutic theories, and psychology are wonderful and fascinating, but, all too often, we find that their theories fail. For example, Sigmund Freud, the well-known Austrian neurologist and founding father of psychoanalysis, created a theory on the development of a child and childrearing that was esteemed and practiced in its day with questionable results. Another example is when, in the 1950's and 1960's, it was theorized and accepted that thalidomide was safe to use for morning sickness. It was an anti-nausea drug and sedative. Women took it to find relief, but it soon proved to only cause more heartache as those who used the pill gave birth to babies with a wide range of birth defects. The pill was pulled from the shelves to prevent further damage.

Sex-change surgery became the go-to answer for asexuals, intersexuals, and hermaphrodites. The results, however, were disastrous. There are many cases of those damaged from sex-change surgery, but perhaps the most famous case is that of David Reimer. Born an identical twin, his circumcision resulted in the loss of his penis. A famous psychologist, sexologist, and author, Doctor John Money, determined that he would be better off changed into a girl. Years were spent in feminizing this little boy—from his behavioral habits to his appearance. They even performed a full castration. Session after session was spent attempting to persuade him to have a vagina surgically created. Dr. Money clung to his theory that genitalia and nurture made you male or female. He held to this fact as truth even though the lives of those who had undergone sex changes gave a different story.

In his teens, David, born Bruce until his conformation to a girl (which is when he became Brenda), was told of his botched circumcision, and he decided to be who he had always suspected himself to be: a male. Of postoperative and preoperative transsexuals treated at John Hopkins, John Colapinto notes that "none showed any measurable improvement in their lives." He concluded that "sex reassignment surgery confers no objective advantage in terms of social rehabilitation."[128] Most of the media and writings during the time of David's case carried positive reports concerning sex-change theory. Doctor Money himself presented David's case as highly successful. Money did not report the fact that David reverted back to being male; rather, he presented it as a case with which he lost contact with the subject. David Reimer committed suicide in 2004.

All of these more subtle approaches to sexual indoctrination are not in any way a call to hide from society. Hiding from society is, in some regards, the cause of many of the issues we struggle with today; however, it is important to turn and face the truth of what is going on in the world around us. Sex is everywhere. That is understood. Telling youth to "just say no" and to "not have sex or else" has long proven futile; however, since we now have a more solid understanding of society's opinions, we can move forward in the quest to dismantle the lies and embrace the truth, and the best place to find truth is in the one place where it has endured throughout the ages—the Bible.

Chapter 7: Sex in the Bible

Many people cannot fathom the words sex, God, and the Bible in the same sentence. For some Christians, it is wrong to utter the word sex or anything of this nature, particularly in church. On the other hand, today's society thinks that Scripture is irrelevant. If anything, the Bible is viewed as a book that lists all the things we are not allowed to do. The Bible would, then, in that mindset, tell us not to be having sex because sex is bad! That is not the case. The Bible is full of sex. From Genesis to Revelation, there is every kind of sex; the good, the bad, and the very ugly.

People do not really want to look into what the Bible has to say about sex. Our natural reaction is to fight against boundaries, and the Bible is the place where we see the boundaries God commissioned for our lives—boundaries for "good and not for disaster."[129] Sex is a particularly touchy subject biblically because it has become the height of societal happiness, and when that happiness is called into question, our quest for truth and wisdom becomes skewed. We want to make the Bible fit our lifestyles so that we will not have to question, submit, or change; however, "Everything in the Bible lines up. The context of all Scripture is to put God first in your life,"[130] and if we "live a life that allows God to complete His will in us, then He will provide all the things we need, both the physical and the spiritual."[131]

God promises that joy in Him will be our strength[132] and that if we delight ourselves in Him, He will give us the desires of our hearts.[133] God is and always will be our ultimate source of happiness. He knows how awesome sex is; He created it for us! "Sex. God. They're connected. And they can't be separated. Where the one is, you will always find the other."[134] He wants us to enjoy sex, but in order to enjoy sex, we need to know the truth about it and God's intention for it. There is a lot to cover regarding the Bible and sex, and the best place to start is with a brief look at some of the instances where sex is the focal point in the Bible.

Old Testament Sex

The Bible contains so much that is relevant to all mankind regardless of era. God shows in His Word how sexuality is woven into people's lives. He does not skimp on the truth. The Bible has many examples of sexual activity as a result of man's decisions. In reading just the book of Genesis, we can see that there are no new sexual issues. It was all there at the beginning, and God has a lot to say on the matter.

The servants of God who lived during the Old Testament era were no strangers to sex and sexual scandal. Though Israel lived set apart from other cultures, they were still surrounded and influenced by those around them. Many cultures in the Old Testament had sexuality and temple prostitution as integral components of their spirituality and religious ceremonies. God gave Israel a set of laws that were meant to help them live differently from the cultures around them, but that did not stop the scandals from happening, and God did not neglect to mention some of the worst in His book.

Genesis

From the very beginning, sex is blatantly on the scene of human interaction as a great point of motivation. When Adam saw Eve, he called her "bone of my bones and flesh of my flesh; she shall be called 'woman,' for she was taken out of man."[135] Adam obviously liked what he saw and he was not just looking at her eyes. They were both unclothed. In Genesis 2:24, it is written, "For this reason a man shall leave his father and his mother, and be joined to his wife; and they shall become one flesh."[136] This one flesh includes the intimacy of the sexual relationship. In Genesis 2:25, the writer further notes that Adam and Eve were naked with each other but felt no shame.[137] Jump ahead a few chapters and a few hundred years, and we find in Genesis 16:4, depending on the translation, that Abram slept with or had sexual relations with Hagar. Nothing is left to interpretation here; it blatantly tells us that the two had sex.

Genesis 38 contains probably one of the most scandalous sexual stories in the Bible. Judah's son, Onan, refused to "have a child who would not be his own heir" with his brother's widow,

Tamar, as was custom in those times, thus, whenever he had intercourse with Tamar, he would spill his seed on the ground instead of inside of her.[138] This act is called coitus interruptus, and it is something that God did not look too kindly upon—perhaps for the reason that is was the early days of mankind and the earth needed to be populated. Onan died because of his actions. This event drove Tamar to, some years later, seduce her father-in-law, Judah, by dressing up as a prostitute and waiting for him to travel past. He liked what he saw, slept with her, and got her pregnant.[139] Incest is in the Bible, and we are still in the first book!

Leviticus

The book of Leviticus contains several rules and regulations regarding sex. These rules and regulations are all important; God had them included in His Word for a reason; however, one must use discretion when reading Leviticus. The Bible remains the infallible Word of God and is and always will be relevant to all eras. Leviticus is the representation of the Old Law—the strict lifestyle God put into place in order to set His people apart from the rest. Jesus fulfilled the Laws when He came and died on the cross.[140] His sacrifice brought freedom from the strict, impossible rules of the Old Testament, but that does not mean we disregard these laws completely. We can always learn from the past. In saying that, there are some more obvious parts of Leviticus that we can read with a grain of salt. For example, in Leviticus 15:19, Scripture refers to the necessity that a man and woman refrain from sexual intercourse when a woman is menstruating as she was considered unclean at this time of month. This is not necessarily a deal-breaker with God now-a-days. We should read the rules of Leviticus with an open heart and an ear tuned in to what God is saying. Let Him be your teacher.

Joshua and Judges

The book of Joshua contains the remarkable story of Rahab. Rahab was probably a prostitute in the city of Jericho. When the people of Israel were on her borders, she risked it all to help the Israeli spies hide from the authorities. She and her family were spared the impending slaughter and were welcomed into the Israeli population. Rahab is mentioned in the New Testament in the lineage of Jesus and in Hebrews, where she is described by the writer as a woman of faith.[141] These two honors shock most people. Why would God do such things for a supposed prostitute? God is not giving people permission to live Rahab's lifestyle, but we see that God examines the heart and can redeem anyone from any situation.

In the book of Judges, we read of the lusty affair between Samson and Delilah. This story contains nothing regarding commitment or relationship building. All that is there is physical attraction and sex. Samson gives in to his lusts, and he pays a heavy price for his actions.

King David

King David, as discussed, was a polygamist who repeatedly married to gain favor with neighboring kingdoms. He was also an admirer of female beauty. When he first saw Bathsheba, "he noticed a woman of unusual beauty taking a bath."[142] It was then that he started down a path that made him an adulterer, and then a murderer in an attempt to cover his sin of adultery.

David's son, Amnon, raped his half-sister Tamar in 2 Samuel 13. This does not seem too surprising considering David's actions toward Bathsheba and her husband, Uriah. Amnon despised Tamar after this event and wanted nothing to do with her despite her pleas for help. This is one ramification of David's compromised standards regarding marriage and family.

The Song of Solomon

The Song of Solomon is falsely believed to be the sole sexual book of the Bible. It is, indeed, filled with descriptive words that describe the body parts beyond regular terminology. The Song of Solomon was a book highly esteemed in its time. The poetry of this book is filled with the love and desire between a man and a woman using middle-eastern language and imagery. The king tells his bride that "your two breasts are like two fawns, like twin fawns of a gazelle."[143] The king is comparing her breasts to the softness of two fawns and so he states that he desires to caress her soft breasts.[144] In verse 2:17, Solomon talks of the "mountains of separation" which is a reference to the woman's cleavage. In verse 2:6, we read, "Oh that his left hand were under my head and his right hand embraced me" which is a description of the man and woman lying with each other.

The pleasures as well as difficulties of married love are recorded in this book. Both the king and queen are highly praiseworthy of each other. They describe the uniqueness of their love in passages such as Song of Solomon 2:2–3. There is no trace of the negative comparisons to other sexual experiences that we often hear of today. On several occasions, Solomon repeats the words "Don't awaken love early." This is read in Song of Solomon 2:7 and repeated throughout the song. He states that sexual love is not a casual act. Chapter 4 contains the private but tender lines between a couple built over years where tenderness has bred trust and no inhibition. Sex is sacred, involves respect for another, and is a secret between two people.

Final Words of Old

Proverbs is a book full of wisdom and instruction for life. It includes words of wisdom for marriage and sexual practices. In Proverbs 5:18, one reads, "May your fountain be blessed, and may you rejoice in the wife of your youth." This is a description of conjugal love. It advocates the long-term practice of intimacy with one spouse. Solomon further advises that men avoid the adulterous or immoral woman but continue to find satisfaction in their wife found in their youth.[145]

The New Covenant's Views of Sex

The New Testament contains many books to various churches. Through writers such as Paul, God continues to reveal His love for marriage and sex as a part of marriage. The early church had much to learn regarding proper sexual interaction. Many of the new believers were from cultures where sex was rampant, thus most books of the New Testament have a lot to say about sexual misconduct and boundaries for sexual relationships.

Jesus had no qualms with sex or with those who had sinned sexually. In the book of John, chapter 4, there is a story about Jesus talking openly with a Samaritan woman who had had several husbands and was living with a man to whom she was not married. Again, in John 8, Jesus is making his opinions of sexual sin known when He offers forgiveness to an adulterous woman and informs the crowd to not judge her. The New Testament writers used the anticipation of a bride and groom to express the love Jesus has for His Church; the term is "the Bride of Christ" and is unique to the New Testament.

In 1 Corinthians 6, Paul discusses sexual sin, and in Ephesians 5, Paul provides wisdom for husbands and wives as he does also in Colossians 3. In 1 Timothy 5, Paul informs widows on living a godly life. Peter instructs husbands and wives on holiness in 1 Peter 3. Much of the wisdom of these two apostles will be discussed in the latter chapters of this book, but I would also encourage you to explore the Scriptures referenced throughout this chapter and in the rest of *God Sex*. God challenges us to test Him.[146] Take a look at what the Bible has to say as you continue to read this book.

The examples in this chapter are just the tip of the sexual iceberg. God did not limit His instructions on sex to just the moments where His people happened to be having it. His Word goes much deeper and gives greater insight into all aspects of sex, for God knows the far-reaching effects sex can have. When staying within God's framework, sex has so many wonderful rewards; however, when sex is done outside God's original plan, the damage caused is great. We have discussed some of the consequences. Now, we are going to explore just how dark inappropriate sex can become.

Part Two: Inappropriate Sexual Behavior

The Bible is specific on certain things; there are others that God leaves for us to discover; and still, buried deep in His Word, are truths that speak into multiple situations. Sexual misconduct falls under all three. "In the New Testament, the Greek word porneia (from which we get the word pornography) is translated into English as 'sexual immorality' and encompasses all sorts of sexual sin."[147] Paul speaks in detail regarding the dangers of sexual sin. He pastored many converts from the Greco-Roman culture and had to teach them how to live a sexually redeemed life. The Old Testament, as displayed in the last section, has detailed accounts of nearly every kind of sexual immorality. Amidst the detailed accounts are Scriptures that, though they do not specifically use the word "porneia," can be applied to the situation.

This next section begins the journey into what can happen when we stray from the boundaries God placed upon sex. God rarely places limitations on our lives, but when He does, it is meant to "protect your life, to enhance your life, and to bless your life."[148] The situations and stories shared in these next few chapters relate the pain caused when we disregard God's precautions for the supposed freedom society promises us should we indulge. In this section, we will be discussing some of the sexual sins that are on the edge of being acceptable. We will see what society has claimed are the facts regarding these issues and will take a deeper look at what the Bible has to say in response. Be warned. It is about to get real!

Chapter 8: Promiscuity

A Quest for Love

It was a quest for love. I lived on the streets, did not know my father, and had a poor role model in my mother. Wherever or whatever it took in my quest for love, I would do it. I was date raped and lost my virginity at twelve; though it took a long time for me to realize that that was what had occurred. Maybe it was my fault? I kept blaming myself.

I was sodomized around this same time. At thirteen, I started sleeping around, but it wasn't about achieving an orgasm. It was about catching the guy. I'd do it in parking lots and sometimes would have sex with three different guys in one night. By the age of sixteen, I was doing threesomes.

My promiscuity was an attempt to change a core issue, that of abandonment. I wanted acceptance, approval, and I wanted to fit in. I felt unwanted and so sought to fill this void with sex. It was a cycle of getting the catch so I could feel wanted, but then abandoning him before he could abandon me. I was afraid to have relationships and to open myself to someone. If I did get close to another, he might leave. Therefore, my answer was to sleep with guys and get rid of them before they left. It did not work.

Today: I have watched this lady overcome incredible obstacles—a past of abandonment and abuse. Several years ago, she came to one of our churches and asked Christ into her life. Bit by bit she is overcoming her issues of abandonment and is making drastic changes in her life. – JS

Promiscuity

Like most young girls, I often thought how my life would be when I grew up. Would I get married, have children, live in a big house, travel? I especially wanted boys to like me. Not having a lot of balance in my life, I wanted to have a boyfriend and fall in love. At the age of 16, I thought I was in love and became pregnant. I didn't consider myself grown up at all, and I was scared to have a child and what that would do to my life at the time. My boyfriend and I decided to get married much to the concern of both our parents, but we were in love after all, so what could go wrong? The marriage lasted three years.

During those three years, we pretty much stopped having sex on any regular basis. I felt like it was all my fault; I wasn't pretty enough or sexy enough or, heaven forbid, I was doing it all wrong! Everything I tried failed. I thought love and sex should go hand in hand. Not experiencing sex was like I was not loved. In a few desperate measures, I turned to pornography to either get some tips or get a reaction out of my husband, but that did not work and only added to the shame and rejection I felt.

On one occasion, I asked a close male friend of mine if he would have sex with me because I was certain I was doing something wrong. After a long discussion about what in the world I was thinking, he finally agreed, just once. That sexual encounter left me feeling worse, even though he said there was nothing wrong with me. I still wanted to work on our marriage, but, with the confusion I felt, I didn't see any way to make it work, and I couldn't see myself living like this for the rest of my life. We divorced, and my life spiraled out of control.

On the outside, it looked like I was doing okay, but I had no direction. When I moved back home to live with my parents, it was so I could save money and go back to trade school. Taking control of my life is what I thought and with that thought came taking control of men. I was not going to get hurt again, so I would start a relationship and have sex if I liked him enough. Feeling like I was in control, if the relationship got too personal and close, I would end it and start again with someone new. I made excuses—convincing myself it would never work, I didn't want to be tied down, etc.

This became a habit for me, even though I didn't consider myself a loose woman. I had a lot of sexual partners. One time I even had a one-night stand, just to see what that would be like; no commitment, just sex. It seemed exciting at the moment, but it was not at all like I had envisioned. I felt more empty, and it brought a whole different level of shame into my life. I tried to convince myself that I was just doing what everyone else had done and I was still a good girl. A few more years went by, more men, and the same cycle. I could truly love 'em and leave 'em. When I had my salvation experience, it was so overwhelming with God's love I knew I didn't want to ever forget what that was like. I had little knowledge of the Bible at that time. All I knew is that something had happened to me and Jesus was really real. I now wanted to change but had no idea how to do it. I still really liked sex, but as I read my Bible more, I realized it had a place, and that was in a committed relationship of marriage. The desire was still strong and I did have sex one more time after Jesus came into my life, but it ended there. I didn't want to mess up my relationship with God, so when I was tempted I just kept saying, "Lord help me," and He gave me strength for that moment. The more I studied and prayed, the stronger I got in my commitment. I opened up my life to my other Christian friends and found a lot of strength in fighting temptation when I had others praying for me and with me. Two and a half years went by and I kept my commitment to God to not have sex before I was married. It was one of the best things I have done. He makes all things New!

Today: This is one of my dearest friends. She is one of those essential people whom every church needs. She loves others as few do. When she tells her story, it's astounding! She is such a different person today! –JS

We have established in the early chapters that many think that sex outside of marriage is good. When this trend is adopted as a lifestyle, it becomes something more complicated. Promiscuity is a term applied to taking "sexual freedom" beyond simply giving in to the chemistry of a pre-established relationship. A person who is promiscuous may have sex just to have sex. Questions like, "Does there need to be commitment in the relationship or is being a friend with benefits okay?" or "Where does one draw a line regarding what is and is not okay in a premarital sexual relationship?" are ignored and replaced by questions like "Your place or mine?" Ignored are the physical diseases that have been known to accompany multiple sexual partners; ignored are the cries of those who know that they have given away something personal of themselves that can never be returned. And what of the comparisons made of encounters present and past? Are we all right with the most intimate parts of our lives being on display to numerous people whom we may not know well? Are we okay with these same people discussing the intimate parts of our bodies with others who may be little more than strangers to us?

Paul, the man believed to have written a large percent of the New Testament, wrote probably the best argument against promiscuity there is. He wrote for the benefit of Christian converts who had grown up in the sexually open Roman Empire. Many of these converts may have engaged in the religious sexual practices accepted by this culture. Paul brought a revolutionary standard of celibacy to a predominantly sexual world and revealed to the believers God's true intentions for sex.[149] 1 Corinthians 6 provides key information regarding human sexuality. Paul writes:

> God honored the Master's body by raising it from the grave. He'll treat yours with the same resurrection power. Until that time, remember that your bodies are created with the same dignity as the Master's body. You wouldn't take the Master's body off to a whorehouse, would you? I should hope not.[150]

These two verses, verses 14 and 15, state "that our bodies are actually parts of Christ."[151] Paul had to be very straightforward with the believers regarding their bodies and sex. When they accepted Jesus into their lives, they became connected to Him. Christians are referred to as "the Body of Christ" throughout the New Testament.[152] Paul built on that imagery to convey the truth about sex.

> There's more to sex than mere skin on skin. Sex is as much spiritual mystery as physical fact. As written in Scripture, "The two become one." Since we want to become spiritually one with the Master, we must not pursue the kind of sex that avoids commitment and intimacy, leaving us more lonely than ever—the kind of sex that can never "become one." There is a sense in which sexual sins are different from all others. In sexual sin we violate the sacredness of our own bodies, these bodies that were made for God-given and God-modeled love, for "becoming one" with another. Or didn't you realize that your body is a sacred place, the place of the Holy Spirit? Don't you see that you can't live however you please, squandering what God paid such a high price for? The physical part of you is not some piece of property belonging to the spiritual part of you.

> God owns the whole works. So let people see
> God in and through your body.[153]

Paul's revelation about sex is as true now as it was then. "Sex between two people is a joining of more than the flesh. It is a spiritual union."[154] This union is meant to be sacred, and yet, society has cheapened it by making it openly available. Bell writes, "When it's just sex, that's all it is. It leaves the person deeply unconnected. You can be having sex with many, and yet you're alone. And the more sex you have, the more alone you are."[155]

Promiscuity in Men and Women

Society already puts pressure on people to be sexually active. Promiscuity is similar to addiction. We search for that sense of feeling good and crave to be loved and accepted. It is built into our very being to want to be loved, and that desire can be enhanced in those who had minimal parenting. Young girls especially will fall prey to the thought that being desired sexually is the same as being loved, because someone wants and desires them. The chase and perhaps the sexual climax act as highs. The low emotions occur when the sex is done and they face the consequence of the lonely feelings.

The pressure of promiscuity falls heavily on men. It is a sort of badge of honor, men are told, to have multiple "conquests" in their sexual history. Multiple sex partners are supposed to be the mark of a true man; however, this sense of manhood is shallow and false. Men who live a promiscuous life pretend to be real men without having to commit to any one relationship. Some men take great pride in their sexual conquests when, in fact, they are running from commitment to one woman. They fear that they don't have what it takes to lay down their life for another.

Women, subscribing to society's code of independence, are pressured to be promiscuous in order to be viewed as normal. There are those who feel that if they are not having sex, then they must be ugly, boring, or not normal. "I sleep with these men to prove I'm not ugly, I'm normal, I'm 'mature,' and I have this sex life so people won't, you know, make fun of me or think there's something wrong with me…"[156] Women may go from partner to partner in order to try to prove to themselves or others that their "don't need a man" policy is actually satisfying, but that sense of false freedom only deepens the loneliness. In private conversations that I've had with women, many reveal that they wished that they had kept their bodies for their husbands. The many sexual experiences have left them feeling less of a person. One woman said regarding her previous partners, "Once you meet someone you really love, the other ones don't mean a thing, and then you're sort of disgusted by them."[157]

Men have no real sense of direction when women act out of their supposed independence. Rousseau says that "each sex needs the other, and when women pretend to be men, men tend to need them less."[158] There is a disconnect between the sexes caused by this combination of male showmanship and female freedom that makes both rethink the need for commitment. Why would a man commit to a woman if she does not need him? This is not to say that a woman who achieves much is wrong; however, the beauty of interdependence is that much more can be achieved than can be achieved through independence. On the same note, why would a woman commit to a man who will not step up and be the man her heart truly needs? Men can acknowledge the strength of women without forfeiting the position of leader in the relationship.

When we engage in a promiscuous lifestyle, we all face the facts that there is little connection with this other person with whom we have had sex, and that we have given ourselves in a way that cannot be undone. Shalit quotes eighteenth century German Philosopher Immanuel Kant when she notes, "Sexual love makes of the loved person an object of appetite; as soon as one has the person and the appetite has been stilled, the person is cast aside as one casts away a lemon which has been sucked dry."[159] Shalit goes on to say, "The young woman, instead of being treated as an end in herself, is treated as an object. Instead of telling our girls that they are right to want to wait for love, we tell them that they are wrong."[160]

The Effects of Disconnect

The sense of disconnect formed due to skewed views of gender identity has transitioned into our communication methods. Our world is becoming dominated by shallow relationships. Twitter, texting, instagram, and facebook, among other things, allow easy connection, but there is little depth in these connections. Texting and facebook are a convenient and effective means of communication; however, they demand little from us. It's easy to write "love you," "praying for you," or "let me know if I can help." More than eighty percent of teens over the age of seventeen own a cell phone, and sixty percent of twelve-year-olds own a cell phone. It is far too easy to make friends and create superficial relationships in this manner and even easier to take those relationships too far.

Sexting

There is a trend that needs the attention and care of parents and guardians. It is called "sexting." Sexting "is the creation, sharing, and forwarding of sexually suggestive nude or semi-nude images (Pew Research Forum, 2010)."[161] Recent studies have revealed that one in ten young adults "between the ages of 14 and 24 has shared naked images of themselves with someone else; up to 30 percent have received such pictures on their cell phones."[162]

The nude images are used for a variety of reasons. One reason is that the sender hopes to jump-start a relationship with the receiver. Sexting is also used as an exchange between intimate partners and is meant to be private. Sadly, these private exchanges are too often shared with others outside of the relationship. There is increasing concern with the use of sexting, and it can be regarded as pornography with offenders facing charges.

Sexting and promiscuity go against our deeper needs and desires. "Without love, sex taken by itself—is a degradation of human nature."[163] There is a need in each of us to develop relationships where we truly know the other person and they know us. Such a relationship will inspire us to make sacrifices for the other. Rather than exchanging random terms of endearment, these relationships are built upon time spent in getting to know the other, and, therefore, a decision can be made as to whether the relationship could result in a lasting commitment. These types of relationships are not built through promiscuity.

Promiscuity, Biblical Cultures, and Christianity

Sex before marriage is not God's intention for us. Paul made that clear in 1 Corinthians. He needed to address the issue of promiscuity because the same thoughts that we have now that lead us away from God's boundaries were also in the biblical cultures. Some cultures in the times of biblical writings did not expect men to remain sexually pure before marriage, nor after marriage were they expected to have intercourse with one woman only. Rahab, as described in the Book of Joshua, may have worked as a prostitute. Her culture probably thought prostitution was a normal occupation. Promiscuity was likely normal for the men of her city.

Christian men and women are now known for saying that sex is natural and so it's fine that they fulfill this appetite before marriage. Funnily enough though, many young people with whom I have spoken say that they regret this choice of sex before marriage. For example, one young girl moved away from home and chose to live in her new city with her childhood boyfriend. After all, this was a cheaper option, and they supposedly loved each other. As part of a band, he was not allowed to reveal that he had a girlfriend. He didn't want to appear unavailable to his admirers. Now, several years later, she is still living with him (his name is on the lease); he is often on the road; and there is little love in the relationship. This beautiful young woman, who believes in God and yet thought that Scripture was outdated, now regrets her initial decision.

Disappointment hit me like a ton of bricks one day when I read the following tweet by a young person: "Broken-hearted by my break-up. Better to settle any day for one-night stands." This young man exposed his heart on the Internet, but tried to sound so tough by his second declaration. He attempted to make the situation seem such a nonissue, but his words betrayed him. This young man made his sexual relationship sound as if he were going to the supermarket. He cried out for acknowledgement and recognition. Recognition in its greatest form comes out of knowing who God is, and then we know who we are. When we know who we are, we are less afraid of being hurt, and we are unafraid of commitment.

The Strength of Celibacy

It is considered today virtually impossible, and some would say wrong, for one to remain celibate outside of marriage. This world tries to make out that everybody is having sex, so if you aren't, you are the strange one; that abstaining from sex until marriage is "old fashioned" and not relevant to this generation. Believe it or not, though, a life with no sexual intercourse does not kill a person, does not make them ill, nor does it mean that they will have a non-fulfilling life. Jesus managed to live a sexually pure life for thirty-three years as a human in a very lustful culture. Do not discount this fact. He is the Son of God, but He also was tempted in every way we are today.[164]

I love the fact that I know many great single people, both young and old, that live their lives with no sexual involvement. They maintain close friendships because they provide accountability and encouragement to do life well. They live in a world that tries to push on them that casual sex and promiscuity is fun and harmless. They will often be criticized and teased for choosing to live this way; however, the people who tease them in public will often, in private conversation, confess to the same people they were criticizing that they approve, admire, and even envy their lifestyle. They may even question the single person as to how to live such a lifestyle. It's funny that what many verbally criticize publicly is their personal cry internally.

That sex is natural is not an adequate answer for promiscuity. We are hungry for food, but good health dictates that we eat healthy meals and portions of food. The body also needs physical activity and so we become responsible with its care. In the same sense, the mind is affected by what it sees and hears. We need to understand that there is a benefit in the monitoring of our natural desires. As Paul noted in 1 Corinthians 6:19–20, our bodies are "temples of the Holy Spirit;"[165] we are beings in which God resides. Paul attempts to elevate human thinking and open men's eyes to a higher view of what it is to be human.[166] Romans 12:1 states that our bodies are "living sacrifices" that are "holy and pleasing to God."[167] When we view ourselves in that manner, the truth about promiscuity and the warning against it become rather clear. Our bodies were made for more than just sex; sex was made for more than just "doing it." Multiple partners invite heartache, mistrust, and painful separation. The need to find worth in sex diminishes when we find our worth in Christ and realize we are more than just a body of natural urges.

Chapter 9: Pornography

Overcoming Pornography

If someone were to ask me how many sexual partners I have had, I could honestly say over one hundred. And yet, I am still a virgin. Jesus said that looking at someone with lust in your heart is the same as having sex with them, so I guess that applies to me. I was in seventh grade when I started reading porn. Yeah, reading it. It was easy to justify even at so young an age because porn meant looking at pictures of naked women and/or watching them have sex with people. I was simply reading stories that happened to have graphic sex in them. I don't remember how old I was or even what the exact date was, but I remember my first porn. I remember how it made me feel. I remember why I read it. I guess the reason is not so important now, but I want to share it so that others can understand how and why this happened, and that those who are going through what I did know that someone in this world understands.

First off, I acknowledge that my vice was mine. I chose it. Was I forced into it or coerced? Of course not! No one forced me to click the link that said "Rated NC-17." I was a social outcast with no friends, living in a small world filled with petty people who saw me as a very easy target. Not that I blame them. I was rather entertaining when made angry. I digress. I was the youngest in a poor family and was easily shuffled to the end of the line and forgotten. So, to say that I was lonely was an understatement. I was certain that my life meant nothing and was worth nothing. I found solace from the world on the Internet. That was where I met a young man in college whose life was about as bad if not worse than mine. He told me that reading sexual stories (they were called "lemons") was perfectly alright. That was all I needed to pull back the veil of mystery, so to speak. I was curious about "lemons." I wondered just how bad they could be. He said they were okay, so they must be okay. I pulled up my first porn only moments after that conversation.

I was a porn addict for six years or so. The days blurred together. Life for me sucked; porn made me feel better. And when it stopped making me feel better, I looked for a higher grade. Nothing was sacred. I read it all—heterosexual, homosexual, lesbian, incest, twincest, bestiality, masturbation, three-somes, four-somes, toys, bondage, rape, and even child porn. It didn't matter because the stories made it all so beautiful, and I wanted it so so badly! It was not strange or disturbing that I was reading about two prepubescent boys discovering "a new game" to play with each other or that a teenage girl desired her werewolf lover even in his wolf form. It was romantic. It was true love. It was my entire world.

When I was not reading porn, I was thinking about it. I lived in my head, lost in my fantasies, and, as a result, lost track of the world. I don't remember my childhood. I don't remember high school. I remember sitting in class daydreaming about sex and wondering when I could get home to read more "lemons." Every night, I imagined myself wrapped in the arms of my quintessential lover, feeling all the wondrous sexual things the stories I read promised me I would feel once I found "the One." The love and acceptance I felt in my head was so much better than the hate and rejection I lived with in my world, and the lessons I learned in the stories I read became the truths I applied to my life. If guys were not looking at me, it was because I was not sexy—aka: thin, tall, blonde, long-legged, and physically fit. If no guy chose me before high school was over then I was unfit as a woman. Ergo, the obvious conclusion must be that I would have been better off as a man. I certainly related to and found a stronger connection with the wounded male souls seeking the redemptive touch of their perfect sexual equal. That or I was meant to be a lesbian instead, because I certainly was not succeeding as a heterosexual female.

I reached my breaking point in my sophomore year in college. I had always known that what I was reading was wrong. The conviction was like a dull echo in my soul. Every time I opened a new porn or read an old favorite, I heard the whisper in my heart to stop. That voice got quieter and came at fewer intervals the longer I reveled, and as it grew more distant, the lessons of my upbringing screamed louder. You see, here is the kicker: I was a Christian. Born and raised; saved at a young age and constantly surrounded by church. I went to a private Christian School and transitioned to a private Methodist college. God was central in my world, but He was not central in my life. My family and I were never part of a healthy church; though the churches we attended, we attended with devout loyalty. So, I knew I was sinning, and I knew the voice urging me to stop was God, and, above all, I knew that if He was stopping His warning then I was very, very far from Him. I tried several times to leave my addiction at His altar, but, as I said, the churches were not healthy, and our relationship—His and mine—was not the best. I feared more than loved Him, and trusting Him was never an option.

But His hand never left me. While in college, He led me to a girlfriend who brought me to my first Spirit-filled church service. That night, I had my first real altar experience and met God face to face. I cried as His grace poured out over my broken soul. I knew that this was it. This was the end. I either give Him the porn and all it had done to me or I die in it. There was no other option. That night, after we returned to the dorms, I removed from my computer my personal collection of pictures and stories; I got rid of my books and comics that contained graphic sex; and I deleted all my bookmarked websites.

I would love to say that after that night, I never read porn again, and I never spent the nights dreaming about sex. I would also like to say I can fly. That does not make either true. That night marked the first of a very long journey that, seven years later, I am still walking out. The damages done by something as innocent as a story echoed in my life. I had to face relationship issues, sexual-identity issues, gender-identity issues, and even the frightening battle of untangling myself from an unhealthy emotional attachment to my sister (my best and only friend) that had turned into an unnatural sexual attraction. This all happened after I laid my addiction at the altar. I say these things simply to make a point: the journey was hard...but I will never say that I regret it; because, through all the pain, shame, and tears, there was God.

His grace met me at every turn—whenever I gave in to the loneliness and read a new story or glanced too long at a sensual image or willingly gave myself to a sexual fantasy. He was there when I cried over my sexual confusion or wondered if my relationship with my sister would ever be redeemed. He gave me the courage to open up to a pastor and even more courage to go see a counselor. He surrounded me with fantastic Christian female friends who taught me what it meant to be a real woman who lived in a real world. He led me, step by baby step, out of my head and into real life. He restored my relationship with my sister who remains my best friend to this day, and He placed a promise in my heart that, when the day comes and I make my vows before Him to love and devote my life to the man He will bring to me, that my past will not ruin the promise of a fulfilling sexual future with that man.

There are days I wish I had never read porn. There are other days that I am grateful that I did. That decision brought me closer to God than I ever thought possible. I experienced firsthand His redemptive grace and His keen skills in the art of regeneration. The woman I am now would shock the girl I was then. Am I afraid I may fall again? Yes. Do I fight the urge to fantasize at night? Yes. But, every time those thoughts and fears and doubts come at me, I rejoice because it was much longer between bouts than the last time, and that means, we—God and I—are winning. And if He can get me out of my addiction, He can get you out of yours. So, don't give up. Don't give in. Walk with Him. And it will be okay.

Today: I have great admiration for this young lady. She is one of the most talented women that I know and I love her dearly. While facing up to an issue that few do, she serves God with a passion and honesty that is rare. –JS

From a Porn Star

My career in the porn industry started with me working as a $200-a-week costume designer. I moved from this into the position of a publicist. I had many friends in the porn industry and saw the money they made. I felt that getting into the porn industry would open doors for me as a stripper. The first time I illegally danced, I was seventeen, and I began a journey of change. I'd convinced myself that I would not do certain things, but I did. I would never take my top off, but then I'd need money and so the top came off. I thought that I'd never go nude, that I'd never do porn, that I'd never do girl-on-girl or girl-on-guy. I thought that I'd never participate in a gang bang, prostitute myself, or do private shows. There was not a thing that I wouldn't do as money was a constant lure. It was also about getting credits to tour strip clubs where I could be a feature entertainer. I could make more money.

Most of those in the porn industry are "loaded." It's a coping mechanism. I had been sexually abused and had already been promiscuous. Doing porn was another way that I could feel wanted. I also thought that it could give me a sense of importance. There was a type of stardom attached as it involved signing autographs. People would throw money at me. Porn made me someone and meant that I was beautiful, sexy, and wanted.

The emotional toll was taxing. While I made a lot of money, I spent it in an attempt to feel better. I'd make porn movies to feel good, but that did not work and so I'd spend the earnings to see if that made me feel good. It didn't and so I'd get loaded and go back to making more porn to make more money. It was a crazy cycle. Some of the scenes were so degrading, and it was all just a show. I remember being taken to one party and was raped multiple times because I was the porn whore. I woke up eighteen hours later after being drugged. I don't know how many men had used me.

My mom partied and prostituted herself, and I grew up on the streets. I felt that I had no alternative but to live this lifestyle. My grandparents were too old to care for me, and my step dad was in jail as a drug dealer. Mom was only eighteen when she had me and would simply just disappear from my life. At one stage, she left me alone with no food for two weeks. We were evicted from our apartment and so I ended up on the streets. At other times, my mom did drugs with my friends. Feeling constantly let down by my mom, I felt that I was better off living on the streets than being at home. My journey into the porn industry was about survival, but I thought that also it would make me someone.

Today: This lady's story opened my eyes to a life that I'd never seen. For me, her life was one that was read about rather than seen personally. She accepted Christ several years ago and has radically changed her life. She entertains me as few can as she reiterates the past and the distance that she has come.

–JS

Pornography is a widespread problem that affects male and female, homosexual and heterosexual, and young and old. "57 percent of pastors say that addiction to pornography is the most sexually damaging issue to their congregations."[168] Men can be named the primary violators in regards to pornography, for men are more prone to visual stimulation than women; however, women have their own personal brand of pornography in romantic and erotic literature. In some ways, pornography may have become a part of everyday life. We check out at the supermarket and there are sexually explicit magazines on the shelves as we stand in line. We walk through a mall and images in clothing shops are highly sexual. It is difficult to find a movie, television show, or any form of entertainment that does not have sex or hints of sex in it. Sex is everywhere in our culture, and pornography is just another extension of society's sexual freedom.

Pornography is, to put it simply, the viewing of sexual activities either through images, videos, stories, or other visual media. Society is beginning to view pornography as a necessary evil and has even come to accept it as almost a natural part of life. Teenage boys are believed to extensively use pornography; it is an enjoyable experience and could be easily considered to be no big deal. After all, pornography is viewed in the privacy of the home without anyone to question. There are even those who believe that pornography has no real negative effect on a relationship. It could even be considered an enhancer to the sex! I have been at parties in which various pornographic websites were recommended between couples to spice up boring marital sex lives. Shalit wrote, as a counterpoint, however, that when a woman found out about her husband's use of pornography, it started to ruin their sex life, because she felt so angry and turned off to him.[169]

Many women are threatened by pornography—at least when they discover their men are viewing it. Men are not so threatened by the idea of their women viewing sensual images. That, though, does not stop men from their jealousies. One young man kept copies of a magazine containing pornography in his apartment that he shared with his girlfriend. To him it was harmless to their relationship as it was only visually stimulating; however, he removed the materials after she threatened to have coffee with male friends because this would be conversationally stimulating to her.[170]

On the point of pornography as a relational enhancer, this thought is extremely untrue. Women feel the threat of losing their men to this unrealistic view of sex and beauty. It shakes their sense of security. There is no realistic way a normal woman of natural build can compete with the images viewed in pornography. A woman wants to be the beauty of her man's life. If the man is overly enjoying another woman's looks, he is breaking her heart. It heightens her fears regarding her importance in his life and shakes her sense of security in the thought that he will still desire her after the aging process and children run their natural course on her human body. It's fascinating today the number of women who purchase breast lifts and enhancements. While these things are not wrong and help a woman to feel more attractive, the images that we view do influence our thinking. We compete and want to keep our man's attention and so are willing to pay a high price to do this.

How It Begins

Addiction to pornography almost always begins at a young age. "Ninety percent of children between the ages of eight and sixteen have viewed pornography on the Internet, in most cases unintentionally. The average age of first Internet exposure to pornography is eleven."[171] Children are exposing themselves and being exposed to unreal images and unreal pictures of sex with dire consequences. It is a sad fact that pornography becomes their primary exposure to heterosexual activity.[172] Pornography skews the truth about human interaction. These children, who are only beginning to learn how to develop and maintain relationships, are being taught that life is about how you look and how you stimulate others physically. "One of our culture's powerful lies—fueled by pornography, sinful lust, and marketing—is that having a standard of beauty is in any way holy or helpful. God does not give us a standard of beauty—God gives us spouses."[173] The children being exposed to pornography—intentionally or otherwise—are fed the lie that people are not relational but are, instead, objects that can fulfill one's desires.

Australian researchers have found that "children were turning to adult films because schools were not handling the positive aspects of sex. A rising number of children are learning about sex from watching pornography because sex education lessons are inadequate, researchers have found."[174] It is the parents' responsibility to teach children about sex; not the educational system's. Parents need to be aware of what their children are being exposed to in school—all the different types of sexual innuendoes, talk, and images—as well as who their friends are and what they are looking at via computer and phone. Parents need to keep the lines of communication open with their children so that they can help them understand the importance of sex, love, and relationships.

The Trade

Pornography is an unrealistic image of sex that, when viewed, is burned into memory with little hope of it ever fading. It is an exposure to an idea of what a relationship should be like that sets up the viewer for addiction and relational disappointment. It promises great and glorious sex without commitment or effort; however, pornography effectively breaks down the bonds of sex in a relationship by substituting intimate connection with indifference. It even drives some to seek sexual stimulation elsewhere by way of an affair because the sex they are having does not live up to the promises made in pornography.

The person who immerses himself in pornography exposes himself to sexual distortion. The people in the pornography movies and magazines are seen as nothing more than an object. The viewer then transfers that idea to other people. Suddenly, humans are no longer tri-part beings with spirits and souls; they are only bodies. These bodies are then compared to the false standard of perfection portrayed in pornography and played out in the secret, one-dimensional world created by the viewer.[175] The person involved in porn carries a totally unrealistic view of sex. The images seen are out of context with no love or commitment attached, and the person viewing the porn burns with desire and suffers the frustration of nonfulfillment.

Pornography then becomes an addiction. At the core of this addiction is the warped attempt to find love, but this pursuit disappears in the deceptive and all-consuming cycle of addiction. Pornography addiction strips the addict of his humanity as well as strips those around him of theirs. Bell talks of a friend who exploited women for sex. Of these pursuits, he writes that exploiting the women "for sex didn't just rob them of their humanity, it robbed him of his as well."[176]

When a person is so thoroughly diminished, relationships suffer. The pornography then transcends from being an action to an attitude. As an example, pornography in marriage can change the addict's view of his spouse from being a three-dimensional partner in life to a one-dimensional sexual object. When the sex becomes unfulfilling, the addict returns to movies and magazines to dull the pain. Pornographic sex is used to fulfill and change the mood, but it fails time after time. The addiction cycle takes effect, and the addict falls further and further into an unrealistic lifestyle.

Truth Behind the Lie

The following article was released in August of 2012 regarding the production of porn films:

> The lobbying group for the adult-film industry is calling for a nationwide moratorium on shooting in the wake of a syphilis scare. Last Thursday, the adult industry trade publication *XBIZ* sent shock waves through the porn world by quoting two agents announcing that the unidentified performer

> had tested positive for the STD and allegedly worked for weeks shooting scenes, using a doctored test. By the following day, LATimes.com was reporting that the Los Angeles County Health Department was looking at a cluster of five possible syphilis cases related to the adult industry.[177]

According to the Mayo Clinic, syphilis is a bacterial infection usually spread by sexual contact, starting as a painless sore—typically on your genitals, rectum, or mouth. It spreads from person to person via skin or mucous membrane contact with these sores and can lie dormant in your body for decades before becoming active again. Without treatment, syphilis can severely damage your heart, brain or other organs, and can be life-threatening.[178] The above article is just another example of the horrible outcome of pornography, but from the other side, from those who are involved in making it. Behind the "beautiful images" is a world of lies, deception, and disease. It is a false world that only brings destruction.

Overcoming Pornography

The viewing of sex is outside of God's intention for both men and women, for genital sexuality is supposed to be experienced rather than viewed. God's purpose is that "sex expresses a love and commitment that have already been established. Sex cannot of itself be the raw material that fuels a relationship."[179] Overcoming pornography can seem insurmountable just as does any sin that contains enjoyment; however, it can be overcome as a person allows God to affirm him of his sexual worth. The key for healing is obedience to God. Sin comes between God and us and, therefore, causes disappointment; however, failure can be a part of overcoming. The desire to read pornography will be there, but God gives us the power to choose to resist. Matthew 6:22 and 23 encourage us to stay focused; the verses read, "The eye is the lamp of the body. If your eyes are healthy, your whole body will be full of light. But if your eyes are unhealthy, your whole body will be full of darkness. If then the light within you is darkness, how great is that darkness!"[180] We need to take responsibility for our lives. The pornography must be destroyed, computers wiped clean of all history and content, and friends must be trusted with access to our Internet content. This is so humbling but is a necessity. To objectify the true representation of the material is crucial, and then count the cost daily of avoiding pornographic outlets.

Pornography and the often-accompanying masturbation should be seen as an addiction. Addiction warps the pursuit of love. Even when in an addiction, the need to be loved and to give love remains, thus the giving and receiving of real human love and grace are a necessity. It is also a vital key to have trusted friends to share the dark secrets and receive encouragement regarding slipups, grace, and perseverance. The person seeking freedom should find healthy activities that keep him occupied. These activities will honor God and allow Him to increase the self-worth of the recovering addict. Church is also a very important asset because it provides teaching, relational support, and opportunities to serve, love, and help others.

Pornography can act as a doorway to deeper levels of sexual impurity. It is the easiest form of inappropriate sexual conduct in regards to the fact that it can be found anywhere. It can be easily accessed, easily hidden, and easily denied. It is an activity that affects the soul first, and, as all parts of a human are connected, the degradation of the soul begins to manifest in the body. Those who are addicted to porn soon find themselves at least tempted if not falling easily into another addiction: masturbation.

Chapter 10: Masturbation

Overcoming Masturbation

Thinking back, I have a hard time even remembering when it all started. I believe I was 7 or 8. I stumbled across masturbation while taking a bath one day. I didn't know what was happening, I just knew it felt good. It started off sporadically and became more and more frequent. By the time I was 9, I was masturbating 2 to 3 times a day. Knowing what I know now, this is not particularly normal for a young girl. Around this time, I had "the talk" with my parents and had pieced together what was going on. As a teenager I had asked the question on "How far is too far to go with a boy?" or "What is a safe boundary?" at a church weekend retreat. We got to write down questions anonymously and our leaders would answer them for us. My leader had given some specifics but said to mainly stay away from anything physical if it turned us on. She also said that masturbation was much safer than actually having sex so, in a way, it gave me the green light to carry on with my addiction. I wasn't having sex, so I wasn't hurting anyone, right?

I managed to stay a virgin until I was married, but fooled around a lot and was still masturbating at least once a day in high school. I couldn't stop. It was like my body needed it, and I couldn't get that nagging feeling away until I did it. Every time I did it, I would tell myself that that would be the last time. It never was. I didn't like the control it had over me but, moreover, the lack of control I felt since I couldn't bring myself to stop. I felt dirty and wrong. I didn't know any other friends that were dealing with an addiction to masturbation and felt like there was no safe place to talk to someone about it. That is the thing about Satan that is so strong—if he can make you stay in the dark with your guilt, he can isolate you. I know now that when I am dealing with something, the best thing to do is talk with someone and get it out in the light. A lot of times that is what needs to be done to overcome it: just saying it out loud.

I finally kicked the habit after high school when I went to do a DTS with YWAM. There was no way I was going to do that with so many people around all the time and especially on a mission trip. It was hard; a minute-by-

minute, day-by-day struggle to choose God over my own desires. It was on that trip that God took me through a re-purification process. He helped me put the past behind me, forgive myself, and commit to staying pure for my future spouse. No masturbations; no fooling around; not even a single kiss until my wedding day. It was freeing—scary, but freeing.

I don't believe it is a coincidence that I ended up marrying a man with the same addiction. By that point, I had overcome it, so I understood it, but I was still disgusted by it. It interfered with our marriage for the first couple of years. There are so many people addicted to masturbation these days that they get so used to pleasuring themselves that they have troubles with their spouse pleasuring them because "they aren't doing it right."

I had heard my mom tell my brother and myself in high school that masturbation was the lesser of the two evils compared to sleeping around. She said this to me again recently since I have a lot of adult single friends, and she wanted me to pass that along to them. My response to that was: "In God's eyes, all sin is equal." I then asked her if Jesus would have masturbated, and she said "No." If Jesus wouldn't have done it, then we shouldn't either. It's not pure. We won't die from not having an orgasm.

Sexual immorality is the only sin in the Bible it says to flee from. We are not to try to get up close to battle it; we are to run. There is no better way than God's way. He wants us pure. Our only addiction needs to be Him. I'm very careful now with what I watch and read. I don't watch sex scenes in movies or read sex scenes in books. I need to guard my mind. I have no desire to fall back into something that has a hold on me; something that makes me feel disgusted with myself and out of control. There is no way I am saying it was easy, but it was worth it.

Today: This young lady has a wonderful marriage and family. She and her husband are great members and leaders in a thriving church. –JS

Overcoming Pornography and Masturbation

As I approach the topic of my own addiction to Pornography and Masturbation, I recall a point of clarity that hit me in the midst of a dark season in my family's past. My father-in-law and I were sitting on the balcony of a cruise ship cutting through the night on the waters of the Eastern Caribbean. Our conversation was sparked by that evening's admission by my father-in-law that he was going through withdrawals as an addict to pain medications. As we stared out into the blackness of the night sky, I prayed that God would give me something to say to him that would help him in some way. God gave me a question and I posed it to him, "What do you do when you cannot even trust yourself?" I felt the move of God in that moment, and we both realized we are addicts. Not only did his abuse of narcotics necessitate an honest admission of his weakness to it, but I also realized in that moment I was addicted to my own drug: Sex.

As Christians, we have a standard of righteousness that we attain to. The choice to do the "right" thing pervades our ideology. In that same thought, we know that all fall short of the glory of God. Jesus gives us grace, mercy, and seemingly unlimited re-dos through the sacrifice of His life on the cross. This is where the Christian addict often gets stuck. I convinced myself that grace was sufficient to allow me the grey area I needed to be righteous and to stay addicted to pornography just like every other guy. Fooled to believe I'd not have to make the hard decision to give up porn all together. Surely God would bless me despite the death I was sowing into my marriage and my life. I needed help, and it wasn't until I admitted I was an addict that I was able to see that grey areas aren't grey.

Truth be told, in the state I was in, I didn't want to give up porn. I loved it with the sick love of an abusive relationship. I was introduced to pornography when I was 9 in my cousin's basement. Days later I saw my first sex film. My craving for porn and masturbation escalated from there into a daily habit on the Internet, TV, or print. The way it made me feel, the "beauty" of the female form, and even the habit of life told me that I wanted it in my life. Certainly, I wasn't "that guy." I'm not that sick-o in the trench coat on the streets of urban America paying for depraved pleasure. I had fragile boundaries I set in place that somehow made me different in my mind from the "real addicts." This is the thinking of an addict. You love the very thing that is killing you. Rational thought betrays you at every turn when you are a closet addict. Even when you try to make a stand for what's right, you've probably already sabotaged yourself in advance to get what your flesh wants.

I got saved in college, and you'd think that I would be miraculously delivered from my addiction. However, God wanted me to CHOOSE Him over porn. I was so deep into the excuses for my addiction; I chose to play down the call to stop. Men's meetings, revivals, and conferences all challenged me to stop the compromise. I'd cry and say yes to the call. To an addict, compromise is a simple process of telling yourself, "Jesus still loves me and I'll be stronger next time." I even told my accountability partners, "Yeah man, I do this and I'm going to stop." They'd inevitably say that they struggled too, often without victory. It is difficult to hear that the men you trust aren't having victory either. This type of compromise stunted years of my life.

Every addict must come to a place in his/her life where they realize that the consequences of their actions are greater than their selfish reward. For me it was the potential loss of my marriage at the bottom of the descent. My wife is a passionate believer of God. She also has a resolute sense of justice. We had difficult conversations about masturbation and pornography early in our relationship. I assured her I was going to stop. That just made me more careful to hide what I did to satisfy my addiction. I hid it for years. Sometimes hinting at indiscretions here and there, but never getting truly honest. I was afraid to tell her, as I knew it would hurt her, and I didn't want to stop. The confessions of my father-in-law inspired me look at my "habit" as what it truly was, an addiction. That night on the balcony of the cruise ship I realized I couldn't trust myself to make the right choices while viewing them as a habit, and I needed to address my sickness in the light of my greatest potential of loss. I didn't want to be an addict any longer. When we returned home, I went on XXXChurch.com for resources on how to get started toward recovery, and I told my wife everything. I learned that the pain of confessing the truth is better than the discovery of lies. I can count on one hand the number of times I made my wife cry. This was one of them. I realized that all the love I have for her couldn't make up for the rift my actions were causing. She felt betrayed, lied to, and insufficient as my mate. I had to make the decision to view porn as the marital infidelity that it is. I had to just stop. I had to risk the loss of my wife to have truth be the basis of our relationship, not my addiction.

It has taken me years to rebuild what I lost that day, but we needed the brutal truth for me to position myself for success. I have had a few lapses of judgment that have led to solitary moments of compromise, but the communication I created with my wife allowed me to recover quickly and keep the light shining. An addict will always be an addict, and the temptation to look and do may always remain. It has gotten easier though. Through honesty with my spouse and wisdom for myself I am able to avoid compromising situations before they arise. The restriction of movies and images that contain sexual content is a necessity. If I have a day that gets me charged up, as the culture of the day is sexually charged, I tell my wife so that those feelings don't result in dangerous behavior. I am walking in freedom that I never believed possible because a person I loved held me accountable to the truth. I also allowed the truth to take hold in my life. A faith-filled life is a series of choices that point you toward God, and I am more vigilant to look out for the choices that lead me into compromise. I am forever thankful that I am free to live the life God has for me without the bondage of guilt and fear.

Today: This guy is wonderfully free of his past and has a beautiful wife and family. He is a faithful leader in his church. –JS

Whether masturbation is right or wrong is not an easy question to answer. Masturbation is seen by many as...

> a safe sexual activity and is a positive sexual behavior. It helps a person become familiar with his own body, is an effective treatment for premature ejaculation in men and orgasmic disorders in women, and is a way for older people to fulfill their sexual needs. For younger adults it allows them to release sexual tension.[181]

Jay E. Adams, one of the premiere voices in biblical counseling, writes in regards to this that "even those things that are right must not be allowed to get such a hold over a Christian that they become his master and he becomes their servant."[182] Masturbation is commonly defined as the "erotic stimulation especially of one's own genital organs commonly resulting in orgasm and achieved by manual or other bodily contact exclusive of sexual intercourse, by instrumental manipulation, occasionally by sexual fantasies, or by various combinations of these agencies."[183] Men are more likely than women to masturbate.[184] Recent research has shown that "the highest prevalence of masturbation was found among those aged 25 to 34 and was particularly high among divorced and single men."[185]

Masturbation often starts at a young age when we are beginning to discover the more intimate parts of our bodies. These parts are activating, so to speak, and we begin to experience sexual desire. We, as fallen creatures in a fallen world, begin to crave sexual fulfillment, and masturbation acts as a supposedly safe and easy fix with little to no consequences; however, anything that is easy is rarely without consequences. Masturbation gives pleasure to self only. Sex, on the other hand, was designed to share pleasure with another. It is an act of giving.

The Dangers of Masturbation

Masturbation is another sexual immorality that is believed to have no adverse effect on other people; however, this, like so many others listed in this book, is a lie. For one thing, if masturbation becomes a long-term habit, it becomes a problem. It sets one up for an unfulfilling sexual relationship. The partner of the one masturbating is left to guess their way through what his or her partner finds fulfilling. Masturbation awakens a giant, so to speak, of sexual desire that damages the soul, the body, and how we relate to others in all stages of relationships.

Pornography and Masturbation

Masturbation tends to be the next step taken by those who view pornography. The erotic images viewed in pornography stimulate the body. "Sexual fantasies are the most common fantasy or daydream in which people engage."[186] The beautiful, oversexed person is viewed, there is no person with whom to deal afterwards, and much is left to the imagination of what is to come. All of this arouses the desire to masturbate. There is a compulsion linked to both activities as well as a feeling of inferiority. The unrealistic images portrayed make the viewer feel like he will never live up to that sexual expectation, thus he retreats into personal pleasure instead of seeking to share sexual pleasure with others.

Sexual pleasure becomes very physical and associated with good looks and big body parts. "Pornography and masturbation 'hook in' to a person's homosexual vulnerabilities and actually strengthen those tendencies. The person who is already weakened in gender identity will easily become hooked by the exaggerated sexual symbols found in pornography (e.g. big genitals)."[187] These things therefore enhance one's sense of inadequacy. This increases one's fear of failure, and performance anxiety intensifies.

Inferiority

Masturbation is counterproductive. It is meant to release sexual tension and anxieties but, instead, it increases both. After the act, there is disappointment, confusion, and more anxiety. Masturbation is a selfish act which leads to guilt and shame and can be a result of feeling inferior to others. This feeling of inferiority creates an addict's cycle. Inferiority complexes can often drive one to masturbate so as to avoid the fear of failing in a sexual relationship; the act of masturbation then causes further senses of inferiority accompanied by shame and guilt. Shame and guilt drive one to seek "feel good" outlets like sexual pleasure, thus the desire to masturbate returns. The deed is done, the feelings return, and the cycle continues.

Loss of Intimacy

Compulsive masturbation can prevent one from becoming intimate with a spouse. While orgasm is the desired result of masturbation, this causes a greater frustration as orgasm is only a part of a greater picture. Sexual yearnings are connected to deep desires which should be shared with another. Mary Steward, who overcame masturbation, wrote the following:

> We must realize that only in *relationship with a member of the opposite sex* (within the commitment of marriage) can real, long-term pleasure be found. Sex is meant to be savored, not sought out furtively in darkness. That kind of sexual potential involves discipline, insight, tools for harnessing that insight, a desire to grow relationally, and stepping out in opportunities to do so.[188]

This brings that sense of isolation to a conclusion. Masturbation on the other hand, while bringing one to climax, merely leaves one in isolation and frustration.

Paul writes in 1 Corinthians 7:3–4 that "one's sexual capacity does not exist for himself."[189] Masturbation teaches us to fulfill ourselves, and, as a result, we become impatient when in a relationship with another. A masturbator does not need to think of another when seeking fulfillment. He already knows his body well and knows how to fulfill himself. It is a shallow shadow of what true intimacy and sexual fulfillment really are. Paul writes in 1 Corinthians of marital sex that we should "stop depriving one another, except by agreement for a time, so that you may devote yourselves to prayer, and come together again so that Satan will not tempt you because of your lack of self-control."[190] God designed sex so that we give to and satisfy our marriage partner. It takes time to develop a good sexual relationship. We need to learn each other's bodies and what brings our lover to sexual fulfillment.

Loss of Control

In 1 Corinthians 6:12, Paul says, "All things are lawful for me, but I will not be mastered by anything."[191] This verse acts as a guideline for sexual activities and can be easily applied to masturbation. As previously stated, masturbation seems like a harmless fix for premarital sexual need, but it becomes another form of bondage. We combine sexual fantasy with selfish pleasure. The more we masturbate, the more we depend on it, the more we want it, and the more we feed the need. Masturbation provides a sexual release, but it begins to own us. "Masturbation can gain such a tenacious control over them that it saps their energies, takes their minds away from their studies, and sets them to thinking about sex everywhere they go and with every person they see."[192] Masturbation is a selfish act that sets us up for disappointment. Only marital sex can give us the satisfaction we crave while teaching us to serve another in the most intimate way.

Parental Advice

Some parents ask, "What do I do if I catch my child masturbating?" As written earlier, masturbation may occur as a part of growing up. Children can begin to discover that certain areas of their bodies are pleasurable to touch. They are curious, and if they are not given a healthy outlet for that curiosity, they will seek answers elsewhere—like sexually explicit magazines or staring openly at well-endowed individuals. As parents, we have a choice in these moments as to how to handle this situation. Dean and I raised two boys. We made sure to keep the lines of communication open with them regarding relationships, sex, and sexual boundaries. When we talked, we would keep our comments light and fun without being crass. In this way, we taught them respect for boundaries and why these boundaries are important. The older they got, the deeper the conversations became until they decided to live within the boundaries we taught them and not simply because we had said so.

Some parents would say that masturbation is better than having sex with another. This is right, to a degree; masturbation can be helpful in some regards unless it becomes an addiction. Things that can help prevent addictive behavior are encouragement in various areas including healthy family conversations as mentioned above, healthy friendships, a strong involvement in both church and church activities, close relationships with church leaders, and encouragement to develop a relationship with Jesus Christ as Lord and Savior. This means that as parents we should have these things too.

Parents are and always will be the primary teachers. It is an awkward moment for all concerned if a parent walks in on their child in the middle of "the act." The parent must, in this moment, be the one to continue the conversation at a later date. Be understanding, open, and listen; refrain from any sort of accusation. Being caught masturbating is an embarrassing thing. Making sure the child does not feel like a failure or dirty is important. If the parents exemplify healthy physical touch—hugs, caresses of the hair or shoulder, and appropriate kissing—in front of their children, their children will be more receptive to lessons in respectful boundaries.

Parents do need to be aware that a child who has experienced sexual abuse can masturbate as a way to escape the pain. This does not mean that all children who masturbate have been abused, but parents do need to be aware and not pretend that nothing is wrong. If a parent suspects that the child has been abused, there are signs for which they can look. A sexually abused child often shows behavior that is unusual for their age; behaviors that include withdrawal, certain fears and bedwetting. Ask a trusted friend regarding the child's behavior and see what they say. Parents should not avoid talking to their children about sex. Children are sexual beings. Parents need to be bold, relevant, and understanding when guiding their children into a proper sexual life.

Masturbation, like pornography, can be difficult to deal with for many reasons. Those who indulge can become lost in this world of masturbation so easily. What is done in private is not known. These things, though, put one in bondage. In Proverbs 28:13, we read, "Whoever conceals their sins does not prosper, but the one who confesses and renounces them finds mercy."[193] God understands the pull of sexual desire; that is why He instructs us in 1 Corinthians 7:9 to marry rather than burn with temptation.[194] His compassions are new every morning.[195] If we let Him, He will help us find freedom.

Chapter 11: Adultery

A Story of Adultery

Our marriage only lasted one year. It was difficult to discern problems since my husband traveled extensively. So even though unfaithfulness was occurring even in this time, I was oblivious to it.

I did know that a relationship that my husband had with another girl was inappropriate. It did not stress me much, and, when I asked him to not contact her, he agreed. Again, because of his travel schedule, it was easy for him to hide his activities from me.

When we had the opportunity to move closer to family due to a work transfer, I was ecstatic as I thought that we could have a more normal life. Soon after this, though, I discovered that he was still corresponding with this same girl through Facebook. Each time that I brought this up, he grew more allusive and defensive, and his comments caused me to feel that I was the one with the problem. He accused me of paranoia and not trusting him. He accused me of being crazy and imagining things. I could not trust him!

My husband also had an alcohol problem, and so one night I was able to check his phone. There were numerous inappropriate texts regarding the intimate relationship between him and this same girl. The day that I found out about his cheating was the day after Valentine's Day. Oddly enough, I still was not one hundred percent sure that their relationship was sexual. I was in shock and even asked my mother if his behavior with this girl was normal. I needed someone to tell me that I wasn't crazy. From this point, I knew our marriage wouldn't work. The adultery was not the only issue. Looking back, I realized that many of his issues tied back to his upbringing in some way.

When I confronted him, his initial response was defensive. He was angry and amazed that I had found him out. He also felt that I would get over this and that we would work it out.

When I kicked him out, I commenced attending church. My brother was also instrumental in helping me rebuild my life. One of my struggles was with being divorced and the shame I felt concerning this. I wondered if God could forgive me. Over time, I realized that it was not this that was so wrong but his behavior that led to our divorce. My ex was still trying to persuade me to work our marriage out. There was a lot of confusion, but my family reassured me of no wrongdoing. I quickly filed for divorce. I knew it wouldn't work nor did I want it to.

Looking back, I realize that our sex life wasn't what I'd hoped. He was more concerned with his pleasure than mine, and soon after our wedding, I discovered that he used pornography. I'd buy sexy lingerie to try to please him, but he still was not that responsive. I felt so unattractive, and it felt like continual blows against me.

On the discovery of the adultery, I was depressed. I hated going to bed, and it was worse in the mornings. I'd cry my eyes out and dreaded having to get through the day. Meanwhile, I went back to school and started working out at the gym. I'd go early in the morning so that I would not have to cope with conversation. The emotional pain was so intense that it was hard to concentrate.

Over time, I found that God gave me peace and courage. I had loved my husband and was heartbroken at the loss of our marriage. I was not vengeful, and when we separated our belongings, I handled it while he couldn't look me in the eye. He was ashamed and sorry and wanted to spend time together. To me, this was pointless, and I was firm in my decision to not do this.

Looking back, I am still amazed that this transpired. Marriage was a life commitment, and commitment means faithfulness to each other. To commence dating again was terrifying. After my divorce, I determined that I'd remain single, but when I saw other married couples being affectionate, I knew that one day I'd want to marry again. Now, I am in a new relationship where I'm learning to trust. He is a completely different type of guy, and I am facing the insecurities from my marriage. I am learning again to be vulnerable and honest about myself. I also have new ideas about marriage since I am in church learning about marriage and am surrounded by great examples. I also no longer feel guilty about my past as I realize that I didn't make the wisest of choices, but I gave my marriage everything that I could.

Today: This beautiful young woman is engaged to a fantastic young man. She is excited for her future and serving God with a passion. –JS

Story from an Adulterer

Looking back in my life, I cannot believe what I did. I always thought that anyone who committed adultery or obtained a divorce was an awful person.

Here I am though. I am one of those people who committed adultery. At the time, I was working hard, trying to build a business and support my wife and children. I convinced myself that by earning the money, I was an excellent husband. I realize though that I gave my wife and children little attention or support. I would arrive home and sit in front of the television, remote in hand, and expect my wife to tend to everything. That's, after all, how my parents had lived their lives and it seemed to work for them.

My wife did care for me. I began to see her, though, as one who was demanding from me rather than respecting and loving me. Looking back, I understand that she was frustrated since I was not tending to her needs. Therefore her cries for attention became more like whines. Our children were also young and so she had little time to spend on her appearance. Coming home to a whiny, pajama-clad wife was not an enticement in marriage.

At this same time, I could afford to put on a woman to help with my business. I realize now that a wise person would include his wife in this decision. In my arrogance though, I did not do this and employed someone who filled the voids in my life at that time—attractive, optimistic, complimentary, and oblivious to my faults. She spoke a language that was the language that all guys love to hear—never-ending compliments.

I found myself working longer hours. I enjoyed spending time with this young woman while she was attentive to my every need. She challenged me in my goals and yet had solutions for problems. After a time, we found ourselves having supper together and working into the late hours. We'd have coffee breaks and we started to share private thoughts.

I didn't realize it at the time, but the devil was playing havoc with my thought life. Regarding my marriage, "I've married the wrong woman. She's interfering with my business." I felt nothing for my wife, but allowed myself to believe that I'd never loved her. Although I called myself a Christian, I convinced myself that divorce was an option. After all, many Christians were now divorcing.

The friction intensified at home. I didn't want my wife to touch me physically nor speak to me. She knew that something was amiss even though she never met my employee. I wanted to be alone so that I could be free to fantasize about my business and this wonderful new lady in my life. If I'd only realized that love is a choice. Fantasies are not reality. I was not laying down my life for my wife as Christ tells us.

As time passed, boundaries that I once had for my life drifted into the past. I believed that my marriage vows were a mistake. I convinced myself that I could be a great father even though I did not want to be married to my children's mother. I told myself that my wife did not love me. A whining woman could not love her husband!

At the same time, this new woman was always ready to pay me attention. This new woman was the perfect one for me, and so we had sex. While I'd love to say that I felt awful, I didn't. In the midst of my thoughts, it felt great but I also felt so guilty.

Several weeks passed. This woman and I had several sexual encounters. This drove me further from my wife, probably due to the guilt that I felt. I finally told my wife in a fit of rage. She would not stop confronting me regarding my absences, both physically and emotionally. My mind swung between blame for her and my terrible guilt. My emotions were so confused. I could not walk away though from my family, friends, and church.

I wish that I could say that the following period of time was easy. It was not. I had to look long-term at my life goals to carry through my decisions. If I had purely acted on my emotions at this time, I would not have what I have today. Therefore I gave up my business and found another. I had to remove myself from all influence of "the other woman." My wife understandably needed to know where I was twenty-four hours a day. This was necessary and understandable. We both went to a Christian counselor who walked us through the difficult process of reconciliation. My wife's confession of her faults made this process easier, but I can never blame her for my idiotic actions. Time passed and life became better.

Today we have been married for nearly forty years. I was a Christian when my adultery occurred, but I was lukewarm in my faith. I had received salvation but had done nothing with this. I attended church when it was convenient despite my wife's wishes.

This episode in my life changed me as I realized that God's plan for marriage was very different from mine. Consequently, due to a miracle-working God, I am still married to this same most beautiful and forgiving wife in the world and will be for the rest of my days.

Today: This wonderful guy is the most gracious counselor that I have ever met. Due to his marriage breakdown, he went back to school to become a therapist and now helps countless marriages that are in crisis. –JS

Adultery is increasing in society. The message that an adulterous affair is to be expected saturates the media. Shows like "Law and Order," "Revenge," and "Pretty Little Liars" contain broken marriages, bitter spouses, and the "glories" of affairs with one's true love. The Kardashians are paraded across television as an example of "real life"—even though common sense tells us their lives are unrealistic, we still get the sense that the problems they face are problems we should expect in our own lives. There are even websites that specialize in helping us have an affair. They coax with tag lines like, "Life is short. Have an affair."[196] Some people are beginning to believe that having a marital affair is a "sign of maturity."[197]

Adultery is when a husband or a wife engages in sexual relations with someone other than their spouse. It can come in several forms: an adulterous marital affair, the dwelling on having sex with another than one's spouse in their minds, or the simple act of adultery. When I say "simple," I do not mean to lessen the severity of the moment; I am acknowledging that one-night stands where sex is just sex happen in the realm of adultery. Adulterous affairs tend to have a pre-set relationship and emotions attached.

Men and women approach adultery and are affected by it in different ways. It has been stated in early chapters that men are taught to believe that sex is a mark of manhood and that multiple sexual partners increase one's maleness. In this thought, a man that commits adultery may be on a quest to feel more masculine. There is a sense of power and control involved. He is in charge of the affair, how often he sees this "other woman," and how to keep said affair a secret. For a woman, an affair may be birthed out of a feeling of neglect. Her husband is not giving her the love and attention she craves, thus, in her need to feel wanted and desired, she seeks attention elsewhere—perhaps from a coworker who offers both friendship and companionship in her vulnerable moments. Perhaps for the woman also, her priorities are wrong and an affair is the result.

There is a reason why marriage vows include the phrase, "For Better or For Worse." It lets us know that there will be temptation, desire, and attraction outside of this commitment to our new spouse. The desire to want what we cannot have was birthed in us from the beginning of time. God told Adam and Eve that they could eat of any tree but one.[198] Unfortunately they forgot to appreciate God's provision and focused upon the one forbidden tree. God had provided many sources of contentment through numerous trees in the garden, and yet they chose to believe a lie in eating from the forbidden tree. They fixated on the one forbidden thing. Adultery happens when we do the same thing. We forget to appreciate and work on our commitment to our spouse. We dwell on that person who is forbidden to us due to the covenant of marriage. This dwelling feels good, but it is the beginning of a downward path. The eating of this fruit, the adultery, leads to a further downfall or a web of lying and destruction unless we confess our wrong.

Adultery or an affair often occurs because we feel emptiness within our marriage. Our spouse is not interested in sex or is not providing us with enough attention. Maybe he travels a lot and so is absent from the comforts of home. This sense of separation drives us to begin living the single life again simply as a way to survive the solitude. There seems to be a void between the husband and wife. Then, suddenly, someone—perhaps a coworker or old acquaintance—begins providing us with the attention we are missing from our spouse. The idea begins to form in our mind, and the trap of adultery begins to slowly close.

Adultery begins in the mind with the thought of "What if?" Sometimes this thought is concealed as "If only...—If only I had not married this guy; if only she had not wanted children so soon; if only I had met this other person sooner." The *if only's* and *what if's* take on a form in our imagination. In our minds, we imagine what life would be like with this new person. Would marriage be easier? Would the sex be better? Our daydreams can begin to take on a life of their own as we allow our lusts for what we cannot have, to grow. Lust is usually connected with dissatisfaction in life. "Lust is distorted fantasy and especially unchecked sexual thoughts—objectifying and using sexuality in a way that does not produce intimacy or a more fulfilling sex life."[199] If we continue to allow these thoughts to invade our minds, we enter into an affair of the heart.

Most people have heard of an affair of the heart. This is a relationship, often sexual in nature, which occurs in our imagination. It is not an affair we carry out, but our spouse is often aware of it. Our preoccupation with our fantasies creates an unpleasant tension in our relationships. The tension causes annoyance and continual dissatisfaction that, if not dealt with in a Godly manner, drives us to distance ourselves further from our spouses and live more and more in our imaginations. We may think that these daydreams are harmless as they only involve us, but we have already discussed the lie of personal secrecy in pornography and masturbation and seen what depths of pain are actually caused in this lie. In Matthew 5:27–28, the writer makes a compelling statement regarding our thought life. Jesus says in these verses that if anyone so much as looks at a woman lustfully, he "has already committed adultery with her in his heart."[200] He is showing that "God also considers the inward thought-and-consent of the heart to be adultery."[201]

Adultery can continue to grow in our hearts and cause us to begin searching, so to speak, for an outlet. This search is mostly subconscious. We have fixated on how disappointing our lives have become and have compared it to our fantasies. We are living out of a place of unhappiness that leaves us vulnerable to the draw of another. When we become attached to another, we may not have the resolve to resist. This is why the phrase, "The affair just happened!" is strikingly untrue. We sought out the attention, even if we were unaware that that is what we were doing, and then allowed it to continue. We wanted this new relationship to be our salvation because that is how we crafted it in our minds. It is for this reason that Paul teaches in 2 Corinthians 10:5 that we are to "destroy arguments and every lofty opinion raised against the knowledge of God, and take every thought captive to obey Christ."[202]

I am not saying that when we look at another person in admiration, we are inevitably going to have an affair. Jesus is not saying that either. Everyone will experience sexual reactions because we live in a world that continually presents sexual images. Jesus is simply warning against letting such thoughts linger. He knows that the eyes and the mind are linked. Douglas Rosenau is a licensed psychologist and Christian sex therapist.[203] He notes that "the Greek word 'look' used in Matthew is in the imperfect tense, which is an action that starts in the past and continues into the present. It could be translated 'continually look.' Christ emphasized the importance of guarding the mental fantasy life."[204] By continually looking at another and allowing the thoughts to churn and grow, these thoughts can lead us to betray our partner in our heart and may even lead us to betray them in our actions.

Should the worst happen and we act upon our thoughts, then the battle of secrecy begins. We often hear from an adulterer who is hiding his actions from his spouse that "what my partner doesn't know won't hurt." This ignores the fact that love does no wrong.[205] Honestly, if our spouse would not have an issue with the affair, why not tell them? The answer is simply this: the adulterer does not wish to lose what he already has. Men who are mixed up in an affair will often claim that they love both their wife and this new person. Between the two relationships, all needs are fulfilled. The wife provides the loving home environment, and this other woman provides the excitement.

Affairs may fill a void in our marriages, but they do not enhance a marriage. Open marriages that allow the spouse to have another sexual partner are not fulfilling the marriage covenant. Marriage was designed for two people only; for a man and a woman. A marriage is built on love, trust, and commitment to another. Many of the characteristics that define true love are found in 1 Corinthians 13:4–7:

> Love is patient, love is kind. It does not envy, it does not boast, it is not proud. It does not dishonor others, it is not self-seeking, it is not easily angered, it keeps no record of wrongs. Love does not delight in evil but rejoices with the truth. It always protects, always trusts, always hopes, always perseveres.[206]

We understand the inadequacies and imperfections of our spouse. There is no perfect person that will fulfill a person in every way. It is through these things that we learn patience, mercy, perseverance, and honor. Love is protective of the other and is not self-seeking.

Fighting for Marriage

I remember a time when my husband sat with another man of middle age whose marriage had deteriorated. Unbeknownst to his wife, he was having an affair. It had been a difficult marriage where the spouse worked hard at her commitment, yet he seemed uninterested. With my husband, he gloated over a picture of his newfound attractive love. My husband refused to look at this picture as he knew of the wife's devotion to this man. She was not perfect, as is no one, but she provided a loving home, bore him children, helped him build his career while also working to aid the family income, and was sexually willing. This new woman, though, was enticing. She admired him while presenting adventure and freedom. This husband failed to realize that his non-commitment, criticisms, belittlement, and lack of attention had added to his wife's faded appearance. He also failed to understand that birthing several children alters a woman's body.

Willard Harley writes on the issue of infidelity in his text, "His Needs/Her Needs: Building an Affair-Proof Marriage." Harley shows us how we do all that we can to attract and win the person of our desires when we are dating and even through the engagement period. In marriage though, we suddenly forget that the battle for commitment is only just beginning. We neglect the things that made us attractive to our special someone in the first place. For instance, we may have learned to love a sport he likes or a show she watches, but then, once the marriage vows were made, we tossed that shared activity to the wayside thinking it did not matter anymore. Romancing our spouses is crucial to keeping a marriage strong. If we fail to meet the needs we were meeting in dating and engagement, the discontentment that may lead us down the thought-road of adultery begins.

Marriage needs to be fought for; that is why commitment in a relationship is so important. Commitment means that we choose to resist the temptations that are present all around us. We choose every day to stand by our marriage, "for better or for worse." Paul in 2 Timothy 2:22 instructs us to flee youthful lusts. No matter our age, married or single, desire for others is real. It does not disappear just because we are having sex on a regular basis. Sexual desire might diminish over the years, but the mind can stay active. 2 Corinthians teaches us to choose our thoughts carefully. Do we indulge in our fantasies or do we dwell on what is true, noble, right, pure, lovely, excellent, or praiseworthy?[207] I have been married for nearly thirty years. I often think, "Would Dean be offended if he knew my thoughts?" We all must decide daily to walk away from situations that could damage our marriage, take the steps to not take our spouses for granted, and make the enhancement of our married life the main goal.

We can protect our marriage from affairs in many easy ways. The first is to determine that our marriage will be our one and only. We will not even consider the "get out of marriage free card" that society presents through easy divorce. We will hold true to our vows despite our doubts and fears. If there is struggle, we will commit to work through it even if that means going to a Christian or biblical counselor for help.

We can learn to discipline our minds. It has already been established that all sinful actions begin as a thought. Adultery begins as an indulged mental scenario. The Bible teaches about renewing the mind.[208] We can and often will find someone else more attractive than our spouse, but that does not give us permission to dwell on him or her. This brings comparison, dissatisfaction, and the like. Acknowledge that that person looks good, move on, and let your fantasies star your spouse.

The way we talk about our spouses is on par with how we think about them. Media all too often portrays women sitting around a table complaining about their idiotic husbands. This is just as damaging as daydreaming about someone else. Our words have power, thus we need to refrain from negative talk and criticisms about our spouse to others, particularly to those of the opposite sex. We are human and do need a sympathetic ear from time to time, but this ear should be attached to a trusted friend who can give sound advice after we are done lamenting. Marital complaint should never be the topic of a girls' or a guys' night out.

Being honest about marriage is equally as important as committing to make it work. If there is an issue neither of us can work out, we need to seek help. Secrets too are a bad idea in marriage as adultery and affairs are built on secrecy. We can feel cheated if and when we find out that our spouse has kept a secret from us. Secrets, particularly of a sexual nature, create problems, thus open communication is key. It is also invaluable to have a network of trusted friends who have insight into our lives and can give an honest assessment when we cannot.

Marriage is strengthened by our trust in one another. We keep our spouse's most intimate secrets as they keep ours. Set limits to protect that trust and do not assume that your spouse is on the same page as you regarding these boundaries. Talk it out. Agree upon them. Hold each other accountable to them. Some boundaries may include not allowing yourself or your spouse to take car rides alone with a member of the opposite gender. Coffees or work-related lunches of the same situation are rarely a good idea, especially if the subject of marriage and relationships can so easily be brought up. All casual relationships can become intimate relationships if boundaries are not set, and adultery can occur as a result.

Sadly, church membership does not make us immune to affairs. This, however, does not mean that church should be taken out of the equation altogether. Twenty years ago, I remember standing in a church, and I was aware of two married couples across the room from each other. One of each couple had had an affair with one of the other of the couple. Both were on a journey of forgiveness and reconciliation. Both believed in the covenant of marriage. This kind of healing can only come from a community of believers who are serving God together. The community built within a church should be one of acceptance and love. It is here that we can find those close, trusted friends that aid us in keeping our lives together. They help us deal with guilt perhaps born from keeping secrets or in addressing an aspect of our attitude that is unknowingly causing damage to our marriage. A good church provides biblical teaching and guidance for a marriage that can help us not run to a counselor whenever there is a problem.

No marriage is invincible. We are all prone to temptation especially in areas where we are the most vulnerable. That is why having an open and honest view of self is imperative to marriage. We need to know our strengths and weaknesses; how these traits come into play in the marriage; do they add or detract? We also need to understand what kind of person tempts us so that we can be on alert and "flee from youthful lusts"[209] when the pull calls. These safeguards help to spare those we love and ourselves from pain and harm.

Adultery, like pornography and masturbation, begins in the mind. It is a trait of our society that has become too familiar. It is almost expected. The hope of happiness in marriage is almost mocked by those who "know better." That is why some people do not bother getting married at all. Why take the risk? Live-in couples can enjoy all the perks of marriage without the struggles; they are not tied together by law, so they can escape at any time. This is a commitment-less attitude that breeds affairs and selfish pleasure. When left unchecked, people get hurt. When left unstopped, the mind and the lies that are allowed to brew within turn to darker outlets—outlets that even society calls great evil.

Part Three: Sexual Misconduct

Despite the culture born out of the "If it feels good, do it" mindset, there are things that will resonate within us as being wrong. These things usually have one defining trait: they violate the deepest part of our humanity. No matter how much we can analyze, debate, or dissect any particular sin, it still causes us to cringe when we think about it, and when the evil event involves sex, the disgust runs deeper.

Sexual violations remain one of the top standing evils that even society cannot argue into acceptance—not that any person would try. This next section takes an honest look at the darkest side of sex where choice is forcefully taken away and the very nature of our humanity is assaulted. Know that these next few chapters deal with very real issues that run rampant in not just our society but throughout the world and even in our churches. Calling it "misconduct" is almost too kind. These are real, deep, sexual sins that are easier to ignore than face, but when we face what we fear most, we find truth, vision, and redemption from the only One who can make all things work out for good.[210]

Chapter 12: Sexual Addiction

Story of a Sex Addict

At one time in the history of our church, Dean and I welcomed an older gentleman into our congregation. He had a sad story that contained all types of regret and hurt. As typical young ministers, determined to grow our church and have mercy, we welcomed him and wanted to help him enjoy life again. He was a highly educated doctor, and I thought, despite my misgivings, that a man who works as a caretaker would not be anything other than good, right? I determined that I would be gracious.

Over time, though, few congregational members enjoyed this man's company. Mostly it was the decent women in our church who were repelled by him. Fortunately, our congregation let us know their thoughts; the result being that, though this gentleman wanted a greater platform for ministry in our church, we withheld this privilege. On the other hand, the more we held back ministry influence from this man, the less he was in the church.

Finally, a woman approached us with the information that she had been having a sexual relationship with this man, spending days in hotels around the city with him even though she was married. Her confession opened up a plethora of lies in which it was found that he was involved in sexual relationships with various women around the city at the same time.

When confronted by Dean, this man disappeared from the area, leaving a trail of devastation behind him. He did, though, later end up in court on other charges. To this day, I do not know if he was repentant. He used his education to enamor and coerce women into his bed. It was sickening that someone who people should be able to trust turned out to be one of the least trustworthy people that I have ever met.

Sexual addiction is a frightening term for someone addicted to sex. Addiction is no worse than any other sin, no matter what it is that the addict is craving. Christians tend to see addiction as a habit to which one succumbs, and it becomes a priority above all other things.[211] The ASAM defines addiction as the following:

> A primary, chronic disease of brain reward, motivation, memory and related circuitry. Dysfunction in these circuits leads to characteristic biological, psychological, social and spiritual manifestations. This is reflected in an individual pathologically pursuing reward and/or relief by substance use and other behaviors.[212]

People usually develop an addiction in order to escape the pain that is the result of some sort of loss in life. This loss can range from the mental loss of confidence due to rejection to the physical loss of a loved one through death. Annette Comiskey of Desert Stream Ministries describes this loss as a hunger or desire that needs to be filled.[213] She continues on to say that addiction is a symptom of a deeper brokenness.[214] Brokenness of the soul is something only God can heal; He restores the soul and guides us into righteousness.[215]

The concept of sexual addiction has only been around since the 1980's. It includes labels such as "nymphomania, hypersexuality, sexual addiction, sexual impulsivity and compulsive sexual behavior."[216] Hypersexuality is the most extreme end of the sexual pendulum; it is when a person engages in frequent sexual activity.[217] Sexologists "simply refer to unregulated sexual behavior as 'out of control sexual behavior' (Bancroft & Vukadinovic, 2004)."[218] Men can "experience this addiction more erotically in terms of concrete patterns of sexual behavior, whereas women may tend more toward a powerful preoccupation with another that could be labeled an emotional addiction."[219] Sex to a sex addict is the drug of choice. [220] It is what they hope will cover their pain and raise them out of their darker moods; however, like all drugs, the addict will experience the high of release for only a brief period of time before the low hits and the craving to get high again returns. The craving is so strong that the person caught up in the addiction will feel that he has lost all sense of control.

Understanding Addiction

Addiction is a self-rewarding cycle that is being classified as a disease because of its mental and biological factors; however, not all addictions are diseases. Christians especially believe that there are deeper needs which are being overshadowed by the power of the addict's drug of choice.[221] Sexual addiction can be equally defined as a persistent preoccupation with fantasies, behaviors, and emotions that culminate in orgasm that, like any addiction, results in an uncontrolled appetite. This appetite manifests in many ways, each of which conflict with our moral values. Lower levels of sexual addiction can be pornography, masturbation, and promiscuity.[222] Each aspect of this addiction—like all addictions—causes the well-known addiction cycle. The high of the drug results in a crash that is fuelled with guilt, shame, and anxiety as well as that burning desire to experience the freedom of the high. The more the cycle is indulged, the stronger the desire to repeat, and the deeper the guilt and the shame. Addiction promises so much, but these promises are dark lies meant to ensnare and never let go.

Defining the Addict

Sexual addiction in many ways seems to be a deeper wound than others. It is more difficult to admit because of its sexual nature. Though addictions are the same at their core, sexual addiction has a few defining traits that make it stand out. The sexual addict is often a victim of some form of sexual abuse and is now repeating "the victimization, only now being the perpetrator."[223] Addicts may have been exposed to sexual behavior such as pornography or assault at a young age. The root could even be something less severe like watching as a parent engages in an affair. Whatever the trigger, the addict is handicapped with a deep pain before even reaching an age of sexual understanding, and if that pain is not addressed, the addict will act upon his or her need to escape the pain.

The sex addict battles feelings of inadequacy and the loss of and lack of purpose. He feels it is impossible to love himself due to the pain living inside of him. These feelings are heightened when around other people. The addict can be socially isolated, awkward, and all too often have very few friends. Any relationship they may have—whether simple friendship or a marriage—is shallow. The addict fears intimacy, most likely due to the betrayal of intimacy that occurs in sexual abuse, and this fear causes him to not allow people to get too close. Addicts hope that sex will create the intimacy they crave and that it will drown the pain that they feel.

The addict leads a double life. He has his front-facing world that is filled with lies and deception meant to cover his addiction. Behind that is his addiction. He keeps it to himself because he fully believes that if others truly knew him, they could not love or accept him. His "addiction violates important values and beliefs"[224] that would define a human. Sex is the desired drug of the sex addict; because of this, the addict objectifies sex, stripping it of all intimacy and connection. It is a shallow drug that results in guilt, dissatisfaction, and shame.

The sex addict does tend to be impulsive and is a hard worker. There is a restless energy that drives the addict to accomplish fulfillment in whatever he is doing. This energy is rarely satisfied and can result in compulsive inconsistencies in life. The addict will seem distracted because he is thinking of ways to keep his addiction going while keeping it a secret. The addict has a deep need to live on the edge. There is an adrenalin rush in the fear and even anticipation of exposure that causes the addict to play out on more risky levels because of the stress and the pressure. With the growth of the addiction, there is an increase in energy needed to keep the addiction a secret, and the more energy he is pouring into his deception, the less energy he has for other things. So, the addict is both driven and distracted.

Sex addicts are selfish. Their addiction is all about taking. They blame others for their issues and demand relief from those issues without giving anything in return. This selfishness adds another level of objectification to the sex, making the high even shorter and the low even longer. The need to fulfill their desire becomes compulsive, even excessive. Sex replaces everything in their lives and robs a person of their appreciation of things.[225] They love and hate what they do. They have given themselves over to sensuality. Paul writes in Ephesians 4:19 that "having lost all sensitivity, they have given themselves over to sensuality so as to indulge in every kind of impurity, and they are full of greed."[226] They become manipulative and controlling of others, hoping to draw out sympathy and compassion while hiding the guilt and shame that will not fade.

Addicts often insist that they can stop their behavior at any time. Lust, however, always wants more. Addicts operate "under the assumption that lust can plateau at a certain level and simply stay there"[227] but this is not true. After a high comes a low. This leads to anger and despair. Amnon was not a sex addict, but his actions followed a similar cycle to that of a sex addict. His story is read in 2 Samuel 13. Amnon's lust for Tamar led to anger and hatred.[228] He lusted after and raped her and then hated and abandoned her.

Sexual addiction can destroy an individual. The needs that the addict seeks to meet cannot be fulfilled in the way that he hopes. Paul writes in 1 Corinthians 6:12, "'I have the right to do anything,' you say—but not everything is beneficial. 'I have the right to do anything'—but I will not be mastered by anything."[229] Needs that are rightly met should maintain and enrich self-respect, thus the addict realizes that, in the addiction cycle, the behavior is of no benefit and the addiction is controlling him. Paul further notes in 1 Corinthians that the body is not meant for sexual immorality but is meant for the Lord.[230] Addiction is not something that glorifies God nor does it fulfill the addict in any way.

Those Who Suffer

It is easy to judge the friends and family of an addict, claiming that they should have known. This is an unfair assessment for, even though there are signs, there is no definite profile that makes someone a sexual addict. A spouse, for instance, could easily explain away the addict's care-giver mentality or the sporadic nature of their sex life; missed family events always have an excuse that is believed despite plausibility; and the spouse can and will ignore the cracks in the relationship in hopes of salvaging what there is. Only when the addiction is brought to light are the clues made clear. The journey for the friends and family becomes hard at this point.

The immediate response to the revelation of an addict in the family is to cast him out and be done with it. This is easy advice to give for someone who has never been in this sort of situation. For the family members caught in this situation, it is a different story, especially for the spouse. The spouse has to face losing a commitment that had defined his or her life. The spouse must be given the right to choose how to proceed. Will the spouse stay to support the addict through the rough days ahead or will he or she leave? It is up to the spouse only to make this decision.

There are certain situations that will determine if others need to step in to help separate the addict and the spouse. These situations include environments of physical abuse or where the spouse has been kept in a codependent lifestyle. Not all women can immediately take care of themselves. They may not have access to the money nor know how to be financially successful on their own. At this point, gentle intervention is important. Offer help as it is needed and take it one day at a time.

Close and trusted friends are crucial when dealing with a sexually addicted spouse. The marriage vows have been betrayed. The remaining spouse goes through a gambit of emotions that need a healthy outlet. Anger at the addict is the first reaction. All the lies and deception hurt the spouse so deeply that he or she cannot help being angry. Fear of the future soon follows. Will the marriage last? Does he or she want it to last? What will happen next? Then, there is grief for what has been lost. The spouse no longer knows what was real in the marriage. Friends need to be nearby to help with the emotions. They need to understand that the loss that the spouse is feeling is very real and very deep. The spouse may not have the strength to forgive. Forgiveness is the key to redemption. If the spouse hopes to recover what was lost, forgiveness will be a daily battle. The strength and support of friends can be the turning point in this process, especially if the road to redemption passes through divorce.

The Road to Recovery

Desert Stream Ministries sets out the following steps regarding the discovery of a sexually addicted spouse. If a spouse discovers that his or her partner is a sex addict, let someone know immediately. Gentle intervention can be attempted such as writing a letter to the addict informing him or her of your awareness of the addiction.[231] Try to bring truth.[232] Another route is to go to a trusted friend and let them know about the letter that has been written.[233] Let those know who can provide immediate support and accountability. These also need to be people whom you trust enough that you can release your spouse to their care.[234] While a counselor is important, these trusted people should be those who are willing to listen, be company, and be committed to you.

Trust needs to be reestablished during this time of healing. Intimacy that was betrayed and then neglected needs to be created anew. It is very important for the marriage connection to be healed first. It is almost too easy for the addict to return to the role of parent; it is harder to return to the place of spouse. Open communication and established activities are also crucial to the healing process. The recovering spouse needs to know that he or she can be heard by their partner. Sex may not be immediately reestablished even though those needs have been neglected. The couple may need to start off on a smaller level of intimacy like talking together after the children have gone to bed. A couple's counselor may also need to be brought in at least for the first parts of the restoration process. Lastly, God must be in the center of it all. He brings the grace and mercy needed for the couple to live as one again. He brings the strength needed to allow forgiveness to run its course.

Keys to Recovery

Sexual addicts who want to be free of their addiction must first repent.[235] That is the key to the entire process. When the addict repents, he or she is submitting to God. God brings clarity to the situation. He helps the recovering addict to see that he or she is more than the addiction and that they can change. Anger at God or at self is natural and needs to be dealt with in a safe environment—such as with a counselor or close friend. God brings healing and encouragement with every daily surrendering.

There is a difference between self-pity and remorse.[236] Those chosen to help the addict must listen to what he or she is saying. Examine their goals. Be aware of trading one addiction for another. A repentant addict needs to understand that all addiction is wrong.[237] The problem is not the addiction but inner issues. Core values and beliefs will need to change rather than just altering behavior, and this will take time. This cannot be done alone. A support system and accountability are needed.

Finally, a recovering addict should be encouraged to volunteer and to serve, particularly in a local church. These actions tie back to Ephesians. One is urged to stop stealing but then to put his hands to good use.[238] In other words, the addict who had lived strictly for his or her own pleasures learns to be selfless by serving and helping others and begins to learn new, healthy behaviors that combat the addiction cycle. They are to do "'something useful with their own hands.' The word *useful* is the Greek word *agathos*, which is also translated 'good' and 'benevolent.'"[239]

Overall, sexual addiction is a difficult issue. The above points are a very brief summary of the recovery process. Some addicts enjoy their addiction and feel no shame; others are quick to repent and seek aid; still more, in fact most, are too afraid to step forward because of the stigma attached to sexual addiction. There is deep shame that stops them from fighting to be free. As believers, we are called to have grace and mercy on those who need help. Christians can be the ones who offer the support system needed in helping an addict overcome this type of problem.

Chapter 13: Sexual Abuse

Sexual Abuse by a Family Member

It started at four. Previously, my uncle would send me gifts from overseas, and, thinking back, it was probably his way of winning favor with me. Whenever he stayed with us, he would pull me on top of him and tickle me. The next year, I moved to live with him and his family, and the touching escalated. I hit puberty, and the touching became more obviously sexual. My life was so sheltered that I did not understand what was happening in my body, and, when I developed breast buds, I asked my uncle to look since I did not know that these changes were normal. My uncle was protective to the degree that we were not even permitted to see Disney movies. We didn't watch television, listen to a radio, or go to the movies.

The abuse escalated in high school. I was an early developer. One time when I was twelve, we were away at a friend's vacation place, and because I was hot, he told me to take off my clothes and lie down with him. He fondled me. I did all of this because it made him happy. If I wanted something from him, I would let him touch and fondle me. I think that his wife was very naïve and suspected nothing. Sometimes, he would let me stay home from school, or he would pick me up from school and take me to his office and play with me at his desk. He would make comments such as, "Imagine if we could run away and be together." "Don't tell anybody. It will ruin our lives." As I grew up, this seemed a good idea as our secret needed protection.

I was about sixteen when I realized that none of this was normal. My uncle said that when I was eighteen, I could date and have a boyfriend. Things were no different at eighteen, but rather, he was extremely protective and possessive. He would rub his penis against my vaginal entrance. After the encounters, I would be very angry. Part of it felt really good, and I could feel my body stirring sexually when he touched me with his fingers, even at twelve. It was as if my uncle had two personalities. He would present himself as a loving father around other people but then he was a different person around me. On occasion, he would cry and apologize profusely but then the abuse would commence again. Twice over the years, my grandmother asked if my uncle was molesting me, but I denied it both times.

When my friends at school started experimenting with boys, I'd pretend that I hadn't commenced menstruating because I wanted to maintain my innocence. I knew that I wasn't innocent, and I was scared of my uncle. I tried to hide any male friendships from him even though they were not dating relationships. At one time, when I was still eighteen, he found out about a phone call that I had made to a guy friend, and he started to hit me. It was two o'clock in the morning and so I ran away. I had no family contact details and so on waking my neighbors, I phoned my pastors. I was able to contact my uncle's brother who provided a home for me. I couldn't press charges against my uncle. I could not break up the family.

I, then, entered a time of promiscuity. I'd have a new boyfriend every month in which I let each one do what my uncle had done to me. If this is what made a man happy, then that's what I did. I'd allow everything but penetration. I'd then become really angry with the boyfriend and break up with him. It was at this time that I took a huge step in which I moved away and attended a Bible college. In this place, I began a journey of faith. When I left my uncle's home, I, in a sense, had left the security behind of nice cars and things.

It was now time to build my own life, and this meant that I get my life in order. I stopped dating and decided that it was time to start a journey of healing and trust. I had to also begin the journey of forgiveness. I now see God as a loving father though, at times, I fight an obsession that I must do good things to please God. One thing that I love about God is that He reveals things to me about my situation. It is faith and trust at each step.

My uncle still blames me and our relationship is very strained. I am not sure who in my family is aware of the truth of our situation. If my uncle expresses any physical touch toward me, it brings back memories. He wants to pretend that our relationship is normal as if nothing ever happened. It's as if he's attempting to be a Godly parent.

I'm now dating a great guy who is caring, respectful, and patient. He encourages me to be me, and he does not push anything that is sexual. While the future contains uncertainty, I'm looking forward to marriage and building my life step-by-step. Yes, I do fear having a daughter because I worry that what happened to me may happen to her. Step-by-step, though, I'm moving forward. I'm trusting God.

Today: This wonderful young woman does outstanding work with the youth in her church and is deeply loved and admired by many. She is still involved with the great guy that she mentioned and is excited for her future. –JS

Sexual abuse is a very real, very widespread problem that covers both a broad spectrum of activities and an unbiased list of victims. Sexual abuse can be viewed as "any behavior, attitude, or verbal response that hinders normal sexual development, bringing distortion and inhibition to personal sexuality and married lovemaking."[240] It includes:

> ...fondling of the breasts, buttocks, or genitals; vaginal, anal, or oral intercourse; exhibitionism; forced masturbation or forced viewing of masturbation; obscene gestures or comments; prostitution; or any other sexual activity that is harmful to the [victim's] mental, emotional, or physical welfare (Finkelhor et al., 2009).[241]

Sexual abuse can occur without touching. Long, suggestive stares and comments can be just as damaging as overly strict rules in a family setting regarding the discussion and/or handling of sexual education. If a family forbids talk or discussion of sex, or sees it as sinful, a youth's sexual development can be stunted, and, thus, the restrictions can be viewed as abuse.

The term "sexual abuse" must be used with care because it can be easily misconstrued. Those in caregiving occupations or in situations where a dual relationship forms are particularly vulnerable to accusations; in fact, boundary violations are a concern for all professionals.

> Determining appropriate from inappropriate forms of physical contact is sometimes challenging. Mental health professionals have been advised that non-sexual physical contact can be misinterpreted, especially with clients who are paranoid, obsessive-compulsive, labile, confused, depressed, hostile, and easily aroused (Houston-Vega et al., 1997).[242]

Hugs, hand pats, or a touch on the back can all be misread. We are influenced by past and present experiences; however, while there are those who have experienced great damage due to abuse, we must also take care to not misuse the term.

There is no bias when it comes to the victims of sexual abuse. Whether male or female, young or old, abuse can happen. There is a fluctuation in the "attitude and beliefs concerning the prevalence of sexual offending;" however, "what is common to most constructions is their gendered nature: the offenders are inevitably male and the victims inevitably female."[243] This can be a fact for most cases, but it is dangerous to ignore the probability of women committing sexual abuse as well.

It is a socio-culturally accepted idea that women could not possibly sexually abuse anyone.[244] This common idea has spread far and wide to the point that it has influenced the law; women are just not seen as sexually aggressive.[245] A survey conducted in 1991, however, showed that women are very capable of sexual abuse. In this survey, seventy-five males convicted of sexual offenses against children were surveyed, and the results revealed that not only were thirty-six percent of these men sexually abused as children, but forty-five percent of the thirty-six percent had been abused by females. Unlike male abusers, case studies have shown that "female victim populations reveal low numbers of females who perpetrate sexual abuse against other females."[246]

Child sexual abuse is also a significant problem that can damage a person for life. Child sexual abuse (CSA) is "any sexual activity that a child cannot consent to (American Academy of Pediatrics, 2010). In cases of child sexual abuse, the sexual contact is often achieved through force, trickery, or bribery and involves an imbalance in age, size, power, and knowledge."[247] Unfortunately, child abuse can be difficult to identify because most perpetrators are relatives (making the abuse incest) or close friends of the family of the victim. Adults may suspect something but do not wish to raise an alarm for one reason or another. They may be afraid of breaking up the family or of ruining a person's life with a false accusation. The child is also too afraid to speak up out of a twisted mix of love for the abuser (especially if the abuser is a family member) and fear of the ramifications should he or she say anything, thus the abuse is allowed to continue while the victims suffer in the shadows.

The Damage is Done

Victims of sexual abuse suffer a number of ramifications, and the younger the abused, the more damaging the abuse. A child is developing his sense of self and how he relates to other people. This sense is crucial to healthy development. Sexual abuse stunts this development. Young children who experience abuse will live out the ramifications as if the handicap forced upon them by the abuse was a part of them at birth. It's as if the abuse has scrambled their brain.[248] The brain is the epicenter of thought and memory, and that is where the most powerful damage is done.

Mental Barriers

Victims of sexual abuse can raise a mental defense in place of a physical defense. The victim can first disassociate from thinking or feeling so that they can escape the shame they feel. The victim is plagued with the disjointed memories of what happened to them. Memories of the abuse are often fractured due to the mind shutting down. It is a defense mechanism that both protects and hinders the victim. The victim is able to forget the worst parts, but they also bury the rest in hopes of escaping the pain.

Emotional Strain

Guilt and shame infect the victim's emotional state. They believe that the abuse was their fault. They struggle with thoughts that tell them they could have prevented it or fought back. The unfair burden of responsibility drags the victim down. Fear accompanies shame—fear of being abused again by the abuser or by new abusers, or fear of rejection should anyone find out. The victim can withdraw from other people and create introverted walls around their heart to keep people from hurting them again. This not only continues to retard the emotional development of the victim but stunts their life advancement as well. The gifts, talents, and opportunities that could have been are wasted behind the walls of fear, shame, and guilt.

Broken Boundaries

All humans need to belong, as Maslow outlines in his hierarchy of needs;[249] however, an abuse victim cannot get past step one in finding acceptance because the very basics of relational boundaries have been betrayed. Children growing up in a non-abusive home are taught the right ways to build relationships and assert boundaries. They are given the right to privacy and have the added benefit of caring family members who can intervene should they be developing hurtful habits. These boundaries and relationships are broken by abuse. In homes of sexual abuse, the boundaries are confused and the guidelines of life for the abuse victim are unclear and distorted. As a result, the victim is uncertain regarding the functioning of healthy relationships and where to set boundaries. The victim tries to mend and erect the broken lines and boundaries but fails.

Touch

Victims of sexual abuse do not know what to do about touch. They wonder what the reasons and motivations are behind even the most harmless touch. They question the look or the hug; they do not trust the people around them nor themselves; and they push people away out of fear. Their sense of physical connection is so skewed that they do not understand non-sexual touch. Pain may become arousing; platonic touch may become painful; and intimacy is almost impossible because the victim cannot bear the closeness. The victim will withdraw further and seek the comfort of touch in another way.

Masturbation can become a form of comfort for the abused. It is a familiar touch; one they understand and control. Young children who have been abused can act out by masturbating because their bodies have been aroused long before they are mentally mature enough to handle it. They have responded to intimate touch regardless of the gender of their abuser. The child knows that his treatment is wrong, but he feels powerless, helpless, and out of control. Masturbation can, to the abused, be a way to escape the sense of helplessness; however, masturbation only adds to the guilt and shame.

Victim to Abuser

Finally, victims of sexual abuse often will act out sexually. They can become promiscuous or, worse, abusers. They can repeat the abuse on those who are weaker than them. Victims of sexual abuse can often find pleasure in sexual fantasies about abuse; they may even feel empowered when they use others the way they were used. Intimacy is foreign to them; sex is used to hurt; thus, they will use it to hurt and in that pain find pleasure.

We know that the abused can become an abuser. We must be careful though in our understanding of this. Young children are innocent in many ways. For example, we tell them to never show or touch another person's private parts but we don't explain why. For the abused child, they have been touched and it feels good. One friend of mine experienced sexual abuse as a child but did not tell his family. While it was pleasurable, he felt guilty and confused. This abuse caused a typical pattern to commence that is at times found in sexual abuse victims. From eight years old on, this young boy would use social engagements with other children as a time for touching, intercourse, and anything else that felt good. He did this behind the playroom doors while his family assumed he and the other children were just playing.

Sexual abuse as a small child opens a dream world. These children are too young to understand "casting down imaginations."[250] Their only guideline is all too often "private body parts are private," but this mantra has been violated. Children don't understand or know the word "orgasm" or "climax," but they have experienced one. Their sexual world has been opened prematurely, and there is a tug of war within them.

When I've talked with those that have experienced sexual abuse, they can explain some reactions and not others. Most battle guilt while other reactions are difficult to explain. Most are embarrassed because the abuse was sexual. We need to know that this topic is complicated. Sex when used outside of God's plan causes great hurt and confusion particularly to children. We, therefore, need to understand that when one who has been sexually abused becomes an abuser, it may be at an age when they are clueless concerning what they are doing.

Sexual Confusion

Sexual abuse can also be a key factor in the development of a homosexual lifestyle.

> Childhood sexual abuse is well attested to demonstrate a correlation to the incidence of homosexuality among those affected by it. A large national survey of almost 35,000 Americans showed that more than three times as many men and women who had been sexually abused as children became homosexuals, versus that of heterosexuals. Another study reported that 58 percent of male adolescents who later became homosexuals suffered sexual abuse as children, while 90 percent who did not suffer sexual abuse identified themselves as heterosexuals. In addition, 43 percent of male homosexuals reported sexual activity with another male during the ages of 10–12, versus 9 percent of heterosexuals.[251]

The ramifications of sexual abuse are widespread and very dangerous. They are also hidden very deeply in the human heart, making it so very hard to heal. Thankfully, God is a God for whom nothing is too difficult.[252] No matter what the pain, He can and will heal it.[253]

Healing the Shame

Many victims of sexual abuse have had a sexual encounter before God's intended time. Sex becomes associated with fear, pain, and control while love, joy, and pleasure are distorted.[254] The victim can try to escape the pain, but freedom and healing come when the victim determines to face the pain and shame. Facing the past is a frightening thing. There are memories of the abuse that need to be dealt with, deep emotional pain that must be worked through, and the positive aspects of life to learn. All of these things can be accomplished through one key step: submitting to Christ.

Jesus is the resurrection and the life.[255] In order to find freedom, the victim needs to release the hurts of the past to Jesus.[256]

Recovery must be looked at in light of the redemptive work of Christ on the cross. Through Christ's resurrection, we have a resurrected life. Jesus promises to be our protector, shield, and sufficiency when it was written, "He will never leave you nor forsake you."[257] It can be difficult for the abused to trust God. The question of "How can a loving God have let this happen to me?" is a common stumbling block. No one knows the mind of God nor will I attempt to explain Him.[258] What I can say is that, through the bad and the worse, God will take care of us.[259] His love endures forever,[260] and His power to restore life is what makes our ruined worlds beautiful.[261] If we trust in Him,[262] He will lead us into our best life. In 2 Corinthians 5:17, Paul writes that we become new creations when we accept Jesus Christ and His Lordship.[263] This, along with a daily relationship with Him, will heal the human heart as nothing else can.

The hardest challenge for a recovering victim may be facing the shame. The shame acts as a foundation for feelings of inferiority and self-hatred. Shame, however, is just an emotion. It is on the same level as happiness, anger, or excitement. When looked at in that light, shame loses a good deal of its power. Shame does hurt; that is not to be ignored; but pain heals; even emotional pain. The medication for shame is reassurance that the abuse was not the victim's fault, love and acceptance by people who will not judge him or her, and trust in both these people and in God. God's purpose beyond the abuse needs to be emphasized, prayed through, and understood. While the abused victim has been sinned against, he or she has to identify his or her sin of hanging onto the guilt and shame.

As the emotional hurts begin to heal, the abused can begin to disassociate with the label of "victim." He or she can begin to see that they are more than their abuse. They can see the truth that God made no mistake in their making, regardless of their experiences. Psalm 139:14 states that we are "fearfully and wonderfully made."[264] Each person is a marvelous work, and when the abused allows that truth to take hold of their heart, they can begin to live in a new identity as one of God's children.

The memories of the abuse can be faced in the safe environment of a biblical counselor. In order to find freedom, the victim will have to face the memories that have haunted him or her since the abuse. Moving on from painful memories is easier said than done. The victim has been violated, and there may be no apology or acknowledgement. There is also reeducation that is needed. Sexual abuse survivors often see sex as uncontrollable, and as a commodity. It is also hurtful, secretive, and has no moral boundaries.[265] "Male abuse survivors sometimes struggle with same-sex fantasies and an arousal by penises."[266] This is not necessarily an indication of homosexuality, but is a consequence of abuse and can be worked through. They, therefore, need to be freed from these thoughts and memories. Talking about the experience helps to remove the power from the memories and allows the victim to see the event for what it is. He or she can then submit it to God and move further into the healing process.

Restoration is a process that takes time. Many of the stories in this book show that healing can take years. It is a daily choice, and it is not always easy. If we hold true to God and His promises, we will find the strength we need to complete the journey.

As written earlier, there is much spoken today regarding all types of sexual abuse. We must take care that these situations are not spoken of lightly and that we do not throw these terms around loosely. Many of these writings show that larger sexual issues are the result of some type of sexual abuse; therefore, that we understand God's design for sex is vitally important.

Chapter 14: Rape

Rape Victim

My 2-year-old son was napping, so I decided to leave my door open and step out on the main balcony to have a smoke. I put my cigarette out and turned to go back into my apartment. I stepped inside of my apartment, and when I put my hand on the door to shut it, suddenly this guy was in my apartment. All I could think of was my son, so I didn't yell or cry out. I didn't want him to know I had a baby, and I didn't want him to hurt us.

He pushed me into the bathroom, and, over the next hour, he forced me to go down on him and do other things to him. It had to be what hell is like. I remember trying to memorize every detail that I could. He came in my mouth, and, for some reason, he immediately left the bathroom. I spit into the toilet. He came back and pulled me out into the living room, and I thought he was going to kill me. He was aggressive with me, and he kept threatening that he would kill me if I yelled or made any noise. He found my cellphone and took it, and he told me to stay put for 10 minutes and that if I called anyone he would come back and hurt me again. After he left, I remember sitting on the floor, crouched down. I didn't have a clock in front of me, and I kept thinking, "Has it been 10 minutes yet?"

I eventually left the apartment and started screaming for help. The asshole had apparently tried to break into another woman's apartment, but she was able to shut him out and call the police. By the time I was running through the parking lot screaming for help, the police were already there. They found him nearby and arrested him.

I did not flush the toilet, so his semen was still in there. I also had not brushed my teeth or washed my hands or face. I don't know how I remembered all of the things I had been taught, but the little things like spitting out his semen and saving it were huge in prosecuting him. He's in prison now, and he won't be eligible for parole for 40 years.

I was a 4.0 student before this happened, and now most days, I barely function. People expect me to just get over this and go on with my life because this asshole is in prison. What they don't understand is that, in one hour, that man took my life. He took "who" I am away... probably forever.[267]

Today: The end of this woman's story remains unknown. Hers was an anonymous story submitted from an outside source. We do not know if she continues to live with her shame or if she has found freedom and healing in Christ. –JS

Date Rape

At thirteen, I was date raped. I said no, but he said yes. He also stole my stuff. I was homeless and felt crushed. No is no. I felt ashamed. Is it my fault? It hurt like hell because I was a virgin.

Today: This remarkable woman recently came to the Lord and has made many positive changes in her life. –JS

Overcoming Rape

I heard the door open and then noticed the hall light on...then it closed. I assumed that my three-year-old was up again, wandering the house. That was, after all, a normal occurrence in my life as a single mom. My two-year-old was surely sleeping soundly in his room. I quickly got up, calling for my three-year-old. That is when it started.

Someone bigger than me had grabbed me. I punched hard and kicked him and tried to scream as his hand covered my mouth. He said, "You don't want to do that…I have seen your kids, both of them." My heart stopped and fear gripped my throat. I felt the metal of the barrel of a gun as he held it to my head. I stopped fighting. My thoughts were wrestling with each other…fight…no, don't…my boys could be killed…were they already dead?…GOD…where are you…why is this happening… should I try and get the gun and kill him…pain…fight…fear… guilt, had I somehow brought this on myself??? Wait…what is he saying to me??

Again, my heart stopped as I realize it is not him talking…it is my three-year-old. He is awake and in the room. I felt the gun shoved into my face. I begged him to let me get my child back to sleep. He hit me, but for some reason, he agreed. He rolled off of me and allowed me to settle my oldest down…miraculously...he fell asleep, while the abuser held a gun to my head.

He became more and more aggressive and angry with me, threatening to kill me if I could not satisfy him…WHAT??? Again, I begged God to please let this end…help me. In what seemed like hours, it finally ended. My body was numb and my brain was screaming in pain. Even as I write this, the feelings return.

God had let me down. He had promised to keep me safe and protect me. I trusted Him.

As the guy was getting dressed, I heard God speak to my heart…Forgive. Again, forgive…WHAT?? But I knew that the only hope I had at making any kind of emotional recovery was to begin now…and forgive. I chose to run to God rather than become angry. I closed my eyes and embraced God.

As he crawled out of the window that night, I quickly found my boys and held them tight. They were safe. And so was I.

The police came, the "evidence" was collected, and reports were written. And just like that it was done.

My life returned to normal quickly, and, somehow, I did find a way to forgive what had happened to me. I was free...so I thought.

It has taken time to heal the physical aspects of rape; the scars are real. It is the unseen scars, the ones no one can see, that have taken the most time to heal. A noise, a smell, a move of my husband's hand, a closing door…all of these can cause the throat-crushing fear to appear. Sex can take on two very different paths…one of pain…one of pleasure. Sometimes the confusion can happen at the same time.

But then I remember…forgive. And I close my eyes and embrace God.

Today: This lady is truly remarkable. She is one of my closest friends. She and her husband have impacted hundreds of people for God and led many on paths of recovery from various types of addiction and abuse. –JS

Rape is the most prevalent form of sexual abuse and is far too familiar in society. Young women are told when they enter college that they have a 1 in 3 chance of being pressured or forced into sexual relations; the studies backing this warning are terribly true.[268] Society is so aware of the dangers that all too often someone cries abuse and rape when nothing is truly amiss. Too many young people are confused now as to what activity is rape, for they have been encouraged through their parents, peers, and education to be sexually free, thus when the thought of saying "No" comes into mind, it is a novelty, and the one refused does not take it lightly. Girls are taught to dress sexually in hopes of drawing in a guy through attraction. They are not warned that attraction backfires, and the girls who need to sound the alarm of rape and abuse seldom do.

The definition of rape does vary but not for the reasons one would think. Men and women in different races and ethnicities can disagree as to what rape is due to the differences in cultural sexual norms.[269] The laws regarding rape even differ according to each individual state in the United States of America; however, each state agrees that it is a criminal offense.[270] Despite the unnecessary debate, rape is "oral, anal, or vaginal intercourse or other forms of penetration by one person (the accused) with or against another person (the victim) without the consent of the victim (Federal Bureau of Investigation, 2009)."[271] A black-and-white definition will never encompass all that rape is and does. It is the testimonies of those who have suffered it that bring the stark truth. Even the Bible does not hold back when telling the truth about rape.

The book of 2 Samuel contains the tragic story about a young woman named Tamar. She is the daughter of King David who is raped by her stepbrother, Amnon. The Bible is very clear as to what is going through Amnon's mind. He was so obsessed with her that he became ill.[272] Amnon constructed a plan that would lure his sister in unsuspectingly, and, when her defenses were down, he used his strength to overpower and rape her. The author of 2 Samuel states that after the rape, "Amnon hated her with intense hatred. In fact, he hated her more than he had loved her."[273] After he took what he wanted, he hated and blamed her and cast her away into a life of disgrace. He did not love her. His desire was selfish and it cost Tamar everything. Bell writes that obsessive lust of this kind drives us to do frightening things and can own us. It takes up mass amounts of head space and causes misery.[274] The fact that God places the story of Amnon and Tamar in the Bible reveals that He is aware of this terrible crime.

In the last chapter, it was made clear that both genders are capable of sexual abuse; however, "physically coercive sex is primarily a male activity."[275] Rape is the "extreme end of the link between sex and aggression" and "although women use many strategies to persuade men to have sex, physical force and violence are seldom part of their repertoire."[276] Rape is not something that only occurs between strangers, it happens in married and unmarried couples, and is common in both hetero- and homosexual circles. Women who have been sexually abused as a child will more than likely be abused as an adult and have a five times higher risk of being raped.[277] Men can be pressured or coerced to have sex from male and female partners. Men as victims are usually less educated, more likely to be ethnic minorities, are from lower income homes, and more likely to be tested positive for HIV antibodies.[278] In regards to homosexual relationships,

> Unwanted sexual experiences represent a prevalent and pervasive problem for men who have sex with men. A complex matrix of substance abuse, disassociation, anxiety, and personality disturbances occur with high-risk sexual behavior in men who have been sexually coerced to a greater extent than men who have not been coerced.[279]

Rape, like sexual abuse and other sexual violations, does not pick or choose. When lust takes the mind to obsession, the rapist will think of nothing other than his or her pleasure. The victim is just an object, and sex is the weapon used to destroy it.

Rape has become so prevalent in societies around the world that certain countries are taking extreme measures to fight back. Dr. Sonnet Ehlers of South Africa invented a secret weapon against rapists, one they would never see coming, literally.

> The woman inserts the latex condom like a tampon. Jagged rows of teeth-like hooks line its inside and attach on a man's penis during penetration. Once it lodges, only a doctor can remove it—a procedure Ehlers hopes will be done with authorities on standby to make an arrest. "It hurts, he cannot pee and walk when it's on," she said. "If he tries to remove it, it will clasp even tighter... however, it doesn't break the skin, and there's no danger of fluid exposure."[280]

Measures such as this show the necessity of intervention; not intervention from the Government or the schools but at the most basic and important level: at home.

Parents will always be the primary teacher for a child; whether the lesson is in how to live a sexually healthy life or how sex can be used to hurt and destroy. Healthy parental relationships build confident and strong adults. Parents cannot rely on the school system to educate their children. Sex education is not taught out of the context of God's perfect design. It reduces sex to a black-and-white definition and strips it of its spiritual and soulful levels. Body parts that should contain a sense of privacy and mystery and be reserved strictly for marriage become no different than an arm or a leg. Sex becomes simple and easy; rape or sexual abuse becomes downplayed as simply being beaten up. A woman who cries over the loss of her pride, dignity, and heart due to rape is almost mocked because "we don't really go for that stuff anymore."[281]

Parents need to be aware of what the education system is teaching their children and be empowered to withdraw their children should they disagree with the lessons. Marriages in the homes need to be healthy, loving, and strong so that children can model their own future marriages after those of their parents. They will know what is and is not appropriate in regards to boundaries and touch and will make the right choices because of it. Parents should no longer fear the opinions of their children and should take the steps to protect their families at all costs. This includes knowing their children's friends and friends' families.

Open communication is the final key. Parents can talk candidly with their children about sex, sexual boundaries, and sexual relationships. All of these steps can help build and develop confidence in a child that will protect them from being coerced, for they will have a strength that drives unwanted advances away.

True beauty and attraction come from strong confidence. A woman who submits to God's ways and protective standards will be able to walk in beauty without needing low-cut tops and short skirts. They will draw good, Godly men who respect their choices and will not pressure them sexually. These men will display the true mark of manhood: submission to God. This kind of man is also attractive in his confidence and strength. That is the result of God's ways coming to fruition in humanity.

If you or someone that you love does experience sexual abuse like rape, don't ignore it. It is easy to cry in the shadows and hope the pain goes away. It is hard to face it and find healing. Remember, the cross of Christ brings freedom from guilt and pain. He empowers us to forgive, and forgiveness allows us to move forward. There is no shame when we come to Christ; He already understands the abuse we experienced. We have a choice because of the cross, and it's in this that we find freedom.

Chapter 15: Pedophilia

Story of a Pedophile

One summer day in the mid-1990s, Spencer Kaplan climbed aboard a bus at the camp where he was a counselor-in-training, sat down next to a little boy of about 9, and thought, "My God, I want to kiss him." Spencer was 14. As a junior counselor, his job was to help an older counselor with the 8- and 9-year-olds. Spencer had noticed this boy before, shy. On the bus, Spencer coaxed him out of his shell. For the rest of the summer, Spencer took the boy under his wing; the attraction he felt was dizzying.

He had felt stirrings of attraction toward other boys. At a school assembly, he was entranced by a boy his own age who struck him as the most beautiful person he'd ever seen. When he was 12, he developed a crush on his best friend. The two would sleep with their arms wrapped around each other, and although nothing sexual happened, Spencer adored their intimacy.

When he got to high school, his sexual and romantic yearnings felt as puzzling. He liked girls, but they didn't make his heart quiver like boys did. He wondered if he was gay but wasn't sure. He was lonely. In his senior year, when he was 17, his regular roller hockey game was joined by "Josh," a 13-year-old, with whom Spencer fell "madly in love." They talked for hours after the games. His high school friends teased him about his "little friend." Spencer realized that he was getting older, but oddly, the type of boy he was attracted to wasn't.

He spent a nervous night on the Internet typing in searches on a word he was beginning to think might describe him: pedophile. He was baffled that the tenderness he felt toward Josh had anything to do with what he read online about predators, psychopaths, violent child rapists, and murderers. He realized that what felt entirely natural to him was despised by society and, that once he turned 18, it could make him a criminal.

Spencer went off to college. He dated both men and women his age, but at the deepest level, he missed the emotional connection he'd felt to younger boys. He spiraled into depression, skipping classes, and spending days smoking pot and sitting glazed-eyed in front of the television. Halfway through his sophomore year, he took a medical leave from school and went home. The feelings followed him there. Walking around the mall in his hometown, he struggled with the effort to look away from young boys.

Spencer decided he had to explain himself to his parents. He sat down with them in the living room and stammered. "The boys at the mall," he started. "I can't stop staring at them. I want to be with a boy. I'm attracted to boys." They were alarmed and insisted on getting him help.

Over the next 10 years, the people Spencer and his family thought could help almost always regarded him as a criminal even though the only crime he had committed was a thought crime. When he shared his attraction to boys with one therapist, she barked: "You can't do that." Another therapist suggested getting Spencer into a sex-offender treatment program. A youth ADHD specialist wanted to medicate him. Confiding his attraction nearly always led to suspicious inquiries about whether he had molested children and gave little help when he answered "No." "Most had not the slightest idea how to deal with someone like me," he says.

Spencer is in his early 30s now. He emphatically states that he understands the law and that he has never molested a child. He considers himself a "minor-attracted person," a term that some prefer to "pedophile," and what he and others like him have been quietly promoting is the idea that society needs to recognize that they exist, that they are capable of controlling their sexual desires, and that they deserve support and respect for doing so.[282]

Today: This man's (whose real name was changed for his protection) story was found whilst we researched this topic. It is unknown where he is now or how he is doing. –JS

Pedophilia is probably one of the most uncomfortable subjects in the world of sexual sins. It is difficult to discuss and even more difficult to face. Believers and non-believers alike would almost prefer to ignore this part, but far too many children have been hurt to let this topic remain in the dark. Pedophiles are known for molesting 80–300 children before being stopped. In one study of male university students, the claim was advanced that

> 21% of their sample reported "sometimes" being sexually attracted to children, 95% reported having sexual fantasies involving children, 5% reported masturbating during fantasies about sex with a child (which, according to the authors,

> defined them as pedophiles), and 75% reported that they would have sex with a child if they were certain of remaining undiscovered.[283]

Though the measures of this trial are sometimes questioned, we can no longer remain naïve on the subject. Pedophiles, either active or passive, are out there, and we need to be aware.

Pedophilia is adult sexual activity or attraction to a prepubescent child. Definitions of pedophilia have included masturbating to a fantasy of a child and/or any adult that has had sexual contact with one who is under the ages of eighteen or sixteen, regardless of sexual preferences and motivations of the older person and regardless of the sexual maturity of the younger person.[284] The term *pedophile* is used interchangeably with child molester, sex offender, rapist, perpetrator, abuser, or victimizer.[285] It is a criminal activity and is listed as a psychiatric disorder in the DSM-IV-TR. "Most state laws identify pedophilia as felonious sexual activity committed with the child under the age of twelve or thirteen (Sperry 2003)." Ephebophilia is "adult sexual activity with and/or attraction to post-pubescent minors; i.e., adolescents less than eighteen years of age (Sperry 2003)."[286] It is not listed as a psychiatric disorder.

In 2002, the media and law enforcement drew attention to a cover-up of clergy misconduct with minors.[287] The USCCB admitted responsibility and then declared the Charter for the Protection of Children and Young People. The document requires that all Catholic diocese and eparchies publish codes of conduct for priests.[288] Apart from this abuse being an occurrence and from clerical circles that should be most trusted, this atrocity stirred much debate regarding homosexuality, pedophilia, and adult sexual activity with minors. Again, though, the tools and environments used to determine these characteristics are highly questioned. There is much still to be learned regarding pedophilia.

Pedophiles, according to some reports, have exhibited a complex set of attitudes. One defining point is that the sexual desire may be subordinate rather than superordinate. Between the pedophile and victim, "interactions between such persons and children sometimes have been characterized as 'affectionate' and inclusive of many non-sexual components, some of which may be experienced by the child as rewarding."[289] Pedophiles almost never force children into sexual acts. They use methods that are referred to as grooming. Desensitizing their victims, they engage them in harmless touching but progress to more invasive acts.[290]

Pedophiles have been described as passive, dependent, isolated, unassertive, and awkward in interpersonal relationships. Lack of social skills tends to be associated with sex offenders as a whole. They can be anxious and depressed, below average in intelligence, preoccupied with religious matters, and ignorant and puritanical concerning sex. They may also be narcissistic and over-identify with their mothers, psychosexually immature, and show an aversion to adult females, the adult female body, and heterosexual intercourse.[291]

Pedophilia is one of those problems that are difficult to confess. Pedophiles live in secrecy within our communities. If they are caught, they rarely confess their potential crime; opting, instead, to make excuses such as being with a child to protect them from predators. It is also difficult to separate the idea of a pedophile from a predator. Not all pedophiles repeat their offenses; not all pedophiles are onetime offenders either. In both cases, damage has been done. Pedophiles are often involved in pornography and/or had something traumatic happen in their lives. They will carry the label of "pedophile" for the rest of their lives regardless of the number of times they acted upon their lusts. We, again, cannot be naïve. Pedophiles need to be known and identified regardless of whether or not they intend to hurt children again.

Pedophilia and the Bible

There is no direct mention in the Bible about pedophilia, but that doesn't mean that this topic cannot be addressed with biblical principles. For example, the sin of fornication can be applied. Fornication is a part of the lists of the "lusts of the flesh" in Galatians 5 and is part of a list of sins found in Mark 7—sins that are born in the hearts of men when they stray from God's ways. Pedophiles are those "without natural affection" as described in Romans 1:31 and 2 Timothy 3:2. The above phrase is taken from a single Greek word that means "inhuman, unloving and unsociable."[292] Pedophiles are people who act contrary to the social norm.

In Matthew 18, Jesus makes a powerful statement about children. He first admonishes His disciples for trying to keep the children from Him. He, then, instructs them in the importance of having child-like faith. Jesus made it clear that children are important, and that "whoso shall offend one of these little ones which believe in me, it were better for him that a millstone were hanged about his neck, and that he were drowned in the depth of the sea."[293]

> The word "offend" in the Greek means "to cause one to stumble, to put a stumbling block or impediment in the way, upon which another may trip and fall, to entice to sin, to cause a person to begin to distrust and desert one whom he ought to trust and obey, to cause to fall away, to cause one displeasure at a thing, or to make indignant.[294]

Regardless of their intentions or motivations, pedophiles hurt children and thus fall under the implied curse spoken by Jesus in Matthew.

Pedophilia and the Church

Pedophile in the Church

There was a time in our church's history that a middle-aged couple began attending services. Sometime later, a parent let us know that the husband was texting their fourteen-year-old daughter late at night. Topics of the texts included inappropriate questions about her attire. Several other parents soon followed with evidence of much of the same. We were aware that this man's past was sexually warped. As a teen, he had attended a church where his senior leader was an adulterer, slept with prostitutes, and took advantage of younger women by pretending to be a counselor. This leader mentored him when he was a young man. It was during this time that he met and married his beautiful but naive wife. Years later, he came to our church and asked for help. He had a deep problem with pornography, and had, over the years, committed adultery and visited prostitutes. He lost several jobs due to use of pornography at work.

We met with this husband and wife concerning the information presented to us. The wife sweetly refused to acknowledge that there was an issue. She insisted that he could not be doing such things even though the texts were still in his phone. He also denied that there was a problem. We firmly insisted that he attend counseling and placed strict boundaries around him in regards to attending our church. After a couple of weeks, they left the church.

Today: This man sits in prison on charges of pedophilia. He denies even to this day that he has a problem. When caught, he said that he was only warning young girls of potential rapists. –JS

Pedophilia is subtle. The husband in the above story was friendly, honest about some of his past issues, and served in church. Often people with deep issues serve in a ministry in the church. It is as if they are trying to compensate for a problem. This husband had friends and a beautiful, loving wife; however, having these relationships in his life did not prevent him from committing adultery on several occasions. Even though he had repented of his adultery, his sexual issues were still present in his life and his forgiving wife seemed only to pretend that there were no problems.

When our church had to intervene concerning his behavior, some of the congregational members struggled with the church's plan of action regarding this man and not for the reasons one would think. Some believed we were being too harsh. One family in particular believed that all this man needed was counseling and prayer; even when he refused to see a counselor, they believed in him and had mercy for him. To them this man was normal, a faithful servant in the church, a generous giver financially, and loved people. Opinions and advice are easy to give out when we are not the ones holding the weight of authority and responsibility. Due to the tight relationships and trust in each other, damage was prevented in our church and in the community. While the outcome for this husband and his wife was sad, he was unable to cause further harm in our church because we acted quickly.

We as leaders cannot afford to be naïve. We must instruct our children and monitor the care that is given to them in our churches. There are children and young adults who come into the church who have suffered at the hands of sexual abuse and therefore do not understand normal boundaries. A simple platonic touch can become a trigger for misunderstanding and pain. Leaders of children and youth need to know what is appropriate and set the standard accordingly. This protects both the congregation and the leadership.

The point is that we need to get to know the people in our churches. Gifts are fine, but it is through relationships that we discover the strengths and weaknesses of each other. Be aware of those that are very elusive or, at the other extreme, overly serve. Sadly, churches are attractive for pedophiles. They are filled with trusting people, families, and children. People walk in and out of churches every day, and we seldom know how they spend their private time. Pedophiles are rarely welcome in churches because of the many children that are a part of the church. Finding people who are willing to work in the children's department is very hard for many churches, but it is vital that children and youth workers are screened and have background checks done or character recommendations from employees or previous churches are obtained. If a pedophile is a part of a church and if families are to feel safe, it is essential that the pedophile is monitored at all times. This seemingly harsh standard is for the benefit of the entire church. Repeat offense is common, thus keeping to a stricter standard is necessary.

Knowledge is power, so they say, and the more we are aware, the more we can help stop things like sexual abuse and pedophilia from occurring. God does not shy away from the darkest aspects of human nature. He does not condemn nor reject us. No one—sexual abuser, rape victim, or pedophile—is outside the range of His help; however, there are those who have been told by Christians that God cannot even save them. These people suffer probably some of the cruelest hate in the world and need the mercy and compassion of a loving God just as much. It is time now to discuss the most controversial sexual issue in the church today: same-sex attraction.

Part Four: Same-Sex Attraction

It is quite possibly one of the cruelest things in life to deny someone love. Love is one of the greatest things we can achieve. From the moment we are born, we are searching for that special someone to make us feel loved. So how can love be wrong? That is the question that is posed whenever same-sex attraction is highlighted. "We love each other" is raised as a battle cry to the point that no one listens to anyone else regarding this issue. Same-sex attraction is stirring so much hate in the name of love. It is a touchy issue that too many are ducking or ignoring or hoping will go away. This section is dedicated to an in-depth study of same-sex attraction. We will explore what society is saying, what science is saying, what psychology is saying, and, of course, what God is saying, and, through it all, see the truth in all its nitty-gritty glory.

Chapter 16: An Introduction to Same-Sex Attraction

Same-sex attraction is no longer the surprising issue that it used to be; all of us know of at least one person who has considered the option of experimenting in same-sex relations. Most people in this generation do not consider themselves immediately heterosexual or homosexual. They are encouraged to explore their options and decide afterwards what "feels right." Children coming into their adolescence are the primary target of this philosophy. Teenage years are a delicate time for sexual development. Confusion is rampant now that sex is so open and available. The media surrounds these young minds with messages about the rights of homosexual couples and how same-sex attraction is no different than opposite-sex attraction. It is all so hip and cool to be "open-minded;" however, society is filled with confusion regarding homosexuality, for it is much more than just a sexual dilemma.[295]

Same-sex attraction is a delicate, complicated, and difficult issue to tackle. There are many layers to it. A good place to start is with the basics. Same-sex attraction begins as all sexual experiences as an attraction. The human body can experience arousal from any source regardless of whether it is a member of the opposite gender or the same gender that is doing the arousing. This thought may not be pleasant to consider, but it is imperative and rather liberating. Many young people experiment with same-sex relations and enjoy them, thus, they get confused about their sexual orientation.

The term "sexual orientation" generally refers to one's sexual preference. We often assume that our orientation would be natural; however, Jim McKnight, an evolutionary biologist and Chair of the Psychology Department at the University of Western Sydney,[296] notes that "How we choose to express ourselves sexually may be quite different from the way nature made us."[297] Arousal is biological. When we accept that fact, we can take it off the table in regards to how we choose our sexual expression. McKnight adds to this liberating thought when he writes, "From a biological perspective a genetic predisposition to homosexuality would be just that, a precursor, or orientation, and no more. Sexual preference on the other hand may well be learned or a matter of personal choice and may even go against one's nature."[298] People can change sexual preferences before they reach full maturity. Same-sex attraction is actually a part of growing up (which is something we will discuss in the following chapters) and, thus, does not need to be a fearful moment when it manifests at a young age.

The APA refers to sexual attraction as "an enduring pattern of emotional, romantic, and/or sexual attractions to men, women, or both sexes."[299] It also refers to one's sense of identity based on these attractions, behaviors, and belonging to a certain community. Julie Harren of Exodus International notes that we do not choose our attractions or desires.[300] The problem with sexual orientation, though, is that it is discussed only as "a characteristic of an individual, like biological sex, gender identity, or age. This perspective is incomplete because sexual orientation is defined in terms of relationships with others."[301] Sexual orientation is closely tied to our intimate personal relationships. These relationships meet our deeply felt needs for love, attachment, and intimacy through non-sexual physical affection, common goals, shared values, support, and ongoing commitment.

Sexual orientation defines one's social basis. From within the basis is the core group of people where one finds the satisfying and fulfilling romantic relationships that are an essential component of personal identity for many people.[302] Females particularly seek out close relationships that can easily become too intimate. How often do young girls lie around a bedroom in which they share deep fantasies and secrets with other girls? They form close emotional attachments that can step over a healthy line, particularly in this day and age where parents tend to be more absent, and the media and the Internet are the primary sources for relational information. The socially accepted standards of relationship taught through the media and Internet place pressure on the young to conform and cast confusion regarding living a healthy lifestyle.

Human sexual responses are not random nor are they the result of biological heredity, genes, or chromosomes. From the first year of life, each person is taught about sex whether directly or indirectly. Ward B. Powers, currently Dean of New Testament and

Ethics, Tyndale College, The Australian Open Theological College,[303] notes that instinct impels the average human being toward some kind of sexual expression, but they themselves determine the sexual activity in which they engage.[304] He believes that it is conditioned by upbringing, training, accepted standards, and patterns of sexual behavior in their society as well as their own moral code.

Morality is a lynch-pin point in the understanding and handling of same-sex attraction. Those who have become too overzealous in their standards have caused more damage than help. Prejudice and outspokenness have probably ostracized the homosexual community from the Christian community. The AIDS epidemic was a bigger picture than being strictly a gay issue. Panic and fear were excessive while "public opinion studies over the 1970's, 1980's and 1990's routinely showed that among large segments of the public, lesbian, gay, and bisexual people were the target of strongly held negative attitudes."[305] It is little wonder that the retaliation has probably gone to the other extreme.

It is far too easy to forget that all the sexual issues in life—bisexuality, heterosexuality, homosexuality, bestiality, masturbation, group sex—are mentioned throughout historical cultures as well as in the Bible; we have trouble remembering the sins for which we ourselves are forgiven. When we as believers have not struggled with an issue, it is easy to become self-righteous. The best thing that I can think to do regarding the problems of others is to name an area where we struggle. Have we defeated that problem? Most likely we found victory and freedom after a long and lengthy battle, or we are still fighting for that victory. We always have other areas of weakness. We sin every day and do not even realize it at times, thus, when we humble ourselves, we become someone who is more relatable to people and even may be able to help others that struggle sexually.

As Christians, we are not to condemn. God didn't abandon those with sexual sin in the Bible; He redeemed them. We need to be those that offer hope. Rosenau writes the following:

> We are called to compassion and not a fear or revulsion of homosexual behavior. The danger in taking a strong stance on any moral issue is that the persons do not feel we can empathetically

> listen and help them deal with the problem—they are unwilling to tell us the story of their tortuous journey for fear of rejection or past advice.[306]

If you are a parent of a homosexual child, pray and carry hope. It is typical to struggle sexually in some way as we are all sexual beings. Sexual sin is understandable, and it is correctable. Most people who struggle with sexual sins like same-sex attraction know, deep down, that this is not what they want. They do not want to be the way they are! Exodus International, a non-profit, interdenominational ex-gay Christian organization that endeavors to limit homosexual desires, has done much work in this field.[307] Their work has brought light to the fact that people were created for another purpose, for God does not create what He does not like.[308] He is a compassionate God that will forgive all our sins, sexual and non-sexual alike, and will help us manage the struggle. Our victory is dependent upon our reliance on Him.

Chapter 17: Understanding Same-Sex Attraction

Sexual orientation is the front-facing explanation for same-sex attraction. Behind that is where the true confusion is found. Many in the fields of science and psychology have done extensive research on genetics, hormones, development, and social and cultural influences in hopes of finding an answer to why a person is heterosexual, bisexual, or homosexual. Despite all the research, "no findings have emerged that permit scientists to conclude that sexual orientation is determined by any particular factor or factors."[309]

McKnight writes that the actual genetics of homosexual orientation are probably polygenetic depending on the dose that one inherits.[310] Many believe that nature and nurture both play a role. There is vast disagreement, though, regarding the opinion of choice regarding sexual orientation. As previously stated, homosexuality is much more than a simple sexual issue. It goes deep into our very being and begins at a young age. Society has struggled to understand same-sex attraction outside of God's boundaries and has developed several theories that sound right but do not supply a fully satisfactory answer.

Mental Illness

Historically homosexuality was viewed as a mental disorder. The DSM II (Diagnostic and Statistical Manual of Mental Disorders) labeled homosexuality as a mental disorder, but it was later taken out in 1974 after much protest from the gay community.[311] Mental illness is found in many people that deal with other issues. There has been strong persecution against homosexuals, and, in turn, there has been a strong move to negate the association of mental illness and homosexuality.

> Since 1975, the American Psychological Association has called on psychologists to take the lead in removing the stigma of mental illness that

> has long been associated with lesbian, gay, and bisexual orientations. The discipline of psychology is concerned with the well-being of people and groups and therefore with threats to that well-being.[312]

Homosexuality is found in a broad spectrum of people and has little to do with mental illness.

Animal Kingdom

The animal homosexuality myth refers to the current interest as to whether or not homosexual behavior is zoologically "natural."[313] Examples such as "one male mounting another have been used as evidence in the argument that homosexuality is natural and therefore should be permitted in human beings. Gay groups argue that if homosexual behavior occurs in animals, it is natural, and therefore the rights of homosexuals should be protected."[314] Behavior, however, cannot be classed as necessarily moral even if it is natural. The nature of human beings is not necessarily the same as the nature of other species. CMI states that there is "documented proof of cannibalism and rape in the animal kingdom, but that doesn't make it right for humans." Some animals kill or eat their young. Does this mean that humans should allow infanticide or cannibalism? A "healthy dose of wariness needs to be employed in making scientific claims about homosexual animals justifying homosexual humans."[315] We need to remember this as we observe the world around us. It can sometimes be difficult to discern whether a behavior observed in the wild is a homosexual expression or is just being misinterpreted as one, but, "for the most part, homosexual acts among mammals are casual and temporary, not habitual and lifelong."[316]

Dr. Antonio Pardo, Professor of Bioethics at the University of Navarre, Spain,[317] wrote the following:

> Properly speaking, homosexuality does not exist among animals.... For reasons of survival, the reproductive instinct among animals is always directed towards an individual of the opposite sex.

> Therefore, an animal can never be homosexual as such. Nevertheless, the interaction of other instincts (particularly dominance) can result in behavior that appears to be homosexual. Such behavior cannot be equated with an animal homosexuality. All it means is that animal sexual behavior encompasses aspects beyond that of reproduction.[318]

A 1996 article published by the National Association for Research and Therapy of Homosexuality, an organization that is committed to the treatment of homosexuality,[319] has gathered arguments against interpretation of animal behavior as sanctioning homosexuality. It notes that "homosexual neuroscientist Simon LeVay"[320] stated that the evidence of supposed homosexual behaviors among animals pointed to isolated acts, not to homosexuality. Although homosexual behavior is very common in the animal world, it seems to be very uncommon that individual animals have a long-lasting predisposition to engage in such behavior to the exclusion of heterosexual activities. A homosexual orientation, if one can speak of such a thing in animals, seems to be a rarity.[321]

Natural Law

Natural-law reasoning is the basis for almost all standard moral intuitions. For example, it is the dignity and value that each human being naturally possesses that makes the needless destruction of human life or infliction of physical and emotional pain immoral. This gives rise to a host of specific moral principles such as the unacceptability of murder, kidnapping, mutilation, physical and emotional abuse, and so forth.

People have a basic, ethical intuition that certain behaviors are wrong because they are unnatural. It is from this intuition that we perceive intuitively that the natural sex partner of a human is another human and not an animal. This same reasoning has been applied to homosexuality. "Simply put, the male body is sexually made for the female body. Sperm are by their design oriented toward the egg the way that the eye is oriented toward light. Same-sex sex and any sex other than vaginal intercourse cannot fulfill the purpose 'written' into our physical form;"[322] therefore, the natural sex partner for a man is a woman, and the natural sex partner for a woman is a man. Because of this, people have the corresponding intuition concerning homosexuality. It is wrong because it is unnatural. This stance aligns with the Bible.

There is an argument, though, from the homosexual community regarding this way of thinking. Their perception is that biblical homosexuality was unnatural, but today's homosexuality is natural. There are those that insist, "Homosexuality feels right to us, so it is natural. It is part of our created constitution."[323] It is something that you are rather than something that you do. The "shameful lusts" of Romans 1:26 refer to "reckless *homo*sexual behavior by people oriented *hetero*sexually."[324] In this case, according to those who advocate the natural aspect of homosexuality, heterosexuals were choosing homosexual acts and were in sin. For the true homosexual, however, it is a natural orientation and not a choice. "Homosexual *behavior* is voluntary and subject to control by the human will, just as heterosexual behavior is. Sex and intimacy, though, are basic necessities of human life, and acting on them, whether they be heterosexual or homosexual, is natural;"[325] therefore if the act is natural, God would not ask one to go against nature.

Another question arises concerning the term "unnatural." Were the biblical examples like those in Leviticus uninformed about homosexual orientation? Were they merely prohibiting homosexual acts by heterosexuals? This question infers that practicing homosexuals were involved in homosexuality against their natural inclinations. James writes in James 1:13–15 that "the nature of sin is that people sin because they *want* to sin."[326] People, therefore, were involved in homosexuality in the Bible because they enjoyed it. According to Mark 7:21–23, they were drawn to this by their own hearts. This is challenging information for a homosexual that wishes to align himself with the Bible. The thought then remains as to why homosexuality feels like a natural inclination. Many of our thoughts and behaviors feel natural and do not have to be learned. We don't learn to be selfish nor throw tantrums as does a child; rather, these things are instinctive. Homosexuality can seem instinctive as well, but it is "an expression of the sinful nature."[327]

The problem at this time for the theory of a natural homosexual orientation is that it is not based on any substantial facts. It is neither biblical nor scientifically proven but is based off of personal experience. Due to its basis of feelings and emotions, it will appeal to those who are sympathizers and homosexual. It has been a political premise upon which to gain rights. Because it rests upon nothing, it cannot become a stance that causes others, particularly Christians, to compromise.

Born Gay, Genetics, and Biology

A second theory that can be connected with the theory of natural homosexuality is the theory of being "born gay." Many homosexuals argue that they have not chosen their condition; that ever since they can remember, they would say that they felt a drawing or inclination toward the same sex. The feeling of being "born gay," though, is explained by the Bible. Sin works on a level that we do not choose. "To use Old Testament language, our sin can be 'unintentional,' but that does not make us less responsible for our violation of God's will."[328] This is read in Leviticus 5:14–19 and Numbers 15:22–30. Sin is more than mature, rational, and conscious decisions. It is our moral inclination from birth.

Biology cannot make us sin. While it can frustrate us, biology can be resisted. Because something was not chosen does not mean that it was inborn. Some desires are acquired or strengthened by habituation and conditioning instead of by conscious choice. No one chooses to be an alcoholic, but one can become habituated to alcohol. Scientific studies suggest some people are born with a hereditary disposition to alcoholism, but no one argues that a person should fulfill these inborn urges by becoming an alcoholic or by being irresponsible with alcohol. Just as one can acquire alcoholic desires by repeatedly becoming intoxicated without consciously choosing them, so one may acquire homosexual desires by engaging in homosexual fantasies or behavior without consciously choosing them. Alcoholism is not an acceptable "lifestyle" any more than is homosexuality. Sexual desire is subject to a high degree of cognitive conditioning in humans. It would be most unusual if homosexual desires were not subject to a similar degree of cognitive conditioning.

McKnight writes that the German jurist, Karl Heinrich Ulrichs, was the first person who researched the biological causes of homosexuality. In the late 1800's, he...

> was impressed by the reports of undifferentiated state of embryonic sex organs in early stages of development. He felt their plasticity suggested we might develop into either sex, or perhaps gain a sexual orientation not tied to one's genetic sex (Kennedy, 1980/81). His theory of a third sex, "a female soul trapped within a male body," set the tone of research for the next century, where homosexuality came to be seen as a sexual inversion caused by hormonal imbalance (Wingfield, 1995).[329]

Another of influence in the biological realm was Doctor Simon LeVay. In 1991, LeVay studied the brains of forty-one cadavers which included nineteen homosexual males and claimed that "a tiny area believed to control sexual activity [the hypothalamus] was less than half the size in the gay men than in the heterosexuals."[330] This study was immediately seized upon by many as proof that homosexuality was biological.

LeVay conducted postmortem examinations on the brains of homosexual men and sixteen presumed heterosexual men who all died of AIDS. His results portrayed that the heterosexual brains consistently had more brain cells in a specific area of the brain that is allegedly associated with sexual behavior. The results were far from conclusive, though, since three homosexual brains were indistinguishable from heterosexual and the sample size was too small to draw clear conclusions. His measurements could also have been wrong. His assumption of a relationship between the specified area of the brain and sexual behavior has never really been acknowledged. Another concern is that these results do not allow one to determine if the size of this portion of the brain in a person is the cause or consequence of an individual's sexual orientation.[331] The possible brain differences may as likely result from homosexuality rather than cause it. Maybe a certain brain type is necessary to express homosexual acts, but this is not sufficient to cause homosexuality. Our desires can make us want to do a lot of things, but no influence can remove our personal responsibility from our intentions or actions. LeVay himself says that "It's important to stress what I didn't find. I did not prove that homosexuality is genetic, or find a genetic cause for being gay. I didn't show that gay men are born that way, the most common mistake people make in interpreting my work. Nor did I locate a gay center in the brain."[332]

Dr. Neil Whitehead and Briar Whitehead, authors and editors of "My Genes Made Me Do It,"[333] state regarding an examination of various cultures, "If homosexuality were significantly influenced by genes, it would appear in every culture, but in twenty-nine of seventy-nine cultures surveyed by Ford and Beach in 1952, homosexuality was rare or absent."[334] The practice of homosexuality does seem to be tied to cultural beliefs and practices. For example, homosexuality is rare amongst Orthodox Jews.[335] Baron wrote in the British Medical Journal, "Some cultures—for example, the Assyrian and Graeco-Roman—were more tolerant of homosexuality. The behavior was practiced openly and was highly prevalent."[336] Sexual patterns appear to be to some extent a product of society's expectations, but it would be difficult to envision a change in the prevalence of the genetic trait merely in response to changing cultural norms.[337]

On perusal of this information, one has to wonder how these facts tie back to their history. Herbert Hendin, a professor in the Department of Psychiatry and Behavioral Sciences at New York Medical College,[338] noted that anthropologists had observed that relatively uncompetitive primitive cultures don't distinguish or reward the best hunters in distinction to other men and yet there is virtually no homosexuality.[339] This challenges man's view of femininity and masculinity. For example, does labeling a female as butch damage her feminine identity? Because a male is slighter in build and creative, does that make him less masculine?

Dr. Dean Hamer is an American geneticist who argues that there is empirical data supporting the origin of homosexuality as genetic.[340] In regards to the press trumpeting various findings in genetics-of-behavior research, the journal *Science* stated the following in 1994:

> Time and time again, scientists have claimed that particular genes or chromosomal regions are

> associated with behavioral traits, only to withdraw their findings when they were not replicated. Doctor Gelernter notes that it's hard to come up with many findings linking specific genes to complex human behaviors that have been replicated. They were elaborately announced but are all now in disrepute.[341]

One such claim is that identical twins would both have to be homosexual since their genes are identical; however, the results concluded that both twins being homosexual were fifty percent[342] and that this was more likely due to the strong influence that one twin has upon the other. "It is not unusual for them to share behavior."[343] Hamer noted regarding this research, "We already know that half or more of the variability in sexual orientation is not inherited."[344]

There is no scientific consensus favoring a genetic cause of homosexuality, and the American Psychological Association's assertion is merely that "most scientists today agree that sexual orientation is most likely the result of a complex interaction of environmental, cognitive and biological factors."[345] In May of 2000, the American Psychiatric Association issued a fact sheet stating, "There are no replicated scientific studies supporting a specific biological etiology for homosexuality."[346] Columbia University psychiatry professors Drs. William Byrne and Bruce Parsons stated, "There is no evidence at present to substantiate a biological theory. The appeal of current biological explanations for sexual orientation may derive more from dissatisfaction with the present status of psychosocial explanations than from a substantiating body of experimental data."[347] That homosexuality is affected by environment and nurture has been the historical secular position.[348] It seems that all that is proved so far is that homosexuality is not purely biological. Biology may be necessary for homosexuality, but it is not a sufficient cause in and of itself.[349]

In his 1980 work, *Overcoming Homosexuality*, Robert Kronemeyer wrote the following:

> With rare exceptions, homosexuality is neither inherited nor the result of some glandular disturbance or the scrambling of genes or

> chromosomes. Homosexuals are made, not born "that way." I firmly believe that homosexuality is a learned response to early painful experiences and that it can be unlearned. For those homosexuals who are unhappy with their life and find effective therapy, it is "curable."[350]

Similarly, in a 1989 *USA Today* article, San Francisco State University professor of psychology, John DeCecco, and the former editor of the 25-volume *Journal of Homosexuality*, stated, "The idea that people are born into one type of sexual behavior is entirely foolish. Homosexuality is a behavior, not a condition, and something that some people can and do change, just like they sometimes change other tastes and personality traits."[351]

While it is commonly thought that homosexuality is inborn and immutable, science is yet to prove this. The homosexual community understandably continues to push their creation as natural. If this is proved, the public will become more accepting of homosexuality. LeVay notes that "people who think that gays and lesbians are born that way are also more likely to support gay rights."[352] Overall though, even secular sources state that biology is not destiny, and the human sexual response is too complicated to be reduced to a neuron deficit in the brain.[353]

The Ten Percent Argument

In the 1970s, according to a large survey, approximately ten percent of homosexuals claimed to be "born homosexual." In another survey in the 1980's, with the homosexual rights movement increasingly becoming active, thirty-five percent claimed that they were born that way. If this is the case, then homosexuality should be accepted as normal. Dr. Tahir I. Jaz, M.D. of Winnipeg, Canada, counters with the observation that "the increasing claims of being 'born that way' parallels the rising political activism of homosexual organizations, who politicize the issue of homosexual origins."[354]

This ten percent figure is likely a fabrication. It originated from the 1948 report by the biologist and sexologist, Alfred Kinsey, who wrote *Sexual Behavior in the Human Male*. While Kinsey's subjects were mainly drawn from convicted criminals, "1,400 of his 5,300 final subjects (twenty-six percent) were convicted sex offenders—a group that by definition is not representative of normal sexual practices."[355] Apart from this, the ten percent figure included people who were not long-term or exclusive homosexuals.

More recent studies have reported that "an estimated 9 million Americans—or nearly 4 percent of the total population—say they identify as lesbian, gay, bisexual or transgender."[356] This report was released in July of 2011 by Gates, a demographer-in-residence at the Williams Institute on Sexual Orientation Law and Public Policy, a think tank based at the University of California, Los Angeles. Best estimate, derived from five studies that have asked subjects about their sexual orientation, is that the nation has about 4 million adults who identify as being gay or lesbian, representing 1.7 percent of the 18-and-over population. That's a much lower figure than the 3 to 5 percent that has been the conventional wisdom in the last two decades, based on other isolated studies and attempts to discredit Kinsey.[357]

Jim McKnight claims that homosexual etiology really cannot be determined. Some stay in the closet because of stigma, but there is also "confusion about the nature and classification of the homosexual experience."[358] Most people will wonder what actually defines one as being a homosexual. Are those that fantasize, even just once, included? Are bisexuals included? Are those that have homosexual desire but never have homosexual sex included? What about those who lived the homosexual lifestyle but ceased for some reason? McKnight writes that Johnson's study "shows that the greatest proportion of homosexual contact occurs in adolescence and then declines as the sample ages. Are homosexuals engaging in homosexual sex homosexual, or just displaying developmental immaturity?"[359] There is no black-and-white number when trying to place a percentage on the number of homosexuals.

Not all common behaviors should be considered acceptable, and even if ten percent of the population were born homosexual, this is not proof. All people are born in sin and deal with the desires born from sin. If those desires manifest themselves in homosexuality in ten percent of the population, all that does is give us information about the demographics of original sin. This same answer applies to the drug addict, the porn addict, and the abuser. It applies to the entire population.

Fraternal Birth Order Defect

Birth order has been explored recently in regard to homosexuality. Some studies have "shown that homosexual men have a higher mean birth order (i.e., they have more older siblings) than do comparable heterosexuals."[360] While the studies encompassed a wide variety of cultures and people types, "the collective evidence, therefore, suggests that a high birth order is associated with homosexuality in men, regardless of their other cultural, demographic, or psychological characteristics."[361] In contrast, birth order leaves lesbianism and bisexuality unexplained. Ray Blanchard, a sexologist[362] and Anthony Bogaert, a psychologist,[363] both conjecture that male homosexuality might result from a maternal immune reaction, which is only triggered by male fetuses. It also becomes stronger after each male fetus pregnancy.[364] Various hypotheses have been suggested to prove this theory, but as of yet, no answer has been found.

Overall, birth order and biology affect people in many ways. Birth order, for example, often affects things such as a child's willingness to be assertive or more phlegmatic. Biology has discovered many things. Man lives in an imperfect world, and we are not immune to the vast differences that are shown through biology. This includes the fact that some will experience a desire to act out homosexually.

Evolution

Some evolutionists have proposed that homosexuality is an evolutionary development. In 1993, Professor Miron Baron, the renowned medical researcher and Professor at Columbia University, wrote in the *British Medical Journal* that there is a conflict regarding this theory. Dr. Baron wrote that "from an evolutionary perspective, genetically determined homosexuality would have become extinct long ago because of reduced reproduction."[365] Jim McKnight also notes that homosexuality is a tailor-made rebuttal of evolution.[366] Due to the fact that homosexuals are unable to bear children, homosexuals would have become extinct if evolution were true.

McKnight does write, though, that "in all probability, homosexuality is adaptive in its own right but there is also the possibility that it is merely a vestige of evolution. Intuitively, the reduced reproductive success of homosexuals argues that this is so."[367] This thought leans heavily upon one of evolution's primary teachings: the survival of the fittest. This part of the evolutionary theory explains that "the less fit are selected out by natural attrition and this is a consequence of relatively random forces of natural selection, catastrophe, climatic change, mutation and the like."[368] McKnight continues to say that perhaps homosexuals carry a mutation, having a defective sexual orientation which means they pursue inappropriate sexual partners leaving them unable to reproduce.

McKnight then highlights another point. Perhaps homosexuality involves a differential fertility rate between sons and mothers which is an evolutionary balancing act.[369] He claims that "recent research suggests a genetic basis for some forms of homosexuality and it is against this backdrop that an evolutionary explanation is overdue."[370] McKnight's claim is that "exclusive male homosexuality is an evolutionary byproduct of an adaptive advantage which keeps it balanced in the gene pool against its diminished reproduction."[371]

People's beliefs regarding creation and the theory of evolution appear to influence their views on homosexuality. In the USA, liberals are more likely to believe in evolution as a theory and twice as many liberals as conservatives believe that homosexuals are born gay. Creationist scientists and creationists assert that the theory of evolution cannot account for the origin of gender and sexual reproduction. Biblical belief asserts that homosexual acts are against God's original design of a man and a woman becoming one flesh as read in Genesis 1 and 2. If evolution is true and the earth is truly hundreds of millions of years old, then homosexuals remove themselves from the gene pool and thus are no problem to the future of humans. If, however, the earth is six thousand years old, as is taught by Creationists, then homosexuality could be very dangerous.

Androgen Insensitivity Syndrome

The Androgen Insensitivity Syndrome is a genetic autosomal recessive condition in which genetic males vary in their sensitivity to testosterone. "What is interesting about the androgen insensitivity syndrome is the far more plentiful cases of partial insensitivity to testosterone (Aiman and Griffin, 1982)."[372] The extreme of this condition manifests in those that are born female but then do not menstruate upon reaching puberty.

Some theorists such as Gunter Dorner, a neuroendocrinologist,[373] argue that androgen insensitivity is a part of a continuum. Male homosexuality is classed within this theory as a mild subclinical case of the androgen insensitivity syndrome.[374] This suggests that relative insensitivity to androgen then leads to degrees of brain feminization and a genetic predisposition and an environmental trigger. "Testosterone is the main sex hormone involved in organizing male orientation and activity."[375] This means that male homosexuality sits somewhere between masculinity and femininity. Unfortunately, evidence is still far from clear regarding this theory. Several studies show little difference in freely circulating testosterone levels between homosexual and heterosexual men. Continual research for this particular theory has waned and remains inconclusive.

The Maternal Stress Hypothesis

Gunter Dorner claimed in 1975 that "male homosexuality was a consequence of insufficient male androgens during pregnancy."[376] This was the result of maternal stress, blocking the adequate supply of masculinizing hormones. This type of testing was primarily done on animals until the 1980's when Dorner released findings based off the war years in Germany. Men in Germany "had a much higher incidence of homosexuality than in a twenty-year period from 1934 (Dorner et al., 1980)."[377] Dorner determined that the high stress experienced by pregnant women in these times led to overproduction of stress hormones which stopped the formation of male pathways in the male fetus leading to feminization of the brain.[378] This theory assumes that distinct masculine and feminine sex roles and behaviors exist and are inborn.

Dorner's work gained huge prominence in the magazine "Omni," where it was claimed that "homosexuals are born, not made." This is another theory that is hugely debated and criticized. While there are those mothers that recall great stress, there are others that do not. Apart from this, Dorner does not account for the fact that, in wartime, many children had no father figure and/or, those children whose fathers did return were left with a parent who would be unable to parent effectively due to the effects of the war.

Concluding Thoughts

These theories are not the only theories regarding the development of homosexuality nor will they be the last. Science and psychology will always produce new theories to either bolster or contradict the old. It is important that we understand these facts and theories. It's also important that we understand that theories are often presented as truth. The homosexual voice is a strong force in many communities. Many homosexuals are loving people; this fact makes it difficult to hold a view against their preference.

The common question asked by visitors to our church in Los Angeles is "Do we accept homosexuals?" instead of the common southern question, "Are you a Bible-based church?" Christians must be careful to understand that theories often contradict Scripture. Theories sound so merciful and understandable. God is omnipotent and omniscient. It should not come as a shock that we lack comprehension of His perfect will. We are to align our lives with Scripture rather than vice versa. This alignment provides us with our best life. Do not allow yourself to succumb to the ideas of society. These ideas deny Scripture and play upon our propensity for mercy. Mercy and grace are wonderful things, but they are to be accompanied by wisdom and the standard that God puts forth.

Chapter 18: Social Pathways to Homosexuality

Same-Sex Attraction from a Female Perspective

I was just twelve or thirteen when I commenced attending an all girls' high school. I'd moved from the comfort of good friendships in my elementary school to an environment in which I knew nobody. It was hard making new friends, let alone the fact that this school was an hour and a half from home. I quickly, too, lost contact with my old friends. Here I was in a new environment filled with strict rules concerning dress code, and high expectations of performance, and it was all female.

My parents encouraged my involvement in sports and made the time to transport me to practices and matches. Due to my abilities, I found myself partnered with several girls a few years older than myself. Over time, much to my confusion, I developed strong emotional feelings and even a sexual attraction to one of these girls. I found myself planning to go places within the school where she would be found. Despite the fact that I had experienced infatuations with boys, I fantasized about her day and night, imagining the both of us even embracing, cuddling, and kissing. I'd probably best describe this case as a crush or infatuation. While I'd never experienced this before and had previously and afterwards liked males, this was a strange time for me. It was embarrassing and shameful and so I told no one. I found myself wondering regarding my sexuality. I had been raised believing homosexuality was wrong.

I am thankful that neither one of us acted on this relationship. I do not even know if she was aware of my young crush. I have been happily married for over thirty years with a beautiful family. Looking back, though, I think that several factors contributed to my scenario. I was vulnerable, having been removed from a secure environment into one in which I felt so vulnerable. I would also say that, although coming from a wonderful family, my father was often absent and unavailable while my mother worked full-time and was oblivious to my emotional state. I blame her in no way as I could have made my needs known but chose to deal with them privately and on my own. In fact, I, as many would, look back and understand that many of us are aware of gaps between parents and children that we attempt to fill in alternative ways.

My age also contributed to this situation as, at twelve or thirteen, as a female, this is the time when we are transitioning from girlie relationships to those with the other sex. I found it difficult to make close friends with other girls. Whether male or female, but particularly for females, we are becoming aware of the other sex. However, if needs have not been met through our same sex prior to this period, we continue to try and fill these needs in wrong places. While both parents were emotionally unavailable, and understandably so due to their own demanding lives, I felt stranded and succumbed to feelings for this sixteen-year-old girl who seemed so together and who offered some friendship.

Today: this lady leads a thriving women's ministry in her church and is a trained counselor. –JS

Same-Sex Attraction from a Male Perspective

I always remember being aware of my same-sex attraction. When I say always, I mean from probably around the age of ten or eleven. It was so strange as I was being raised in the South and being regularly in church, I was told it was wrong. I educated myself by reading books without anyone knowing. Learning that one's mind was not fully developed until the late teens gave me hope that I was just passing through a phase.

Looking back, I'm not sure why this happened to me. I wasn't abused. I don't even try to figure it out. I know, though, that I craved the company, reassurance, and acceptance of guys. I remember that I really didn't seem to be getting this from anyone.

At my church, at one stage, I met another fourteen-year-old who was experiencing the same thing. We talked about our experiences, reassuring each other, but he was the only one to whom I did talk. I felt no conviction at this time either way regarding my sexuality; just that the Bible said that homosexuality was wrong.

While I stayed in high school, I didn't date and did not act out on my attraction to guys.

Those that I surrounded myself with, though, were those that others would have thought homosexual. This included the creative and theatrical guys. Nothing was said, though, of my choices.

At the age of seventeen or eighteen, my parents separated and so, having no one to answer to, I decided to explore my options regarding my sexuality. I realized that my attraction was not going away. I felt powerless, as this attraction felt so natural. It was as natural as was the color of my hair. I'd go clubbing and hang out with other homosexuals and transvestites. I was a different person at work than who I was outside of work. I was thinking that I should know who I am by now, and this same-sex attraction had not left me. It seemed easier to embrace this attraction than run from it. I knew no matter what, though, that it was wrong, but I didn't know what else to do. I couldn't shake that feeling that if I embraced this thing that I'd go to hell. However, the attraction was so strong that I felt that there was no way to overcome it. I was going to gay clubs and felt totally comfortable.

About this time, a really good friend took me aside and confronted me about my homosexuality. In some ways, this was a relief as I had kept my secret for nine years. Talking about the problem made it real, and if others knew, I could pursue a relationship. Perhaps I no longer needed to hide my issue. I knew that there were plenty of good and successful people in the gay community. I could become one of these.

It occurred to me, though, that the sexual part would have been a bit weird because I felt still that it was so wrong, but yet it felt natural. At one time, a guy tried to get with me, but I couldn't respond. Again, it felt right, but I knew it to be wrong.

I decided to go to Bible College because, while homosexuality felt right for me, at the back of my mind, something within me urged me to continue being in church. I just kept showing up; Bible College, then to work, then to church on Sundays. At this stage, several pastors and leaders knew, which, to me, were the people that needed to know. By halfway through this year, still I felt no change. In one service though, there was a guest minister, and, while he was praying for individuals, I really hoped that he would not select me. I went home and realized that I should want prayer. I needed to make a decision. Therefore, I prayed a desperate but focused prayer in which I told God that I was ready. I cried out my plea to God to either take away this attraction or kill me. At this, I felt relief. I was determined that I would love God, though I may feel this way for the remainder of life. People can say what they like, but I took responsibility. I was only 21.

I kept praying: "God, remove this desire." There was no immediate change. Three months later, however, while at work, I felt something heavy hit me. I ran to the bathroom and fell to the floor crying. This sounds so strange as I'm not one to hear voices, but I audibly heard God say, "You'll never feel this way again." Throughout the day, there were echoes of this.

After that day, I had no interest in the homosexual scene, and I stopped spending time with those attached to that scene. I stopped everything that was attached to the homosexual lifestyle and just went to Bible College, church, and work. It was a recovery period of being free from this ten-year battle. At times, the devil would whisper, "Have you really changed?" The devil will try to tell you that this victory is not real. I also attended second-year Bible College.

Today, I'm a family man with a beautiful wife and a child. The devil tries to tempt me at times that change is impossible. For example, just before my marriage, the thought that I'd fail my wife worried me, but I have now been married for eight years. Sometimes memories come to me of my past; deep moments of stress seem most likely when life presents its toughest moments. I see it, though, as an attack upon an area which I have overcome. I just keep saying no because God is big. This was my turning point. There's no way I'm going back. For the last six years, I love to focus on others who have the same dilemma. I love helping others, but I feel it also makes me stronger in myself.

Overall, I think that there are a lot of people like me. They love God and feel like this. They are attracted to their sex. It's easier to not change. I think, though too, that it scares homosexuals that someone could admit their same-sex attraction but stay celibate and stand for what is right.

Today: This young man is an outstanding worship leader while being devoted to his gorgeous family. –JS

Same-sex attraction is a complicated issue, as the theories presented in the previous chapter have indicated. What these theories do not touch upon is that homosexuality is rarely what it seems. There are those in our society who experiment with homosexuality but do not choose to pursue it as a lifestyle. One young girl announced to her family that she was a lesbian, even though all her previous romantic relationships had been heterosexual. Her past was full of family mishaps and moving from one place to another. She had ceased being a part of her church and was being wooed by another crowd—the homosexual crowd. Within a month, she decided she was a lesbian. This phase lasted for a mere six months. She never announced her reformation back to heterosexuality, but her choice of partners, all being male, made it obvious. It is often unnoted in scientific and psychological theories that there can be multiple factors that lead up to a homosexual lifestyle and not just one thing that triggers it. Homosexual lifestyles manifest differently in the genders, and the past is where it all begins.

Same-sex attraction is "four times more common in men than women;[379] however, each homosexual seems to be...

> distributed on a continuum from lifelong exclusive homosexuality towards heterosexuality; it is a relatively rare orientation with approximately 1–3 percent of men identifying as exclusively homosexual and having abstained from heterosexual sex over the last five years. Although the rate of homosexual behavior is highly variable across cultures, 30–40 percent of men have had some homosexual experience; for the vast majority this ends at adulthood.[380]

Women are more pliable regarding their sexual choices and "more than 25% of 18- to 25-year-old women who initially identified as lesbian or bisexual changed their sexual identity during the next five years."[381] At this age, young people want acceptance and are vulnerable to both peer pressure and the teachings and practices of their environment. Change such as education and culture seem to affect women more sexually than it does men. In a national survey, "college was associated with a 900% increase in the percentage of women identifying as lesbian or bisexual."[382] Most studies have been done regarding homosexual men while, according to McKnight, lesbian studies are woefully inadequate (there are fewer lesbians than homosexuals, and they are less visible in society).[383]

Most believe that, regarding the etiology of homosexuality, there are two very large categories: "theories that point to nature (that is, biological variables) and theories that point to nurture (that is, the influence of experience, of psychological variables)."[384] Those who tend to believe that nature causes homosexuality argue that early homosexual traits indicate a biological cause. The theory of nurture—occasionally referred to as the psychoanalytical theory—states that psychological forces influence and mold children from birth. Many psychological studies indicate that the parent-child relationship, early childhood development, early homosexual experiences, and childhood abuse foster homosexuality.

The church as a whole has been fast to refute scientific theories that base homosexuality on biological factors. It is easier for Christians to embrace the thought that homosexuality is a choice and/or a learned behavior. If homosexuals were born as homosexuals, as biological theories attest, then how does that fit in with God's creation? It is easy for Christians to default to the mantra that sexual sin is a choice and thus can be easily reversed and/or that a learned behavior can be unlearned. Christians are less swift to counter psychological arguments. Psychological theories have an appeal and at times are overwhelming. The science of the mind sounds so much like truth that it can become confusing and difficult to argue. Christians can become mesmerized by psychological theories and may have difficulty finding Scriptures that can shed light on the uncertainties.

The fact is that science, psychology, and the Christian faith have all touched upon points that, when combined, show how the homosexual lifestyle can develop. Biology can be a factor, but it is not *the* factor. Mental capacities play a part, but these are not the defining moment. Lifestyles are, inevitably, a choice, but choice is not always realized nor is it easy. Homosexual influences can start at the very beginning of life, but no human is simply "born that way." This chapter will now look at the deeper foundations of homosexuality found in the home and in society that science, psychology, and even the faithful have yet to understand.

Disruption of the Family Bond: A Christian Perspective

Exodus International is causing a stir amongst homosexuals because they have taken a stand for the truths of the Bible and have applied those truths to the theories presented in science and psychology. This ministry has researched homosexuality, interviewed and helped those who wish to leave that lifestyle, and have revealed to the world the potential pathways leading to homosexuality. Exodus International "asserts that homosexuality is a result of thwarted psychological development caused by some childhood trauma that twists the psyche and/or a child's failure to bond with a same-sex role model."[385] This ministry maintains that, at some point in the early childhood development, there was a break in the bond with the same-sex parent. That break creates a deep, unmet need inside the child that will affect his or her emotional development. The need for same-sex peer bonding becomes sexualized at puberty, leaving the child isolated and confused.

The broken parental relationship is not always the parent's fault. There was a young man with whom I met with regularly over the years who lived with an over-indulgent mother. His father was not a part of his life mostly due to his parents' poor marriage. His mother avoided his father and doted upon him; needless to say, they were very close. In his teens, he was pursued and molested by a pedophile. This assault opened up a flood of confusion for him. He was both aroused and repulsed by the continual assaults, and his molester told him repeatedly that he was a homosexual. Because of all of this, the young man filled his life with both homosexual and heterosexual encounters in an attempt to determine his preference.

The parent of a failed parent-child bond can feel like he or she has lavished love upon the child, but if the child does not perceive that lavishing as love, the relationship can become stunted and even broken. This child, then, feels obligated to protect himself or herself from further damage. The child is hungry to be loved and desires to finish the business that has not been completed with his or her same sex. I have seen several fantastic Christian families go through this trauma. Nothing seems unusual in the family. Yes, the family and parenting were not perfect, but there is no perfect family. A child, though, is vulnerable to the lures and acceptance of the homosexual community and those that advocate his/her choices. Often to the amazement of all, a child "comes out" and announces his/her gayness. As written by Solomon in Proverbs 27:7, "To a hungry soul every bitter thing is sweet."[386] As parents, it is vital that we discover the ways in which our children receive love. This is not an answer in its entirety, but it does help. A person continues to seek love from the same sex because the initial need was never met.

The Developmental Pathway of a Homosexual

Men and women are not the same. They are affected by familial and social situations differently. The pathways to homosexuality also vary for the genders. Male homosexuality is more straightforward than lesbianism, thus it is easier to explain the basic pathway through the male perspective.[387] A baby (for the sake of this example, the baby boy) does not begin to recognize the differences in genders until eighteen months old.[388] Before this, the child feels one with his mother because in most cases, it is the mother who provides most of the nurturing. For example, she is the one who nurses the child. Between the ages of two-and-a-half and four, a baby boy will begin to look to his father for value and gender identity. He will begin to separate from his mother and attach to his father.[389] Ideally, the father will provide affirmation and attention.[390] He will show an interest in the boy's interests and help him to understand his physical body through fun, rough play and other such forms of male physical affection. If this bonding does not occur, the boy will not detach from his mother nor will he receive the affirmation he is seeking.[391]

This break in the bond may happen because the boy did not recognize his father's affection or was frightened by his father in some form or fashion (for example, if his father had raised his voice).[392] I have spoken to young men that struggle with same-sex attraction who were bewildered by their parents. Many of these young men had a father who was either physically or emotionally absent. Other young men felt rejected by their fathers as their interests did not align with the goals their fathers may have preset for their lives. The boy's perception of life is very important.

Perception is influenced by temperament. Young boys who are emotionally sensitive children are more susceptible to develop same-sex attraction.[393] Sensitive young boys are often artistic, observant, and take life personally. Kelly Welch states, "There is considerable evidence that gay men are brighter, more creative, better communicators and more socially adept and less disturbed than the average male."[394] A father needs to be aware of how his son receives affection. Physical touch is very important, but it may not be the boy's primary form of receiving love. Children can receive love through quality time, affirmation, rewards, and, as mentioned, physical touch. If the father fails to realize how his son receives affection, he can unintentionally reject his son. This rejection, when repeated, will cause the boy to pull back from his father on both a physical and mental level and pull away from the masculinity that his father represents.[395]

A boy who does not connect with his father will begin to learn the feminine traits of his mother, sisters or female caregivers. He soaks up their habits and behaviors while still craving masculinity.[396] If we look at society and families in our midst, we see this occur.

The boy that has little access to mature males seems less robust emotionally. Mothers can tend to be overprotective. Without the interference of a mature male, she makes her son "her little man," a cute but dangerous identity if he is the only man in her life. The boy watches and internalizes his mother's daily habits rather than the masculine traits of the man's world. We see this occur in homosexual communities too. The longer one spends in an environment, the habits and traits become accentuated. Hand actions and body movements often may take on a new level of femininity if homosexual. We imitate those around whom we spend time.

Between 5 and 6 years of age, the boy seeks to bond with his male peers.[397] He is looking for the answers to the questions that were unanswered by his father.[398] He wants acceptance, confirmation, and inclusion. It is difficult to have a healthy relationship with the opposite gender until there is a healthy bond with the same gender. Same-sex bonds created from childhood through puberty build a sense of self that become the groundwork for awareness in the other gender.[399] A young boy who is already lacking in his sense of masculinity may become intimidated by the other boys and default to the familiar company of girls.[400] This feels safe and offers a place of comfort to him. He is already displaying effeminate characteristics due to the female influences in his life, and these characteristics cause people to react negatively. Often society does not mean to be cruel, but what is unusual draws our gaze. The young boy, already insecure in his masculinity, will continue to question his gender. He will continue to distance himself from the male bonds he needs.

By puberty, the young boy is not attracted to girls. He is already familiar and comfortable with this sex. His need for opposite-gender association has been met; however, his need for same-sex connection has continued to go unmet and thus grows into a more intense sexual desire.[401] Current scientific and psychological studies both agree that "the core attractions that form the basis for adult sexual orientation typically emerge between middle childhood and early adolescence. These patterns of emotional, romantic, and sexual attraction may arise without any prior sexual experience."[402] Repeated conversations with those open to discussing this issue have revealed that they hungered so much for male love that their desires, influenced now by hormones and changes in their physical bodies, become very real and very powerful sexual desires.

To the one struggling with homosexuality, this is the end of the pathway; this end portrays that it is naïve to say that homosexuality is only a choice. Many homosexuals plead with God to remove these desires. A man who has developed in this way needs healthy, patient and non-sexual connections with other men. He must have the needs of his childhood met before he can move forward into the full masculine identity God has for him.

The Development Pathway of a Lesbian

According to Christian therapists, lesbianism is more complicated than homosexuality.[403] The main points of the pathway for homosexuality apply to lesbians, but there are other contributing factors that can create same-sex attractions in a female. "Women's sexual beliefs and behaviors can be more easily shaped and altered by cultural, social and situational factors."[404]

Exodus International identifies several additional factors to the pathway that are unique to the development of lesbianism. The first situation is when a young girl becomes an athlete.[405] Athletic girls spend a lot of time with their male peers, sharing in their love of sports. Like the effeminate little boy, the tomboyish girl may begin to adopt the mannerisms of her male companions, thus shedding her developing femininity. She is rejected socially from her more dainty peers, and, upon puberty, she is seen as unappealing to her male peers due to her more masculine demeanor. Her lesbianism can then emerge as a form of defense against the rejection and lack of feminine influence in her world.[406]

The next situation is the break in the mother/daughter bond.[407] A young girl can successfully attach to her mother at the right time in the development process, but that bond can remain fragile all the way through puberty. The mother/daughter bond can break at any point in this timeframe and stunt the daughter's feminine development. Perhaps the mother or the daughter is hospitalized; maybe the mother struggled with depression or an addiction; perhaps there was a breakup in a parent's relationship, and mom was absent from daily life. I have seen a young woman struggle with opposite-sex relationships on a romantic level due to her growing up with an alcoholic mother. Mom was often in her bedroom asleep or intoxicated, leaving her daughter to care for herself. Her father tended to hide in his career. As the daughter matured, friendships were reasonable but intimate male relationships were awkward for her. In this situation, lesbianism is a search for motherly love.[408]

Then there is the girl who has been abused by men. One young acquaintance of mine was raped by a boyfriend. This crisis, on top of a complicated upbringing, brought her to thinking that lesbian relationships would be safer. Her salvation and ongoing discipleship have caused her to break out of this lifestyle, but when she faces difficult situations, she still tends to run back to lesbian connections for comfort. Sexual abuse is a powerful tool that can drive a young girl from the safer male relationships in her life. One man betrays her trust and hurts her in the most intimate way. The girl is left broken, confused, and aching. She will defend herself by burying her pain and withdrawing from men altogether. Her lesbianism is protection; in her mind, women are safe.[409]

Lastly, there is the scenario where two heterosexual females get involved in a deep and dependent relationship that blurs the line between friendship and lover.[410] These two girls can become sexually involved because of that confusion. Often in lesbianism, the lover is a friend first. This situation is not rare. Young females hang out incessantly. They develop intimate friendships built upon shared secrets behind closed bedroom doors. Girls lay in bed together sharing their deepest hopes and dreams. Lines are crossed sometimes in these situations, and best friends become too intimate. This manifestation of lesbianism seems almost innocent and even romantic, but it is equally as damaging as the other three situations. A girl who falls into this kind of same-sex attraction can be hurt on a deep emotional level and lose all sense of proper relational boundaries.

These pathways of homosexual development are a basic outline and will vary on a case-by-case basis. A young man who grows up without a father will not necessarily become a homosexual; a young girl in a healthy family with involved parents is not necessarily safe from becoming a lesbian. Humans are complex beings, and life in a fallen world is complicated. There are still other instances, scenarios, and moments that can influence a young child's sexual development.

Teenage Development

The importance of the parental bond does not end after the child reaches puberty. It becomes even more important. According to current professional understanding, principal attractions that form the basis for adult sexual orientation typically emerge between middle-childhood and early adolescence.[411] Same-sex attraction in adolescence is more common than we think; however, these attractions do not necessarily make a homosexual. Many teenagers will go through a same-sex attraction phase; it is a part of growing up. Adolescence is the period of life where children will emotionally separate from their parents and families and begin to develop autonomy. Becoming aware of sexual feelings is a normal developmental task of adolescence, and sometimes, same-sex feelings can manifest through experimentation and can cause confusion about sexual orientation.[412] This confusion is not new. Paul had to warn believers about it in biblical times. He writes in Romans1:26–27 of how people have "exchanged natural relations for unnatural ones."[413] Youth can fall prey to this exchange because they do not know what to do about their attractions. It is in this moment that the parental bond becomes so important.

Parents are the primary teachers in their children's lives, thus they should not retreat as their children mature. Teenagers do become more physically able, but their emotional needs remain. They need to experience the love of both their same-sex and opposite-sex parents to help with healthy sexual development. If the parents remain involved in their children's lives, the children will be able to move forward into the teen years with less likelihood of tripping up sexually. They feel secure in who and what they are. They will then begin to detach naturally from that same-sex parent and show more interest in the other sex.

Parents are the role models for proper expressions of affection. Sexual education in the home is paramount; it is an active expression instead of a black-and-white summary. Fathers and mothers work together to grow their children's self-worth; they show sons how to treat women and daughters how men should treat them. The parents also act as a living example of a healthy marriage. They can teach and demonstrate love every day of their lives. Believers need to incorporate the standards that God puts forward in the Word. Single parents can give the same lessons through the inclusion of same-sex role models in their children's lives. If parents do not step forward to teach their children, society will do it for them via the Internet, television, and public or private school education. Children are shaped by what they hear. Parents need to be diligent in this area.

Educational Pressures

Public educational systems advocate the western idea that sexual experimentation is liberating and that, if you are not exploring your sexual options, you are old-fashioned or abnormal. Secondary or tertiary schools are becoming places that advocate sexual freedom. Students are utilizing these teachings by experimenting—especially in high school and college. Students who would not dare experiment while living at home may take advantage of their first taste of life outside the rules of their parents by breaking said rules. They may throw out all of their boundaries in the name of maturity and do whatever feels right at the time. These devil-may-care environments breed same-sex experimentation that leaves young people confused.

Younger victims are especially damaged by this process. They may become the targets of older classmates. They get pulled into a homosexual act and enjoy it, even against their will. They, in turn, begin to question why they liked it and could engage in other homosexual acts just to determine if this enjoyment makes them gay. These students become excluded from heterosexual acts while trying to discover their true sexual orientation. In the end, they choose homosexuality because of their feelings. This detrimental result is celebrated by society and, thus, repeated often.

Habit

The idea that sexual identity can be determined by what sexual experiences are the most enjoyable is faulty due to our own human makeup. Our brain is wired to learn and repeat behaviors. Our first sexual experience becomes the blueprint for the rest, thus if our first sexual experience is a homosexual one, we may become prone to that form on a mental level. We, as fallen creatures, sin both against our body and our mind when we engage in sexual sin.

Sexual experiences can alter brain wiring. The brain reacts to a sexual high, calling for a repeat performance. It is a learned behavior. Homosexuality can, because of this wiring, come out of abuse. As discussed in Part Three, sexual abuse arouses sexual desire before a person is ready and leaves lasting damage. The brain records the experience—good or bad—and desires to repeat it. Homosexuality is not always the outcome of abuse, but, while not all sexually abused people become traumatized, homosexuality is found amongst survivors of childhood sexual abuse. The non-abused can follow a similar path when pulled into homosexual experimentation early on in their sexual exploration.

Public Opinion

Public opinion is cruel. It shifts with the winds and gives no regard to the emotions of those who fall on its bad side. Children who have seemingly unbalanced hormonal developments take the brunt of society's opinions in the form of school bullying. There are two stages in life where hormones cause changes in the human body. The first is in the eight- to twelve-week gestation period. It is here that the baby's gender is developed. A male can be born with less testosterone; a female with less estrogen. (This is due to the androgen wash as discussed in Chapter Seventeen.) Hormones make a second transformation during the stage of life we call puberty through the teenage years. It is in these two moments that males and females can be marked as the non-norm.

A young man who, while in gestation, received less androgen, may develop traits that are labeled as feminine. He may be intuitive or more empathetic, which can cause his more athletic peers to view him as weak. His masculinity is called into question by those from whom he seeks confirmation. He, in turn, will question his gender identity and may believe himself to be homosexual as a result. Females who are more athletic due to a higher exposure to androgen may also be labeled and ostracized by their peers. Their insecurities are heightened because they feel less comfortable in the socially accepted forms of feminine expression. They wonder if they would be better off as masculine and can consider lesbianism as their destined route.

This sense of self is known as gender identity. Gender identity is fragile. Society defines it, and those who do not live up to the standard are forced to consider other routes. Hormones can cause males and females to be more or less effeminate or masculine, but these traits do not make one homosexual. God wrote our gender identity upon our hearts when He created us. There are so many wonderful heterosexual men who thrive in their artistic nature; there are athletic women who are wives to great men. God is the One who defines who we are; not our hormones nor the labels of others.

Last One Standing

A lack of heterosexual suitors can lead people to choose homosexuality. The thought backing this idea is that, if we are rejected by the opposite gender then maybe our own gender will accept us. We are supposed to be pursued by the opposite sex; when this does not happen, we may seek love in the homosexual community. This was the reasoning presented to me by one young man. He struggled relationally with women due to a domineering mother toward whom he still held unforgiveness. He felt that girls did not see him as attractive but males did; therefore, he chose homosexuality.

Unrealistic Expectations

Human perfection is painted in the media. Men and women can fall prey to the comparison trap when faced with Catwoman in her skintight leather or Batman in all his buffness. Supermodels represent that to which we aspire. We fail to remember that models are covered in makeup and lighting that accentuates their best features and hides their flaws. The everyday person can feel inadequate by comparison. Insecurity about our bodies can drive us away from pursuing opposite-gender relationships because we believe we are not worthy due to the fact that our bodies are not perfect.

Unhealthy Emotional Attachments

Wrong emotional dependencies or unhealthy emotional attachments can affect one's sexual preferences. Emotional dependence and attachments, for the most part, are a normal and healthy part of life; however, if we do not receive the love we need, we can turn to more unhealthy means to secure it. For example, a mother who is feeling neglected, can try to replace her husband's love with her son's. She can begin to act and speak as if she is the only woman in the world worthy of him. This can cause the son to never detach from her, thus creating an unhealthy emotional entanglement between them. This can also be seen in relationships between a boss and employee, a counselor and client, or even two friends. Emotional needs, however, cannot be completely fulfilled by other people.

There are also those who play out in a homosexual way because they have been emotionally hurt. These people may be married with a family, and yet they get caught in a sexual act. There have been times when a husband or wife randomly plays out in a one-off same-sex encounter that baffles friends and family. This often arises out of life pressures and a past where masculinity or femininity has not been adequately affirmed. The homosexual act provides a sense of conquering and of affirmation, and provides the wanted feelings of being desired.

Society has worked hard to make homosexuality appear as a normal and natural path in life; however, the theories and situations presented in the last two chapters show that this particular sexual lifestyle is far from simple. Multiple factors come together to bring a person to the conclusion that homosexuality may be the only option. The consequences of that moment echo throughout life. Society is only beginning to see what happens when love and marriage outside of God's standards are accepted and allowed to develop.

Chapter 19: Cultural Effects of the Same-Sex Lifestyle

Homosexuality is becoming an accepted part of culture.

> Homosexuality has become an increasingly prevalent part of modern society. It has infiltrated our schools, our news media, our entertainment media, and may soon redefine our concept of marriage. However, homosexuality is by its very nature dangerous to those who practice it. And society is doing homosexuals a disservice when it endorses and promotes homosexuality as normal. In doing so, it is encouraging these Americans to engage in self-destructive behavior.[414]

Despite this warning, there is an aggressive push for people to accept those who pursue the homosexual lifestyle. The gay rights movement seeks to elevate homosexuality to the same level of social and political respectability as heterosexual relationships.

The gay rights movement seeks to remove the stigma of homosexuality by arguing the following:

1. Homosexuality is an immutable trait, and discriminating against immutable traits is wrong (cf. race discrimination).
2. Homosexuality, if not immutable, is highly correlated with personality, and discriminating against such deeply rooted notions of self is wrong, as well (cf. religious intolerance).
3. Homosexuality is perfectly normal and should be respected, despite God's laws against it in the Bible. Gay rights are a favored topic of liberals, and are based on moral relativity, the idea that there is no absolute Right or Wrong.[415]

Advocates of homosexuality are...

> implied to be sexually pure, or at least honest. No one seems to question the sexual inclinations, sanity or integrity of the legislators who are forcing it down people's throats (excuse the pun). One may well wonder how these politicians were enlisted to this unjust cause—some were no doubt complicit (themselves already immoral), but surely many were amoral mercenaries (who would do anything for votes) or moral cowards (fearing popular rejection or ridicule).[416]

Those who oppose same-sex attraction are, in turn, labeled as "homophobic." Homophobia to the average person is the fear of homosexuals.[417] An article from "The Logician" explains that those who stand against homosexuality might be doing so "due to their having subconscious homosexual tendencies, which they want to deny to themselves or hide from others."[418] The accusation of "homophobe" seems an irrational argument and an attempt to divert attention from the real issue. It shifts blame to the accuser rather than looking at homosexuality.

To a degree, homosexuals have been harassed by those opposed to their choices. This, though, does not mean that we should then accept homosexuality as right and beneficial. Despite the stigma now created against those who do not accept sexual choice, we need to explore this topic more thoroughly. Accepting something as good just because it looks good is not going to hold up when the consequences are brought to light. The fruit of the Tree of the Knowledge of Good and Evil looked good and delicious to Adam and Eve, but the consequences of that decision were disastrous. We cannot form our beliefs and standards just because we are told that it is not fair to deny this, that, or the other. We must always come back to God's Word in the face of new social theories. He is still our Creator and the Author of life.

The Homosexual Agenda

The book *The Marketing of Evil* by David Kupelian, an award winning journalist, editor and author,[419] describes a plan to alter American perceptions concerning homosexuality. This book...

> ...reveals how much of what Americans once almost universally abhorred has been packaged, perfumed, gift-wrapped and sold to them as though it had great value. Highly skilled marketers, playing on our deeply felt national values of fairness, generosity and tolerance, have persuaded us to embrace as enlightened and noble that which all previous generations since America's founding regarded as grossly self-destructive, in a word, evil.[420]

One notation is "to inspire potential jammers by providing a juicy list of negative associations with which opponents, usually Christians, are to be smeared."[421] The aim is to utilize the processes that caused America to hate gays to turn them to warm regard concerning homosexuality.

> As part of the liberal ideology in modern education, and as a result of psychological tactics used by homosexual activists, schools have increasingly fostered the promotion of homosexuality, whether as part of official policy (or) through homosexual activists working with or in schools. As a form of indoctrination which begins at the kindergarten level, homosexuality is treated as healthy and normal, with students at very impressionable ages sometimes being influenced to experiment with homosexual behavior. This is often done under the rubric of HIV instruction, of preventing suicide by homosexuals, and preventing homophobia.[422]

Another columnist noted the following:

> I have seen an American university professor, lecturing on psychology at Geneva University, shamelessly manipulating a lecture hall full of eager students with false facts and statistics, or tendentious reading of facts and statistics, to convince them of the naturalness, normality or at least great frequency of homosexuality. I have read a "dear Abby" type newspaper column, where a youth struggling with emotions or feelings he could not fathom was effectively advised by the columnist to become a homosexual.[423]

Alfred Kinsey, who pioneered experimental "sexology" in the 1950's, was himself a homosexual. This fact was not advertised when his work was in the media during the 70's. This relevant fact was cunningly concealed at the time. He was made to appear as an objective, scientific researcher. Among his "findings" was a claim that 15–20% of the U.S. population had had homosexual experiences, i.e., was either exclusive homosexual or bisexual. Certainly the credibility and power to change society would have been much reduced if Kinsey's personal inclinations were publicly known.[424]

Homosexuality and the Civil Rights Movement

One of the stages used to assert the rights of the homosexual community is the civil rights stage. Homosexuals have attempted to align themselves alongside other persecuted minorities such as the African-American community. The best way to refute this effort is to hear from the founding family of the Civil Rights movement, the Kings. What follows is a section from a statement made by Alveda C. King, daughter of the late slain civil rights activist, Rev. A.D. King, and founder of the faith-based organization Kings for America, Inc., regarding "gay rights" as a part of civil rights:

> Thirty-nine years ago, my great-uncle, Reverend Dr. Martin Luther King Jr., delivered to mindful citizens of America a prophetic dream which envisaged all of this great nation's people living in

> the full exercise of all rights granted to them by the U.S. Constitution. My forebear's dream was deeply rooted in the American dream wherein the Founders of our Union saw every lawful citizen standing in dignity outfitted by unalienable rights from God to life, liberty and the pursuit of happiness, free from the tyrannies of personal whim and ideology handed down by kings, dictators, political groups, and yes, some institutions of democratic government....
>
> Yet, there is a larger body of science represented even by the above scientists that agrees that mature behavior patterns rely much more on social shaping and choices than genetic predisposition, such that these behaviors may be successfully modified by a variety of means. The food addict may eat responsibly, the alcoholic may drink responsibly or not at all, and the homosexual may live according to a wide range of choices as well. Thus, binge drinking, overeating, cocaine abuse and other behaviors do not have to be granted public latitude as a matter of right in this great nation. Certainly, these and other mutable behaviors may be practiced; they may be under constitutional protection in fact (under our privacy clauses), but they may not be granted civil rights or public protection.[425]

Again, if behavior or other aspects of personhood may be altered, then those aspects fail to meet civil-rights status. Homosexual practice clearly falls into this category.

Alveda C. King has said, "I have met many ex-homosexuals just as I have met many ex-husbands, ex-wives, ex-drug addicts and ex-lawyers. Yet I have never met an ex-Negro, ex-Caucasian or ex-Native American."[426] The politics of preference does not jibe with civil-rights legitimacy.[427] In short, the distinction is between characteristics that may be altered and thus do not merit civil-rights protection, and immutable characteristics, which do merit civil-rights protection.[428] This is why sexual orientation does not merit civil-rights protection, while characteristics such as race, sex, and religion do.[429]

The plan of the homosexual movement to indoctrinate the world has taken a hold of the recent generations with devastating consequences. Sexual experimentation, as already discussed, is seen as a mark of maturity and the start of great emotional, physical, and mental pain. No form of sex outside of God's standards is perfect or pure. Society has tried to convince the population that homosexual relationships are no different than heterosexual relationships; however, this chapter will show just how different and even damaging same-sex relationships are.

The Question of Love, Desire, and Control

The first difference seen in homosexual relationships is the accepted idea that there is no choice. Secular sources claim that "most people experience little or no sense of choice about their sexual orientation."[430] This idea is a difficult statement upon which to lean a major decision. Homosexuals are human; they want their sexual orientation to be seen as a good orientation; the thought that they have no choice effectively negates an aspect of their humanity. Free choice is one of the things that separate humanity from the rest of creation. Humans can feel desire—both good and bad desires—but many people will choose not to act upon those desires. To strip someone of their sense of choice is to strip them of responsibility, and relationships do not do well without responsibility.

Sexual Standards

The sexual relationships and standards of homosexuals differ greatly from heterosexuals. Homosexual men tend to have an elevated sex drive in comparison to heterosexual men. "Homosexual promiscuity is legendary and there are many studies pointing to an enormous differential between homosexual and heterosexual men's sexual contacts."[431] The second Kinsey report found that in a sample of 685 men, over 90 percent had had more than 25 sexual partners, nearly half had more than 500 different partners, while 23 percent had over 1000 partners. These findings are echoed worldwide.[432]

Many lesbian relationships are quite stable, show a considerable degree of fidelity, and endure over many years. "Lesbians tend to have less permissive attitudes toward casual sex and sex outside a primary relationship than do gay men or heterosexual men. Also like heterosexual women, lesbians have sex fantasies that are more likely to be personal and romantic than the fantasies of gay or heterosexual men."[433] They are less likely than men to become intimate with others outside of their primary relationship. While sexual frequency is decided between the partners, lesbians have less sex than gay men and heterosexuals.[434]

Homosexual Marriage

There is an outcry in the homosexual community to allow same-sex couples to marry. Some statistics show that homosexual couples are happy in long-term relationships and that "the factors that influence relationship satisfaction, commitment, and stability are remarkably similar for both same-sex cohabiting couples and heterosexual married couples."[435] Rob Bell, who is a Christian pastor, speaker and author, speaks for gay marriage. He says that the old way of doing things no longer works.[436] He is perhaps referring to a Christian's literal adherence to Scripture. Recently,

> Bell spoke at San Francisco's Grace Cathedral and openly endorsed marriage equality. Grace Cathedral is the Episcopal Cathedral of the Diocese of California. Bell was speaking to the Cathedral's Grace Forum in an appearance presented in partnership with his publisher, HarperCollins. In response to a question regarding same-sex marriage, Bell said, "I am for marriage. I am for fidelity. I am for love, whether it's a man and woman, a woman and a woman, a man and a man. I think the ship has sailed...I think this is the world we are living in and we need to affirm people wherever they are."[437]

His view is puzzling as it denies the origin of the term *marriage*. His statement implies that those who oppose homosexual marriage should show grace and compassion; however, these virtues go both ways. The homosexual community wants the title of marriage for their union despite the fact that it is a biblical term that describes the union of a man and a woman.

In an interview with an ABC news reporter, well known conservative radio host Rush Limbaugh said marriage...

> ...was not established on the basis of discrimination. It wasn't established on the basis of denying people anything.... No one sensible is against giving homosexuals the rights of contract or inheritance or hospital visits. There's nobody that wants to deny them that. The issue has always been denying them a status that they can't have, by definition. By definition—solely, by definition—same-sex people cannot be married. So instead of maintaining that and holding fast to that, we allowed the argument to be made that the definition needed to change, on the basis that we're dealing with something discriminatory, bigoted, and all of these mystical things that it's not and never has been.[438]

Doug Mainwaring, co-founder of the National Capital Tea Party Patriots and himself an openly professed homosexual,[439] adds to Limbaugh's argument when he says the following:

> In our sometimes misguided efforts to expand our freedom, selfish adults have systematically dismantled that which is most precious to children as they grow and develop. That's why I am now speaking out against same-sex marriage.... Genderless marriage now enjoys an aura of equality and fairness, which suggests that the framers of the Fourteenth Amendment had same-sex marriages in mind as they penned their magnificent giant leap forward for humanity. While this situation is highly unlikely, those who

> selfishly seek additional "rights" for themselves have found their justification in the penumbra they now sense surrounding legitimate civil rights.
>
> Same-sex marriage will not expand rights and freedoms in our nation. It will not *redefine* marriage. It will *undefine* it. This isn't the first time our society has *undefined* marriage. No-fault divorce, instituted all across our country, sounded like a good idea at the time. Its unintended consequence was that it changed forever the definition of marriage from a permanent relationship between spouses to a temporary one.... Same-sex marriage will *undefine* marriage and *unravel* it, and in so doing, it will *undefine* children. It will ultimately lead to *undefining* humanity. This is neither "progressive" nor "conservative" legislation. It is "regressive" legislation."[440]

Marriage is not simply the legal joining of two lives. God made marriage into more than just an "Ok, you can share life and have sex, enjoy" agreement. Marriage originates in the Bible and thus should not simply be redefined on a whim.

God commanded the first man and woman to rise, take dominion, and multiply. Homosexuals can attain two of the four aspects of marriage; there are two that they cannot. They can rise and take dominion, but they cannot multiply and do not fulfill the first statute: they are not a man and a woman. Society may claim that this definition is old fashioned and unfair, but it is the standard set in place by God. "It is unwise to think that one may be more humane than God."[441] This book has already shown just how dangerous the consequences are when the standards He put into place to regulate relationships are disregarded. Marriage is meant to be a true partnership of body, soul, and spirit and can only become so when we submit to God's ways.

Same-Sex Parents

In addition to wanting the title of "marriage," homosexuals fight for the right to have a family. The concept, like the idea of allowing same-sex couples to marry, seems innocent in theory; however, little thought is given to the future of the child. Mainwaring notes the following:

> Sadly, children became collateral damage in the selfish pursuits of adults. Same-sex marriage will do the same, depriving children of their right to either a mom or a dad. This is not a small deal. Children are being reduced to chattel-like sources of fulfillment. On one side, their family tree consists not of ancestors, but of a small army of anonymous surrogates, donors, and attorneys who pinch-hit for the absent gender in genderless marriages. Gays and lesbians demand that they have a "right" to have children to complete their sense of personal fulfillment, and in so doing, are trumping the right that children have to both a mother and a father—a right that same-sex marriage tramples over.[442]

We have established throughout this book that the most important influence upon a child is the parent. This fact is the same in a homosexual union. A child raised in this kind of home will, first, most likely believe that homosexuality is right and true. As the child grows, more practical issues will emerge; such as a homosexual coupling of two men having to explain menstruation to a young girl or a lesbian couple needing to explain premature ejaculation or wet dreams to a young male. These are sensitive issues in an embarrassing time of life. With the child already living in a state of sensitivity, who will have these tough conversations?

It does need to be understood that there is still very much we do not know about the effects of a homosexual couple raising a child because this practice is still very new. "We are only beginning to understand the complex ways in which biology, experience, and culture interact to shape men's and women's sexuality,"[443] and the long-term effects on the child of a same-sex couple are still undecided.

> In a historic study of children raised by homosexual parents, sociologist Mark Regnerus of the University of Texas at Austin has overturned the conventional academic wisdom that such children suffer no disadvantages when compared to children raised by their married mother and father. Just published in the journal *Social Science Research,* this found numerous and significant differences between these groups—with "the outcome for children of homosexuals rated "suboptimal" in almost every category.[444]

Of course each would have their view of suboptimal, and their own value of what is important when raising children.

Another concern for allowing children to be introduced into homosexual unions is the higher percentage of domestic abuse documented in homosexual homes. A study by the Canadian government found that "violence was twice as common among homosexual couples compared with heterosexual couples," and, according to the American College of Pediatricians, "Violence among homosexual partners is two to three times more common than among married heterosexual couples."[445] We can want to allow two people who love each other to either adopt a child or have one conceived through in vitro fertilization, but is it fair to risk that child's life just because we want to believe in same-sex couples?

There is still very much that we do not know about the effects of a same-sex couple raising a child, and many advocates for the homosexual's right to have children would claim that these above statements do not determine the good or evil of the matter. Heterosexual couples do face domestic violence. Single-parent homes do have to face the issue of answering the hard teenage questions. These facts are very true yet cannot be used as an excuse to justify same-sex family situations. There is a lot that needs to be discovered before anyone can say with definite certainty that children raised by a same-sex couple will be more or less than normal.

Health Concerns of the Homosexual Lifestyle

AIDS was once considered one of the highest risks when engaging in a homosexual lifestyle. It was a well-known fact that homosexual males especially had a wide-spread problem with HIV. The homosexual community almost embraced the stereotype as if to say that they did not care about diseases. They would live and be as they were. As time has passed and the sins of humanity have increased, the threat and spread of disease has increased amongst the homosexual community. "Among individuals aged 18 to 59, for example, 21.8% of homosexuals and bisexuals reported that they had an unmet health care need in 2003, nearly twice the proportion of heterosexuals."[446] Homosexuals remain the highest percentage of people diagnosed with HIV within a one-year span, but there are so many more equally as dangerous diseases that are limited to the homosexual community. What follows are real-life, secular statistics that homosexual activists do not want people to know because these studies are claimed by pro-homosexual activists to be discriminative studies produced by supposed homophobes.

According to the Centers for Disease Control and Prevention (CDC), "Both hepatitis A and hepatitis B disproportionately affect men who have sex with men."[447] A separate CDC report stated that 64 percent of all adult P&S syphilis cases in 2004 were among men who have sex with men, which is up by 5 percent from 1999. A recent medical study has noted that, in Europe and North America, there is an outbreak of lymphogranuloma venereum, a sexually transmitted disease that infects the lymphatics, that is limited to the homosexual community.[448] A 2007 study based off results from 2002 has found that "lesbians are at greater risk for morbidity and mortality linked to overweight and obesity."[449] There are other diseases that are increasing in the homosexual community while "the frequency of methamphetamine use is twenty times greater among homosexuals than in the general population."[450] These results plus others portray that there are vital differences between the heterosexual population and the gay, lesbian, and bisexual population in regards to health.[451]

Isolation

There is a new word that has emerged with the rise of the homosexual community. It is "gaydar." This slang word combines the words gay and radar and refers to one's ability to discern another's sexual orientation. Despite the rise in demand for acceptance of homosexuals, there is still a consistent, steady stream of isolation and rejection to the point that homosexuals need to be able to identify one another in hopes of finding some place safe. "Cheryl Nicholas (2004) found evidence that eye gaze may be one of the primary contributors to gaydar."[452] There is the need to associate with others that are like them.[453] This is a touchy subject in regards to the cultural ramifications of homosexual lifestyles. It is never a beneficial move to force people to accept something. There will always be a stubborn streak in humanity; it is part of the fallen nature. We do not like to be told what to do, thus we will buck against authority in all aspects. This is true for the homosexual movement. If we are told we must accept, we will reject, and people will be isolated.

It can become easy to want to justify homosexuality. We may know a homosexual couple that has been devoted to each other for a long time. We wonder how we can love them with the love of Christ if their love is not up to His standards. It is easy therefore to succumb to the unbiblical stance of equal love for all. We do not want to see people hurt; that is not the basis of Christianity; and yet, we pass judgment on the adulterating husband and the sex addict. We justify divorce because that couple was growing apart anyway and the husband seems so much happier with his new lover. We cannot judge love as fair or unfair according to our perspective. We are fallen creatures. We judge according to what we want and what benefits us.

Love cannot be defined in terms of who gets hurt, who is happy, and what is equal. We must love as God instructs us to love rather than on our terms. "If sin were reduced to hurting others, then we could become morally perfect by isolating ourselves from all people. Sin, however, is not primarily a human-against-human action. It is human against God. God defines love as obedience to him."[454] At the end of the day, God has standards that are beyond our comprehension. Who are we to change God's standards? If we align with His sexual standards, then our lives are more likely to be free of disappointments.

Chapter 20: The Church's Response to Same-Sex Attraction

Christians have a very bad reputation for being anti-homosexual. Some of it is unfair propaganda brought about by the activists for homosexuality; some of it we brought upon ourselves for reacting without understanding the issue; and most of it is misinterpretation of what we truly believe. Let it be made clear: the black-and-white, harsh reality is that God did not create homosexuality nor does He condone it; however, the black-and-white ends there. God is mercy, love, grace, and redemption. Just because you fall prey to homosexuality does not mean He hates you, nor does it mean that He rejects you, and it does not mean you are going to hell. Only those who reject Him and the gift of His Son, Jesus Christ, go to hell. Now that that is cleared up, we can discuss the difficult topic of homosexuality and the church.

Homosexuality is probably the most confrontational issue in the church today. There is a wide array of opinion regarding Scriptural interpretation and beliefs. Some people believe that biblical passages regarding homosexuality are no longer relevant to this day and age; other believers would say you cannot be a practicing Christian if you are a practicing homosexual. Christians are notoriously under-informed about homosexuality. There are those who assume that homosexuality is a brain or gene issue; there are those who believe homosexuals are born gay. These mindsets are accepted by younger Christians because the older generation has not taken the steps to understand today's theories surrounding homosexuality and to educate the younger generations about the biblical truths that dictate human sin. Christians are also at a loss as to how to treat homosexuals. God commands us to love everyone as we would love ourselves.[455]

The homosexual community has a broad spectrum of members that tend to fall into three primary categories. The smallest percentage is, sadly, the loudest. These are the militant activists who are pushing for political and social change. Secondly, there are the moderate homosexuals who are happy to live life and who do not want to be changed. Then there are the retentive homosexuals who do not want to be homosexuals. These individuals struggle with their same-sex desires and want nothing more than to be rid of them. In other words, not all gay people want to be gay.

The first category does not want anyone to know about the third category. They would prefer the world to believe the "Once gay, always gay" mantra. This first grouping is affronting, strong-willed, and will do whatever it takes to advance the cause. Homosexuals push to grow their number of supporters so that it can look like their cause is right. If more and more people believe, it is easier to make the resisters look insignificant. This push is dangerous and disturbing. The truth about diseases, domestic abuse, and high drug usage in homosexual communities is hidden. Counselors and therapists are persecuted for trying to help those homosexuals who want out of that lifestyle. People are trapped in the pain and suffering of this life outside of God's standards all because of the small percentage leading the charge.

We all need grace and understanding. All men have fallen short of God's plan for mankind.[456] Homosexuality is a rather obvious manifestation of sin, but that does not make it the worst sin. Jesus says in Matthew that there is "nothing done or said that can't be forgiven;"[457] so, to say that homosexuals are immediately rejected and hated by God is a cruel, evil, and terrible lie! "Once gay, always gay" is also a very big lie. There is nothing God cannot do[458] and no one He cannot redeem.[459] Those who want to change can change when they submit to and rely on God.

Understanding the Basics

Humanity as a whole does not like it when the Bible directly points out our sins. The Bible is very specific about sin. It lists it clearly for all to see. Homosexuality has been raved against as a huge sin, but it is found most often amongst a list of several sins. Yes, homosexuality is pinpointed and discussed on a singular biblical basis, but that is because it was and remains a predominant sin in thriving societies. In order to really clear up a lot of the confusion surrounding how and why Christians approach homosexuality, we all need to understand the basics about humanity's sinful nature.

Human Nature 101

The Bible portrays human nature and behavior. In Genesis 1:31, God called all of creation "very good." He approved of all aspects of the humans He created, including their free will; a free will indicates that man is able to make choices. In continuing through Genesis, we see that, from the beginning, God joined male and female in a life-long marriage and made family a priority. God provided laws for the good and preservation of man. Sin is a deviation from said laws.

Genesis contains the full story of how man disobeyed God. This disobedience affected mankind and all over which he was given authority. Physical decay, suffering, and the natural death of living creatures were all introduced into the world. This is read in Genesis 2:17; 3:17–19; Romans 5:12 & 17; and 6:23. A final result of man's disobedience was man's tendency to sin. This tendency does not mean, though, that a man absolutely must perform a certain type of sin nor does it justify man giving in to the attraction to sin. Genesis 4:7 shows that God gave man the ability to resist sin. God gave formal laws through Moses to help combat man's continual reaction against the basic moral laws they innately knew—through creation, through conscience, and through oral tradition. These laws displayed the unchangeable morality God had for man's wellbeing. We see this in Scriptures such as Exodus 20, Deuteronomy 4:8–9, Leviticus 18, and Galatians 3:19.

Deception

The Bible shows that, while nurture and environment can make one more predisposed to certain types of behavior, man's sinful nature deceives us into believing that sinful behaviors are not sin. As spiritually fallen creatures, our propensity to sin is within us. Yielding to sin reduces our ability to resist temptation (temptation is the urge we feel to do things we know or at least suspect are wrong). The devil (a fallen angel who wants to drag us down with him) will tempt us and try to deceive us. He tempts us to fulfill our desires anywhere other than with God and within His standards.

The devil, and living in this fallen and broken world, will give us many reasons not to trust in our true and loving God. Adam and Eve, the first humans who were perfect in every way, were deceived. If they can be tricked, we cannot think of ourselves as unable to be deceived. There are many times in the lives of believers and non-believers alike that we will rationalize our urge to sin. Rationalization of sin is an attempt to justify it or make us believe it is not really sinning. This excusing of behavior brought Adam and Eve down; it brings us down. One justification leads to another, and the soul is corrupted.

When we are deceived, we don't know that we are deceived; having other believers in our lives is a valuable tool as they help us guard against deception. The homosexual is deceived when he allows himself to believe that he cannot change or that he was born homosexual. Solomon writes in Proverbs 28:13, "Whoever conceals their sins does not prosper, but the one who confesses and renounces them finds mercy."[460] James wrote in James 5:16, "Confess your sins to each other and pray for each other so that you may be healed. The prayer of a righteous person is powerful and effective."[461] Reading and studying the Bible combined with great Christian friends help us to rise above the natural urges of our fallen nature. Strength and change can be found in those around us.

Biblical Reality

In the midst of all the theories and ideas and socially propagated lies surrounding homosexuality, Christians come back to what is written in the Bible. This need for truth tends to get us into trouble, for non-believers do not necessarily understand our meaning or our intent when we try to state the truth.[462] Still, we stick to our standards because we love our God. Jesus said that "if you love me, you will obey my commandments."[463] God tells us to love others; in this love He also commands us to all live up to a standard: no gossip, help others, love those who hate you, sex only in marriage, and no homosexuality. God knew that our sinful habits would not change with the times; therefore, His commands do not change with the times either.

The Foundation of the Standard

The problems regarding homosexuality seem insurmountable and accompanied by judgment because if you have an opinion, you would be considered judgmental. We, however, must commit to a standard rather than living by what feels good. Feelings change as the sun sets and rises and are an unreliable barometer through which to live life. The Bible consistently teaches that homosexuality is wrong, and while Scriptures concerning homosexuality are explained in the next chapter, it is important to understand this truth. God only joined opposite genders together sexually, approving them in marriage. He made man and woman uniquely compatible and complementary. This is seen in Genesis 2:18–24, Matthew 19:4, and in 1 Corinthians 11:8–12.

Homosexuality is a result of man yielding to his sinful nature. It is a perverse form of fornication. The choice of a wrong sexual lifestyle aligns itself with any other wrong choice. Yes, in the end, engaging in a homosexual lifestyle is a choice. According to the Bible, homosexual desires are not in themselves sinful. People are subject to a wide variety of sinful desires, but these are not sinful until a person acts upon them—either by acting on the desire or by encouraging the desire and deliberately engaging in fantasies acting it out. People tempted by homosexual desires, like people tempted by improper heterosexual desires, are not sinning until they act upon those desires in some manner, whether in the mind or flesh. The feelings that draw a person, the environment that cultivates it, and even the genetics that make one predisposed are not choices, but, in the end, every human has a choice as to what they will or will not do about how they feel. It is a way of fulfilling the unmet needs in our lives left by the Fall. We rejected God; we are incomplete; and we choose drugs, alcohol, sex, and even homosexuality in hopes of stopping that feeling of emptiness.

There are several verses that list homosexuality amongst many dangerous and damaging sins. Leviticus 18:22–23 warns, "Do not have sexual relations with a man as one does with a woman; that is detestable. Do not have sexual relations with an animal and defile yourself with it. A woman must not present herself to an animal to have sexual relations with it; that is a perversion."[464] Mark 7:21–22 contains a detailed list of sins, and none of the sins in this list can be debated as anything other than what they are: "For it is from within, out of a person's heart, that evil thoughts come—sexual immorality, theft, murder, adultery, greed, malice, deceit, lewdness, envy, slander, arrogance and folly."[465]

Romans 1:20–27 speaks clearly on man's inability to claim ignorance about their sinful lusts and desires:

> For since the creation of the world God's invisible qualities—His eternal power and divine nature—have been clearly seen, being understood from what has been made, so that people are without excuse. For although they knew God, they neither glorified him as God nor gave thanks to him, but their thinking became futile and their foolish hearts were darkened. Although they claimed to be wise, they became fools and exchanged the glory of the immortal God for images made to look like a mortal human being and birds and animals and reptiles. Therefore God gave them over in the sinful desires of their hearts to sexual impurity for the degrading of their bodies with one another. They exchanged the truth about God for a lie, and worshiped and served created things rather than the Creator—who is forever praised. Amen. Because of this, God gave them over to shameful lusts. Even their women exchanged natural sexual relations for unnatural ones. In the same way the men also abandoned natural relations with women and were inflamed with lust for one another. Men committed shameful acts with other men, and received in themselves the due penalty for their error.[466]

Paul, the author of Romans, continues to write about morality throughout the New Testament. In 1 Corinthians 6:9, he writes, "Or do you not know that wrongdoers will not inherit the kingdom of God? Do not be deceived: Neither the sexually immoral nor idolaters nor adulterers nor men who have sex with men;"[467] and more in 1 Timothy 1:10, "for the sexually immoral, for those practicing homosexuality, for slave traders and liars and perjurers—and for whatever else is contrary to the sound doctrine."[468]

Christians may come across as hateful, unfair, and cruel to the homosexual community. It should not be our agenda to be this way. God, though, created a standard to which to conform for our benefit. The standard for which we live our lives is a high one that we cannot accomplish without God. God made it that way. He wants us to rely on Him. We, as believers, are still human. We still sin; we still make fools of ourselves; but we have God to fall back upon, and our passion for Him is what drives us to do the things we do. The Church is meant to be a place where those who are lost and suffering in their sin can find help, healing, and redemption. We stick to the standard God places before us; it seems harsh, but it is full of His love. I hope this understanding of that standard will help you as you read the next chapter where we discuss in detail all the Scriptures that have become the primary tools in both the Christian and non-Christian arguments of homosexuality.

Chapter 21: Biblical Arguments For and Against Same-Sex Attraction

There are several Scriptures that have been raised as a rally cry for both the Christians and non-Christians in regards to homosexuality. Verses like 1 Corinthians 6:9 are quoted out of context; the intention and motivation of biblical characters are skewed; and confusion is the result as both sides throw verses at each other in hopes of winning the argument. Many of the Scriptures used in these arguments are irrelevant to the cause and, when studied in their context, do not back either side's position. "We must be clear that although the Church *can* err in its interpretation of the Bible and is happy to be corrected, it ultimately stands under the Word of God. We must not give away any ground regarding the authority of Scripture."[469] God's Word is absolute; sometimes we need to take a closer look to understand exactly what it is saying so that it can be used for healing instead of hatred.

The Question of Then and Now

Some people question the reasoning behind the negative view of homosexuality but not of other practices expressed in the Bible. For example, intercourse during a woman's menstrual period was banned as written in Leviticus 18:19, 15:19–24. Why do we not then veto this today? Blood in the Old Testament represented sacrifice and was sacred in the Jewish traditions and way of life. The overall sacrifice of Jesus frees us of this. Another problem is that of slavery. While Scripture teaches of the use and care of slaves, it does not speak against it. Slavery was a popular practice in biblical times, and yet it was abolished one hundred and fifty years ago. It has no place in any civilized culture. Context is important regarding Scripture. Primitive cultures contained many practices that were, with hindsight, abhorrent practices before God.

The punishment for adultery was stoning to death for both the man and the woman as seen in Deuteronomy 22:22. We obviously do not practice stoning today, but that does not negate the fact that God still abhors adultery. Polygamy and concubinage were seen often in the Old Testament; neither is condemned in the New Testament, though it advocates that a husband have one wife. "But since sexual immorality is occurring, each man should have sexual relations with his own wife, and each woman with her own husband."[470] Prostitution was considered natural and necessary. "A man was not guilty of sin for visiting a prostitute, though the prostitute herself was regarded as a sinner."[471] Divorce was permissible in the Old Testament in Deuteronomy 24:1–4, though Jesus forbids it in Mark 10:1–11. His words carry a softer message in Matthew 19:9. These examples therefore make one consider seriously the fairness of the negative attitude toward homosexuality. Scriptures speak against its practice, but it also condemns the above-mentioned.

When Christ's death and resurrection occurred, a new way of living was written—that of Christ's testament, the New Testament. Polygamy is not mentioned in the New Testament, but many passages note marriage as consisting of one husband and one wife. Divorce is rampant today. We live in a world where believers err to God's grace and mercy to justify their sin. Jesus is also seen as forgiving the adulterous woman, showing that adultery is still sin, and Scripture in the New Testament continues to condemn this practice. Some things are not again mentioned in the New Testament and so we are left to form our own judgment.

In this chapter, we are going to explore the verses used to denounce homosexuality, the characters that are heralded as the champions of homosexuality, and the truth within all of these.

In the Beginning...

God set the standard for human relationships from the very beginning. There are many homosexuals who argue that God created them as homosexuals; however, God did not "create" same-gender sexual relationships. Genesis 1:27 writes, "So God created mankind in his own image, in the image of God he created them; male and female he created them."[472] This verse shows that male and female came from God. He created both genders; both genders reflect Him; and His perfect will is reflected when the two parts of Himself as portrayed in each gender are united. "The scientific attempts to demonstrate that homosexual attraction is biologically determined have failed. The major researchers now prominent in the scientific arena—themselves gay activists—have in fact arrived at such conclusions,"[473] thus, in both the Scriptures and the secular world, none can say that "God created me this way."

God enforces His will for the two genders further in Genesis. In chapter 6, verse 19, God commands Noah to preserve only male/female pairings of animals to breed each species. God made it clear that the preservation of the male-female bond is essential even in the animal kingdom. It is beneficial for more than just the procreation of the species. God is a creator; He made the world to create. There is no fruit from homosexuality. Nothing is created from within it save for pain. Pain is opposed to God's perfect intentions.

A Sin of Pride: Sodom and Gomorrah

Sodom and Gomorrah are well-known cities even to those who are not believers. Interestingly research shows that "there was a catastrophe that emptied the area of settled occupation for 600 years. The efficient cause of this evacuation of the cities was probably an earthquake, with an accompanying release and explosion of gaseous deposits. Biblically, and fundamentally, it was God's judgment, remembered again and again throughout the Bible."[474] Jude 7 records that Sodom and Gomorrah "acted immorally and indulged in unnatural lust."[475] There was no sexual sin that was not prominent within the walls of these two cities. In Genesis 19, the city of Sodom is revealed as a place in which men sexually lusted after men, from which the term "sodomy" was derived. Jude 7 refers to Sodom and its region being given to fornication, including that of unnatural relations. Sodom has been used as the example of what God does to those who practice homosexuality. It is an example that can be used out of context if it is not understood.

Genesis 19 contains a story that illuminates the height of the debauchery in Sodom and Gomorrah. "The outcry against its people has become great before the Lord,"[476] thus God sends two of His angels to the city. They are given shelter by Lot, Abraham's nephew. During the night, men from all over the town came to "have sex with them."[477] Lot, in a desperate plea, offers his two virgin daughters in place of his guests. This actually portrays the awful state of this city and the condition of Lot's life. The word used to describe the situation with his daughters means "to know sexually."[478] Lot refers to his two daughters as having not "known" a man (19:8);"[479] they were the quintessential sexual offering, yet the men of Sodom refused. They preferred homosexual acts over heterosexual acts. The angels blind the men of Sodom, lead Lot and his family from the city, and Sodom and Gomorrah are destroyed. The record of Sodom, as well as accounts of nations elsewhere, testify that living within the environment of people where iniquity abounds is conducive to furthering the same iniquity among succeeding generations, resulting in the necessity of divine judgment when nations become given over to such sins. This is also seen in Leviticus 18:24; "Do not defile yourselves in any of these ways, because this is how the nations that I am going to drive out before you became defiled."[480]

Despite the seemingly obvious conclusion of this story, there are those who argue that it was not true homosexuality that was driving the men of Sodom to want to have sex with the disguised angels. It was, instead, a lack of hospitality. Ezekiel does allude to a lack of hospitality in Sodom; he writes that they "did not aid the poor and needy."[481] This argument is "based on the Canaanite custom that guaranteed the protection of those coming under one's roof."[482] While inhospitality is wrong, it is the homosexual behavior of the Sodomites that is especially criticized in the account of Sodom's destruction.

Others argue that it was not just blanket homosexuality being condemned but homosexual rape, meaning it is different from homosexual behavior in loving relationships. Heterosexual males were intent on humiliating strangers by treating them "like women," thus emasculating them. There is a similar case in Judges 19–21. Their awful behavior has nothing to do with the problem of whether genuine love expressed between consenting adults of the same sex is legitimate or not.

God's destruction of Sodom was not only because of the practice of homosexuality. Evidently it was a deciding factor, but it was Sodom's pride, which was sin, that intensified their offensiveness to God.[483] Sin is not just about the act but about the heart also. Ezekiel 16:50 informs us "that the Sodomites were haughty, and committed abomination before me: therefore I took them away as I saw good."[484] The word for *abomination* here is *tôʿêbah*, which is the word often used for sexual sin including sodomy—the slang used to refer to homosexuality (Lev. 18:22; 26–27, 29, 30; 20:13; Dt. 23:18; 24:4; 1 Ki. 14:24; Ezek. 22:11; 33:26).[485] The Bible and secular history reveal that prevalent homosexuality is associated with pride, affluence, increased free time, selfishness, indulgence, and carelessness. "Therefore, rebellion against God's laws and order and the resultant environmental factors are seen to be a cause in promoting sensuality and homosexuality."[486] Sodom and Gomorrah took pride in their sin; thus, though there was more sexual sin in these cities than any other in the world at that time, it was the pride that brought God's wrath. It's interesting to note that today, many gay festivals and celebrations are called "Gay Pride."

The Charge of Leviticus

The Book of Leviticus contains the most misunderstood verses about homosexuality. This book complements Exodus and reinforces the story of the Old Testament.[487] Leviticus is the book that lists out God's laws in detail to His people. George Bush, an American biblical scholar[488] (not the former President of the United States), notes, "The book of Leviticus contains some matters purely historical, yet its leading scope is to record the laws concerning the sacrifices, ordinances, and institutions of that remarkable economy from which it derives its name."[489] God had a lot to say in regards to keeping His people from becoming unclean. In Leviticus 5:3, God "addresses situational moral sins. The word 'uncleanness' is translated from the Hebrew 'tame'."[490]

Sexual contact between males was defiling; therefore God charges the priests and Levites to deal with it as object lessons of His holiness.[491] In Leviticus 18:22 and 24–30, there is an explicit command forbidding male/male sexual relations. Leviticus 18:22 is a direct condemnation of all homosexual unions. "Contrary to biblical revisionists who say this Scripture does not foresee 'committed, monogamous gay relationships,' Leviticus 18:22 is a sweeping condemnation of all homosexual unions."[492] As written in Leviticus 18:22, "Do not lie with a man as one lies with a woman; that is detestable,"[493] and in Leviticus 20:13, "If there is a man who lies with a male as those who lie with a woman, both of them have committed a detestable act; they shall surely be put to death. Their bloodguiltiness is upon them."[494]

"The word 'abomination' is derived from the Hebrew 'toevah,' which denotes a clash of basic dispositions between the righteous and unrighteous."[495] It is the same word that is used to describe homosexual sins in Leviticus 18:22.[496] Such an act was regarded as an "abomination" for several reasons. The Hebrew prescientific understanding was that male semen contained the whole of emerging life. With no knowledge of eggs and ovulation, it was assumed that the woman provided only the place of incubation. Hence the spilling of semen for any non-procreative purpose—in coitus interruptus (Gen. 38:1–11), male homosexual acts, or male masturbation—was considered tantamount to abortion or murder. (Female homosexual acts were consequently not so seriously regarded, and are not mentioned at all in the Old Testament; however, Paul addresses the subject in Romans 1:26).

Some debate whether these Scriptures clearly condemn homosexuality or if the Hebrew terms used were meant to describe the homosexual behavior present at pagan temples.[497] This is far-fetched when considering other Scriptures that also reference homosexuality. Male prostitution was a part of Canaanite religion as seen in Deuteronomy 23:17–18, but this is not the only type of homosexuality condemned. If this were true, then Leviticus would differ from the general tone of biblical sexual prohibitions. If the Old Testament were solely prohibiting cultic prostitution, then there would be no reason for the New Testament to continue along this track. The New Testament is not focused upon distancing the church from the Canaanite religion; rather, it wishes to uphold holiness in sexual behavior and distance itself from general licentious behavior. Leviticus 20:13 is another warning advising homosexuals of the consequences of their actions. God seems to provide opportunities for repentance, but when it is refused, the death sentence is imposed.

Most of the Levitical laws were similar to those of other surrounding nations; Egypt, Assyria, and Babylon all had some form of negative attitudes toward homosexual acts. Israel was set apart from these nations due to the higher moral standard set within their laws.[498] "Unchastity was punished more severely, and prostitution was illegal rather than regulated."[499] It makes no sense then for the Old Testament law to permit homosexuality apart from its prohibition in idol worship. If Leviticus 18:22 or similar passages did have cultic prostitution in mind, the fact that homosexuality was associated with cultic prostitution would make homosexuality in general all the worse.[500]

Sexual Religious Rituals

The book of Judges shows shocking corruption and the worship of other gods amongst the Israelites. This book "describes the history of Israel from Joshua's death to the rise of Samuel."[501] We read of some corruption in Judges 2:11–13:

> Then the Israelites did evil in the eyes of the Lord and served the Baals. They forsook the Lord, the God of their ancestors, who had brought them out of Egypt. They followed and worshiped various gods of the peoples around them. They aroused the Lord's anger because they forsook him and served Baal and the Ashtoreths.[502]

While many would see the worship of other gods as not a big issue, this worship involved the regular killing of children for sacrifice, self-mutilation, ritual prostitution, and homosexuality.[503]

Deuteronomy also contains Scriptures of concern. While it records Moses' farewell addresses to Israel, the title "implies a second law-giving, but in fact the book contains a reinstatement and reaffirmation of the Sinai covenant."[504] The main purpose of this book was to remind the Israelites of their special relationship with God. They were His covenant people and needed to obey His laws.[505] How quickly had they forgotten all that God had done for them. How quickly do we also forget God's greatness and plead only with Him in crises. Leviticus shows that God does not change His mind in His written Word.

In Deuteronomy 23:17, God orders that there be no homosexuals—sodomites from the Hebrew word Qadesh, which specifically pointed to male homosexuals who worshipped false idols.[506] These were specific practices of the idol worshippers inhabiting Canaan. Most of the practices were meant to appease the "gods" and thereby gain a good harvest. Ashtoreth/Astarte was the Canaanite deity who required this type of devotion.[507] Walter Wink, a theologian and important figure in progressive Christianity,[508] points out that this Scripture most likely refers to a heterosexual prostitute involved in Canaanite fertility rites that had infiltrated Jewish worship; the King James Version inaccurately labeled him a "sodomite."[509] This however would go against previous biblical references that we have discussed. "Progressive Christianity" is dangerous and a very slippery slope that actually slides us slowly away from sound biblical principles. In Deuteronomy, one has glimpses of some of the issues of the times as 22:5 prohibits cross-dressing or "transvestism." We see that the culture of these times was similar to those of today.

The Relationship Between David and Jonathan

Homosexuals have sought out a validation point in the Scriptures by way of the relationship between David and Jonathan. 1 Samuel 18:1 notes that Jonathan loved David. In 2 Samuel 1:26, one reads that David lamented Jonathan's death, in which he said that his love for Jonathan was more wonderful than the love of a woman.[510] It is these two passages that some say suggest a homosexual relationship between David and Jonathan.

The Hebrew word for "love" used in these passages, however, is not the typical word used for sexual activity. This word for "love" has clear political and diplomatic connotations as seen in 1 Samuel 16:21 and 1 Kings 5:1.[511] "David's "love" for Jonathan was not sexual (erotic) but a friendship (philic) love."[512] Secondly, David's comparison of his relationship with Jonathan to that of women may be a reference to his experience with King Saul's daughter. Saul promised his daughter in marriage as a reward for slaying Goliath, but Saul continued to add conditions upon this marriage with the underlying desire to have David killed in battle.

This can be read in 1 Samuel 18:17 and 25. Jonathan's love for David was far deeper than anything he could have received from an arranged marriage. Apart from these reasons, the Bible clearly and consistently denounces homosexuality, and so, to proclaim that there was a homosexual love between David and Jonathan contradicts the prohibitions of it found throughout the Bible.

The friendship between David and Jonathan was a covenantal relationship. In 1 Samuel 18:1–5, we see David and Jonathan forming an agreement; according to 1 Samuel 20:16–17 and 42 and 23:16–18, Jonathan was to be second-in-command in David's future reign and David was to protect Jonathan's family. In their relationship, we see several qualities of true friendship. In 1 Samuel 18:4, a sacrificial type of love is portrayed as Jonathan gives David his clothes and military apparel. Jonathan did not strip off all his clothes as some suggest but just of his armor and royal robe.[513] Jonathan recognized that David would be king of Israel, and, rather than being envious or jealous, Jonathan submitted to God's will and sacrificed his own right to the throne. Saul, Jonathan's father, is trying to kill David, but in 1 Samuel 19:1–3, we read of Jonathan's loyalty toward and defense of David. Jonathan rebukes his father and reminds him of David's faithfulness to him

David and Jonathan also freely expressed their feelings toward one another. Jonathan formulates a plan in 1 Samuel 20 that reveals his father's plans toward David. Jonathan's plan was to keep David safe, but, rather than this being a description of a homosexual relationship, it describes true friendship between two men. In 1 Samuel 20:41, the two men kiss which "was a common cultural greeting for men in that day."[514] This is also several chapters from the giving of attire, and it is an act accompanied by weeping rather than being anything of a sexual nature.

According to the Bible, true friendship involves loyalty, sacrifice, compromise, and emotional attachment. While it is a shame that emotional attachment amongst males is seen as homosexual, David and Jonathan portray that men can have a deep affection for each other. In Acts 13:22, David is described as "a man after God's own heart."[515] It would be contradictory to the Bible's repeated condemnation of homosexuality to exalt a homosexual male to such a place of honor. David also had many wives and concubines, not that this is complete proof of his heterosexuality. The Scriptures do, though, speak of his attraction to women. In 2 Samuel 11, we see David's sexual attraction to Bathsheba, who was a woman. He pursued her due to this attraction. Saying that David and Jonathan had a homosexual relationship is merely a quest by the homosexual community to validate their choice.

Lastly, David is addressed by God through the prophet Nathan for his sin surrounding his adulterous affair. In fact, "Nathan's interview with David (2 Sam.12:1–14) is one of the most dramatic stories in literature."[516] On confrontation by Nathan, David genuinely confesses and repents. Why then, does God not similarly address David if he had a homosexual relationship with Jonathan in a time when God condemns homosexuality? It would be odd for God to confront David concerning one sexual sin but not another.

When Society Accepts...

Society's desire to accept homosexuality is not something new. There is a passage in 1 Kings that highlights the rise of acceptance and the impending evil it brings when sin is promoted through the government:

> Judah did evil in the eyes of the Lord. By the sins they committed they stirred up his jealous anger more than those who were before them had done. They also set up for themselves high places, sacred stones and Asherah poles on every high hill and under every spreading tree. There were even male shrine prostitutes in the land; the people engaged in all the detestable practices of the nations the Lord had driven out before the Israelites.[517]

This king, Rehoboam, was strongly influenced by the "diversity" of his mother, Namah of the Ammonites, who were relatives of the Sodomites.[518] He was an evil king.[519]

In 1 Kings 15:11–13, the scribe describes the consequence of weak leadership. Out of thirteen other hideous Canaanite-adopted practices, the practice of sodomy-influenced religion in Israel was particularly seen as a danger to the wellbeing, health, and religious integrity of God's people. "Asa, unlike Rehoboam before him, removed his own mother who also followed 'tolerance' policies. Tolerance is dangerous when it is not based on biblical love."[520]

Jehoshaphat, the head of state, did what was "right" in the eyes of the Lord in 1 Kings 22:43 and 46. As a king, he obeyed God and made peace with the North.[521] He removed homosexuals from positions of influence within the country. "He took positive steps to ensure that the Mosaic law was known and understood."[522] His decision was based on God's commandments. He was a secular leader—in that he was not a leader in the temple or religious realms—that brought blessing and good. He and others following his example refused to allow laws and policies that would damage the wellbeing of the nation.[523]

Jesus: The Champion of the Oppressed

Jesus was an advocate of the oppressed. He fought for the poor, women, and the physically afflicted, all of whom were groups deemed inferior in many cultures in biblical times. He upheld the Old Testament law consistently. He does not specifically talk on homosexuality, but He continually upheld marriage between a man and a woman, and His indication was that the only alternative to heterosexual marriage was celibacy. In Matthew 19:1–12, He issued an extensive disapproval of all sexual relationships outside of the male/female model, described in Genesis 1:27. He was never swayed by others' opinions regarding these things, and so, if He approved of homosexuality, He would have stood for their rights.

Homosexuals and the Kingdom of God

One of the most debated Scriptures regarding homosexuality and the Kingdom of God is in 1 Corinthians. In these times, "Homosexuality was widespread in the Graeco-Roman world; fourteen of the first fifteen Roman emperors practiced it."[524] The city of Corinth "was known throughout the Roman world for its vice and immorality. One of the major influences on that degenerate moral climate was the degrading worship of the goddess Aphrodite (the goddess of love)."[525] Her temple housed approximately 1,000 prostitutes who aided in the worship of

Aphrodite.[526] Homosexuality, therefore, is no surprise in such a city.

Paul writes in 1 Corinthians 6:9–10.

> Do you not know that the wicked will not inherit the kingdom of God? Do not be deceived: Neither the sexually immoral nor idolaters nor adulterers nor male prostitutes nor homosexual offenders nor thieves nor the greedy nor drunkards nor slanderers nor swindlers will inherit the kingdom of God.[527]

Sometimes the meaning of Scripture seems so obvious, but there is debate surrounding the Greek word translated as "homosexual offenders" or "arsenokoite."

> Some say that it is a reference to male prostitutes rather than to two committed homosexuals. Yet, others argue that Paul, who wrote the passage, would not have repeated "male prostitutes" twice. Others argue that the two root words in arsenokoite are the same terms used to prohibit any premarital or extramarital sexual relations, so they may not refer to homosexual relations alone.[528]

However Robin Scroggs, Professor of Biblical Theology and one who is sympathetic to the homosexual community,[529] writes, "The word is derived directly from Leviticus 18:22 and 20:13 and is used in rabbinic texts to refer to homosexual intercourse."[530] Scroggs also reminds us that to solely focus on this verse toward those struggling with homosexuality is cruel. I do agree that we as believers need to show grace; all people are riddled with imperfection and sin, and some sins are more obvious than others. Grace, however, cannot be used as an excuse to neglect the standards outlined in God's Word.

Even if one believes that homosexuality is a sin based upon this Scripture, the next verse says that homosexuals can inherit the kingdom of God upon salvation. Paul writes in 1 Corinthians 6:11,

"And that is what some of you were. But you were washed, you were sanctified, you were justified in the name of the Lord Jesus Christ and by the Spirit of our God."[531] One Scripture must not be taken without looking at its context. We also need to be aware that it is not just homosexuality that is mentioned here but other types of sin as well. Of note in this passage is that Paul celebrates former homosexuals who are attending the church. This verse changes the tone of the passage as he acknowledges their accomplishment by the power of Christ.

The Wages of Sin

In 1 Timothy 1, Paul says of homosexuality that it is a sin "worthy of death" but is forgiven through repentance. Geisler notes, though, that the word used in reference to the sins Paul lists alongside homosexuality "is a broader word for other sexual sins than 'adultery.'" It includes homosexual acts, and is even translated "sodomites" (NKJV) or "homosexual" (NASB). The context in which it is used and the other sins with which it is listed demonstrate the severity of the sin of sodomy."[532] Wink believes that 1 Corinthians 6:9 and also 1 Timothy 1:10 are unclear. It is not obvious whether these texts "refer to the 'passive' and 'active' partners in homosexual relationships, or to homosexual and heterosexual male prostitutes. In short, it is unclear whether the issue is homosexuality alone, or promiscuity and 'sex for hire.'"[533] Wink again is fitting Scripture to fit an agenda.

In Titus 1:16, Paul speaks strongly against those who go against God's created model for intimacy. We claim that we know God, but, when we justify sin, our minds and consciences are corrupted. Once we compromise the standards of God, it is a slippery slope of continually justifying our sin. Jude 1:4, 7, and 19 address the church regarding the allowance of unrepentant homosexuals into the church. The same standards that apply to other sins must also apply to homosexuals. Repentance is the door of acceptance into the Kingdom of God. In Revelation 21:27, John utters a final cry against sexual immorality when he writes, "Nothing impure will ever enter it, nor will anyone who does what is shameful or deceitful, but only those whose names are written in the Lamb's book of life."[534] While homosexuality is not specifically mentioned, it is a part of the sexual immorality that is spoken of throughout the Old and New Testaments that is abhorrent to God. It produces nothing life-giving and is against the nature of God.

The Intuition of the Apostle

In Romans 1, Paul discusses surrender to lust, but the meaning of the actual acts is debated. No matter the lust though, three times in this passage, the statement "'God gave them over' tolls like a death toll (1:24, 26, 28)."[535] The passage reads as follows:

> Because of this, God gave them over to shameful lusts. Even their women exchanged natural relations for unnatural ones. In the same way the men also abandoned natural relations with women and were inflamed with lust for one another. Men committed indecent acts with other men, and received in themselves the due penalty for their perversion.[536]

Whether the passage is describing prostitution or is condemning homosexual behavior is not in question. Most of this passage deals with the male perspective, but in Romans 1:26, for the first time, there is a specific mention of female homosexuality. It is described as a "depraved condition brought on by a sinful nature"[537] and is also considered sin.

Claim Ignorance

Some advocates of homosexuality debate the above passage; they believe that the persons whom Paul condemns are obviously not homosexual.[538] They would state that it is not clear that Paul differentiated in his thoughts or writings between gay persons, in the sense of lasting sexual inclination, and heterosexuals who simply involved themselves in occasional homosexual behavior. They may go on to say that it is in fact unlikely that many Jews of his day knew of such a distinction. Boswell was a prominent historian and a professor at Yale University.[539] He writes that Paul is speaking to those who violate their natural sexual orientation; those who go against their own natural desire. "'Nature' in Romans 1:26, then, should be understood as the personal nature of the pagans in question."[540] Paul probably believed that all people were heterosexual and had no concept of homosexual orientation. This idea was not available in these times. Probably these described relationships were extremely lustful and were not relationships involving faithful commitment to each other and neither were they relationships of integrity.

I believe that this is a strange comment to state that Paul was ignorant regarding the practice of homosexuality. God used Paul to write a majority of the New Testament. I doubt that God would use an ignorant man. Paul's letters are our primary source of early Christianity and the earliest datable Christian documents, many being written between eighteen and thirty years after the death of Jesus.[541] Paul himself spoke fluent Greek and was both Jewish by heritage and had the rights of a Roman citizen.[542] He was not a sheltered or ignorant man. He wrote letters and traveled amongst different cultures. Paul also studied from a young age under Gamaliel who was a leading teacher of the Jewish law.[543] Readers see from many of Paul's letters that he was a learned man and was well informed regarding cultural practices and ways.

Natural versus Unnatural

Advocates would continue to argue that Paul assumes that the condemned were heterosexuals who were behaving contrary to their nature. He uses words such as "leaving," "giving up," or "exchanging" their regular sexual orientation for that which was foreign to them. Paul knew nothing of psychosexual theories or supposed sexual orientation. For such persons, having heterosexual relations would be acting contrary to nature; they would be "leaving," "giving up," or "exchanging" their natural sexual orientation for one that was unnatural to them. These words indicate that a free and sinful choice was made to engage in sinful acts. They would, again, conclude that Paul thought that these people were heterosexual, but they were practicing homosexual acts that were unnatural for them.

These arguments can seem to make sense except for when we look at the word for which the argument hinges. The word "unnatural" leads us to believe that the sin of homosexuality is not just a violation of biblical ethics but also a violation of God's natural and moral standard for man. Paul writes in Galatians 5:19, "The acts of the flesh are obvious: sexual immorality, impurity and debauchery;"[544] He writes in Ephesians 5:3–7:

> But among you there must not be even a hint of sexual immorality, or of any kind of impurity, or of greed, because these are improper for God's holy people. Nor should there be obscenity, foolish talk or coarse joking, which are out of place, but rather thanksgiving. For of this you can be sure: No immoral, impure or greedy person—such a person is an idolater—has any inheritance in the kingdom of Christ and of God. Let no one deceive you with empty words, for because of such things God's wrath comes on those who are disobedient. Therefore do not be partners with them.[545]

Further in this same chapter, written in verses 22–25, Paul describes the intimate relationship of marriage. "In particular, wives should submit themselves to their husbands as the church is submissive to Christ its head. Husbands should love their wives as Christ loved the church his body."[546] Paul gives no room for one to broaden this most intimate of relationships.

He writes to the Colossians, a predominantly Gentile church,[547] in Colossians 3:5–7, "Put to death, therefore, whatever belongs to your earthly nature: sexual immorality, impurity, lust, evil desires and greed, which is idolatry. Because of these, the wrath of God is coming. You used to walk in these ways, in the life you once lived."[548] Paul writes about sexual immorality and uncleanness. Many of the areas to which Paul traveled were very accepting of homosexuality, yet Paul kept communicating the sinfulness of such practices. While homosexuals today state that to suppress homosexual urges is to be untrue to self, rather the Colossians passage tells one to separate oneself from sexual sin and earthly things.[549]

The Thorn

Another view that has been put forth is that Paul, himself, struggled with homosexuality and that is why he was so adamant against the practice. John Shelby Spong, a public speaker, writer, media speaker, and retired Episcopal bishop of Newark in New Jersey,[550] believes that homosexuality is "a healthy, natural and affirming form of human sexuality."[551] Spong "claims he is a Christian yet he champions causes that historic Christianity has often fought tooth and nail against."[552] Spong believes that homosexual desires were Paul's thorn in his flesh, to which he refers in 2 Corinthians 12:7–10:

> To keep me from becoming conceited because of these surpassingly great revelations, there was given me a thorn in my flesh, a messenger of Satan to torment me. Three times I pleaded with the Lord to take it from me. But He said to me, 'My grace is sufficient for you, for my power is made perfect in weakness.' Therefore, I will boast all the more gladly about my weaknesses, so that Christ's power may rest on me. That is why, for Christ's sake, I delight in weaknesses, in insults, in hardships, in persecutions, in difficulties. For when I am weak, then I am strong.[553]

In an article named "Was the Apostle Paul Gay?" Spong writes:

> Paul felt tremendous guilt and shame, which produced in him self-loathing. The presence of homosexuality would have created this response among Jewish people in that period of history. Nothing else, in my opinion, could account for Paul's self-judging rhetoric, his negative feeling toward his own body, and his sense of being controlled by something he had no power to change. The war that went on between what he desired with his mind and what he desired with his body, his drivenness to a legalistic religion of control, his fear when that system was threatened,

> his attitude toward women, his refusal to seek marriage as an outlet for his passion—nothing else accounts for this data as well as the possibility that Paul was a gay male.[554]

Spong believes that Paul's condition was not that of "a chronic eye problem or epilepsy as it is often proposed to be,"[555] thus, the passage in 2 Corinthians has been interpreted as meaning that Paul's struggle was with homosexuality. This misinterpretation has led to many homosexuals justifying their lifestyle because it is considered to be a "thorn in the flesh" comparable to that of Paul's condition.

This view, in a word, is ridiculous. Many people feel that "Paul didn't ask for his thorn and it wasn't taken away when he prayed; I didn't ask for homosexual feelings and they weren't taken away when I prayed. So, this is my thorn in the flesh and I'm stuck with it, but I know God's grace is sufficient for me."[556] This interpretation though goes against the character of God. If Paul's problem was same-sex attraction, given with God's permission, then God would be making homosexuality a thing of edification to Paul—"a kind of weakness that will "improve" him by keeping him from conceit and pride."[557] The Bible always denotes homosexuality as an abomination and idolatry, and not once does it speak of its acts in a good light. I believe this argument is part of the mission to endorse the choice to be homosexual and is, without a doubt, absurd.

Homosexuality leads only to destruction. Even though many of us know homosexuals who are lovely people, the ramifications of practicing homosexuality are deadly. Society depends for its very existence on healthy heterosexual relationships, and this is not a description of homosexuality. No one was ever born from a homosexual relationship. God would not give sin to edify anyone nor does He tempt anyone. This is seen in James 1:13, "Let no one say when he is tempted, 'I am being tempted by God'; for God cannot be tempted by evil, and He Himself does not tempt anyone."[558]

It is easy to misinterpret Scripture when struggling with an issue. The 2 Corinthians passage is one such passage that is commonly used to enforce the fight of acceptance for homosexuality. One desperately desires that God remove homosexual desires and when this does not occur, it is easy then to believe, that like Paul, perhaps this is his cross to bear as "a thorn in the flesh." This though is not God's way of dealing with such desires. These desires are only an outer manifestation of deeper issues, and so if they were to be taken away, the deeper problems would still remain. There are still the unresolved issues of false identity, wrong thought patterns, a false concept of God, arrested development, and damaged emotions. This is frustrating for homosexuals. They have invested much in their personal "belief" system. It is also upsetting and frightening as "the thorn in the flesh" idea makes them appear to need a "cure." There is nothing good in homosexuality, and God would never use it as a state that we must accept for edification or character-building.[559]

Some homosexuals believe that the Old Testament Scriptures were relevant in those times only and not to today. Activists argue that moral constraints from the Old Testament can be dismissed since there were certain ceremonial requirements at the time, such as circumcising male children or not eating pork. These are no longer binding because of the fulfilling of the Law through Jesus' death and resurrection. While Old Testament ceremonial requirements are not to be followed today, its moral requirements are. God may issue different ceremonies for use in different times and cultures, but His moral standards are eternal and binding for all cultures.[560] Homosexuality is a practice due to man yielding to his sinful nature. It is disobedience to God and a misuse of man's sexual abilities. This disobedience itself is idolatry, as whatever becomes one's chief allegiance is one's god. A person given continually to homosexuality is given over to these perverse desires. Apart from this, the individual and societal disobedience to God create an environment which is favorable to spreading and intensifying sin, which if continued, in time requires judgment in this life or the next, but, as the authors of the New Testament write time and again, when we confess our sins to God, He is good and just to forgive us.[561] Homosexuality is not the end; it can be the beginning.

Chapter 22: Hope for the Hopeless

Nothing good comes from homosexuality. Even its statistics are manipulated by those in the homosexual community and their sympathizers in an attempt to hide the awful truth of their plight. Those that have left the homosexual lifestyle admit that they were drawn into the practice by those in it rather than being born homosexual. Homosexuals then tend to embed themselves in the gay scene to affirm themselves of their gayness for five to seven years. They were recruited into the lifestyle and have since left it for a normal heterosexual lifestyle.[562] They often leave homosexuality, though, to harmonize with their values.[563]

Proponents of the homosexual agenda often claim that homosexuality is unchangeable; however, this is untrue. Those who are unhappy in their homosexual lifestyle and have the will to change can leave it all behind. 1 Corinthians 6:9–11 declares that change is possible. A homosexual's orientation varies and cannot any longer be called a fixed state. There are those that have left this way of living and are either living celibate lives or are married. Some have children. A 2006 survey found that men leave the homosexual lifestyle because they want to find healing for the emotional pain that the lifestyle has caused them.[564] "In 1980 a study was published in the *American Journal of Psychiatry* which stated that eleven former homosexual men became heterosexuals 'without explicit treatment and/or long-term psychotherapy' through their participation in a Pentecostal church."[565]

Many of the people who are trapped in a homosexual lifestyle do not want to be gay. Ed Welch outlines how these people can get out. "First, understand the person. Second, distinguish between spiritual and physical symptoms. Third, address the heart issues. Fourth, if it is relevant, address the physical problems."[566] We must understand that the desires and attractions are very real for a homosexual.[567] It is the behavior and actions that are chosen. On the whole, Christian and biblical therapists and counselors tend to believe that homosexuals can change.

Each homosexual who wishes to get out of his old lifestyle must find his identity in God rather than through his sexuality or gender. Before we were born, God dreamed of us. He designed us according to what He imagined us to be; this truth is found in Psalm 139. God can and will redeem us as we choose to relate to Him and to others. The stories in this book help us understand the progressive thoughts of those who chose to honor God's way of living. There are abundant similar stories in which people made a choice to live a life pleasing to God and, therefore, have overcome the temptation of living a sexually driven life.

Change for a homosexual can be a frightening thing. It is an unknown area of life, for these people seeking freedom have lived with their homosexual desires for a large portion of their lives. The first place to start for them in redeeming their self-identity is to submit to Christ. True masculinity and femininity are found in obedience to Jesus. A recovering homosexual is not necessarily seeking to become a heterosexual; the true goal in healing is to obey Jesus and to learn to think like God thinks.

A recovering homosexual must also understand that homosexual acts can stop immediately, but it takes longer for the desire of the heart to change. I have seen many people respond to God at an altar call but then fail to walk out the journey from there. Freedom takes time and hard decisions—decisions like not placing ourselves in tempting situations. Whether the behavior is learned or biological, one's wants and desires take time to change. In Mark 7:21–23, it is written that it is not outside influence that makes us "unclean," but it is the things that come from our hearts. 1 Corinthians 6:11 is the reminder that change is a possibility and that both the desires and acts can be overcome. In James 1:13–15, the author states that there is a battle against temptation; in Titus 2:12, we are instructed to say "no to ungodliness and worldly passions, and to live self-controlled, upright and godly lives."[568] Exodus International states that "the cure is 'redemptive prayer' in which God, as the Ultimate Father, heals the psyche and returns the person to healthy heterosexuality."

A recovering homosexual needs to acknowledge that what he or she has chosen to do previously is sin. Homosexuality is a spiritual orientation that is not godly. It is not a simple physical propensity,[569] but homosexuality infiltrates the soul, body, and spirit. They need to determine to change not only their lifestyles but their attitudes as well. They can seek to know God and understand His ways through diving deep into His Word.

A Helping Hand

We love grace, but we hate obedience. We run to familiar things rather than to what God calls us to: Christ. Biblical teachings are best utilized through a combination of grace and knowledge. We can all too often try to justify the sins of those we love. We convince ourselves that what they are doing is not really wrong. We fall for deception. We are too inclined to just excuse sin and err to God's grace; meanwhile, we allow people to stay in sin.

Faithfulness to Him means maturity, and at times, it hurts. Our vulnerabilities and weaknesses are not offensive to God, but our sin is. If we want to know God, we have to be willing to allow Him to know us. John writes in John 8:32, "And you will know the truth, and the truth will make you free."[570] Jesus visualized the fisherman Peter as a world-changer. If we keep ourselves in God's words, we can love, and we can help the homosexual in need of change to move forward into healing. "The goal is to understand what God says, to learn to 'think God's thoughts.' One way into Scripture is to understand that there actually *is* something deeper than homosexuality."[571]

While most will not be the pastor or counselor for the person walking out of homosexuality, we can be a part of a support system. The church cannot be one that sits back and critiques. We need to be available to be there and hear the pain and hurt without judgment. Church members can offer love, companionship, and encouragement in perseverance. We can love the homosexual and persevere with him in the quest to change. There likely will be mistakes along the way, but none of us is without sin.[572] Possibly we will see our own sin along the way because homosexuality comes from the same heart that generates any other sin.

When helping a homosexual, we must be willing to listen and hear their struggles so that we can know the person behind the sin. At times, there is a grieving process and great emotional pain as one determines to leave this lifestyle. We often neglect to realize that close attachment and deep relationships have been established in homosexual relationships. Heterosexual supportive friends need to be accepting and available. Demonstrations of our support are needed the most. We need to know that change is possible and see this for those enmeshed in homosexuality. Help them to live in a healthy community and let them know that they have much to offer. For lesbians, it is important that they find safe men to escape lesbianism. We need to stand by those who are trying to walk out God's healing and redemption and show them that we, like God, will not abandon nor forsake them. We will celebrate their victories, support them in their failures, and walk with them every step of the way.

Same-sex attraction is a powerful and dangerous draw that has affected nearly every person on earth in one form or fashion. It is a deviation from God's perfect plan. It warps the body's sexual nature; it twists the soul with guilt, shame, and hatred; and it buries the spirit. Society is steeped with a call to accept while Christians are torn between grace and truth. Only God can see into the hearts of those struggling with this sexual predicament and only He can bring them out. Homosexuality is not the end of life. It does not close the door of God's grace. It is a chance to turn to Him and draw nearer than ever before. God's grace is sufficient. He will bring healing and redemption to the repentant heart. So, if you are struggling with same-sex attraction or have decided to live out a homosexual lifestyle, do not despair. If you wish it, God will help you heal.

Part Five: Marital Sex

We have studied many aspects of our sexual society. We have looked at the socio-cultural influences that drive our younger generations to give themselves away too quickly and too soon; we have taken the veil off of the grey areas of pornography, masturbation, and abortion; we have taken a painful look at the sexual sins that still make us cringe; and we have torn open the controversial realm of same-sex attraction. I hope that it has been a journey of help and healing for you. We have looked at all the ways we can do sex wrong; now, it's time to see exactly what God had in mind when He decided to create the awesome act known as marital sex.

Chapter 23: The Marital Sexual Relationship

Story of Marital Sex

My sexual journey in marriage differed from that of my husband's. Previous to my marriage, I'd had two other sexual partners. Not a lot on today's standards but still more than I'd wished. While many think that sexual experience enhances a marriage, I don't believe that it does. While my husband entered our marriage as a virgin, he was the confident one, while I stood there embarrassed and ashamed. I didn't want him to see me naked, and I was embarrassed about my sexual performance. It was hard to relax and be me in spite of many years of previous sexual experience.

Sexual experience prior to marriage makes one no expert. It dawned on me on our wedding night that, yes, my new partner was sexually different from the others, but the reality of the sexual relationship is that it develops over time. Sex is so much more than the sexual act, but it is something extremely intimate and involves deep trust. The joy and fun comes more out of trust and intimacy than actually from the sexual act. This cannot be found in the constant change of sexual partners but only in the long-term commitment of a life partner that has promised faithfulness to one other for life.

Today: This lady laughs at her past as one who understands that marriage is built rather than being instant. She knows the forgiveness of God and has both a wonderful marriage and family. –JS

Have you ever watched an old married couple? They are quite the vision of enduring love. They walk arm in arm or sit together on a bench; they look deep into each other's eyes, not noticing nor caring about the looks they receive from passersby. The awkwardness of aging has done nothing to dampen their love; it actually seems to enhance it. He is unafraid of being a gentleman; she is unafraid to be his lady; and they revel in the love they built over the decades. They are what we all hope to be one day, and yet, when we look at them, it never occurs to us to think about their sex lives. That's because, when all is said and done, marriage is far more than simply monogamous sex; on the other hand, it is also the place where really great sex is created.

Sexual fulfillment is part of the bigger picture of marriage because the sexual part of a marriage is deeply entwined with emotional needs and mutual help for one another. Sex is a disappointing experience when there is no emotional relationship or communication. This means that we are not connected to the other person, and this in itself is lonely. J. John is a Canon in the Anglican Church and dynamic speaker but also a devoted husband to his wife, Killy. He notes, "The best marriages are not held together by any one thing, but instead, by countless little bonds generated over the years. In such a marriage, it is as though a vast web of tiny threads ties the husband and wife together."[573] Sex is part of a bigger picture.

Sexual love is a part of marriage, but sexual love is a lot more than intercourse and achieving an orgasm. It is lying close to another and being conscious of the other's body even without intercourse. It is reunion after being apart, tender loving touches, and the random hug during the day. It is holding hands for no apparent reason and sharing memories while creating new thoughts for the future. It is the tentative reaching out with one's fingers or toes after an argument while there is an ongoing awareness that one belongs to the other. These things are all a part of the sexual relationship that is vastly different from a sexual encounter to gain immediate sexual gratification.

The Truth About Real-Life Sex

Redbook magazine once conducted a survey. It was "found that the most strongly religious women were 'more responsive sexually' than all other women."[574] This is a fascinating result to come from a culture that preaches that religion is boring and outdated and that marriage is oppressive of one's sexual nature, but, as this book has stated time and again, the true potential of sex is only found within God's boundaries. God created sex to connect and break down barriers—it's a fulfilling of "I am my beloved's and my beloved is mine."[575] Two will know each other in ways that no other person ever will. There is vulnerability and nakedness and freedom and protection and trust. The sexual relationship is similar to many other aspects of marriage. It is built, learned, matures over time, and gets better with practice.

One's first sexual encounter can also be disappointing. It's not all that you thought it would be. For some, it is easier "to not have intercourse on the wedding night. Before the wedding day, most young men would say that this is a definite impossibility. However, the wedding day is often so busy that taking the pressure of the first encounter off of both people can be a wise decision."[576] I know several couples who have done this, believe it or not.

A couple's sex life is built over the years as each gets more comfortable with the other and begins to share their likes and dislikes. One learns what the other sexually responds to and does this often until a couple desires to try something different, not someone different. Each is comfortable with the other despite age and body deterioration. Each becomes the deep companion that all crave.

God's Design for Sex

God is the Creator of mankind and made the man and woman to be united in marriage. Some in church history believe that before the Fall, there was no sexual intercourse, but this is untrue. Regarding Adam and Eve, "When our first parents consummated their covenant, God was not shocked or horrified, because He created our bodies for sex."[577] The words that a man is to "be united to his wife" (Matthew 19:5c) are highly significant in their context in the teaching of Jesus.[578] The Greek word translated "be united to" or "be joined to" is "proskollethesetai" and is derived from the Greek meaning "to glue or cement together or to inlay or weld."[579] This word is used throughout the New Testament when referring to physical and sexual conjunction, of social conjunction, and of spiritual relationship. While marriage was created for companionship and mutual help, it was also created to fulfill the sexual natures of man and woman.[580]

God has given sexual natures and needs to both sexes, and in a marriage, both the husband and the wife have equal responsibility for fulfilling the sexual needs and natures of each other. "Good sex is not automatic. It's more of an achievement."[581] Men and women are created differently so that they can share life together. The single act of intercourse does not make one man and wife; rather, being united is a continuous thing and extends itself through the different levels of marriage. A man and woman join in every way in marriage, meaning that decisions are made not for the betterment of one but for the betterment of the marriage, meaning the two as a couple.

Two becoming one is a lifetime. There is no microwave timing in marriage and this includes in the sexual area. Andrew Comiskey is the founder of Desert Stream Ministries, a former ministry of Exodus International, and is considered to be an ex-gay leader. He gives seminars to those who desire to be free from such relationships and behaviors. Regarding marital sex, he says the following:

> Sexuality becomes holy when it is oriented towards two things: first, another's good. You honor him/her with purity; you defile him/her when you partake of his/her choicest parts outside marriage. Secondly, you honor the Creator when in marriage you avail sexual love towards new life. Sexual love glorifies God when it unites two lives for the purpose of creating life.[582]

Marriage based upon mutual commitment rests on the continual consent of the man and woman. It demonstrates the sacred love between a husband and wife—not the actions but purely what love is.

Probably the greatest ingredient for the success of a marriage is each partner's willingness to submit. "It is important to be intentional about living for your spouse in the sense that you are always wanting to serve them and fulfill their needs."[583] In one of His teachings, Jesus said that there is no greater love that a person has for another than to lay down their life for their friends.[584] In Ephesians 5, Paul uses the term "submit" several times when he describes the relationship of marriage. The word "submit" is a Greek word, "hupotasso," meaning to arrange under, obey or put in subjection.[585] It is a Greek military term meaning "to arrange [troop divisions] in a military fashion under the command of a leader." In non-military use, it was "a voluntary attitude of giving in, cooperating, assuming responsibility, and carrying a burden."[586] The Bible tells us to place ourselves in alignment with one another out of reverence for Christ. We are to follow Christ's example who gave His life for ours. In our marriages, we are to, therefore, love each other in this way, not leading lives that depend only on feelings but carrying sacrificial love for each other.

Paul teaches powerfully about the defining points of marriage in Ephesians 5. Regarding the sexual relationship between a man and woman, a husband will find that a wife is likely to be much more interested in sex if he loves her in the sacrificial way described in Ephesians. Often husbands believe that a wife should just submit to his leadership. He fails to realize that his leadership relies on his willingness and heart to serve. If a husband really believes he's the head, then he would surrender his desires and plans. "He would die to his need to be in control and do whatever it takes to serve her, to make sure she has everything she needs."[587] Out of this a woman feels secure and loved and is, therefore, much more likely to respond to the advances and needs of her husband. In the same sense, a woman is to respect her husband no matter what. Respect goes far beyond love; it means honoring him through the good and the bad. This depth of affection empowers and enables him to be the husband she desires.

Sex is not a search for something that is missing. It is rather an expression of love found in marriage. It is the celebration of a love discovered between a man and woman. "When it is said that the man and the woman will become 'one flesh,' the word for *one* in Hebrew is the word *echad. Echad* is oneness made up of several parts or members. So the man and the woman are two people, two separate independent beings, and yet when they come together, they're 'one'."[588] This same word, "echad," is used for "one flesh" in Genesis.[589] The Hebrew word "flesh" in Genesis means more than the physical side of man. "It stands for the whole person, soul as well as body, and mind, emotions and will."[590] According to God, a husband's and wife's commitment to each other is total in every way.

Genesis describes how the man and woman were naked in front of each other and felt no shame. This is the way a married couple needs and desires to be. They want to be able to bare themselves to each other and yet still be loved by one another. This is the last part of the creation of Adam and Eve, and it is a celebration of all the ways in which they have bonded. Our preoccupation with physical appearance affects our sex lives. We should discard media images from our minds and realize that our spouse chose us for a very good reason. Sexual arousal and response need attention and focus, and if we focus upon the look of our bodies rather than the experience, we are unable to relax and be aware of the sexual pleasures of both our self and our partner. We need to forget our drooping breasts and bellies and focus on enjoying the other's body and this act of fun and love.[591]

Proverbs 5:15–19 are Scriptures that refer to sex:

> Drink water from your own cistern, running water from your own well. Should your springs overflow in the streets, your streams of water in the public squares? Let them be yours alone, never to be shared with strangers. May your fountain be blessed, and may you rejoice in the wife of your youth. A loving doe, a graceful deer—may her breasts satisfy you always, may you ever be intoxicated with her love.[592]

It talks of marital sex as a cistern (a device used to contain water); words such as rejoice, satisfy, and intoxicated show that pleasure and fun should be a part of lovemaking. These verses also give one the impression that lovemaking should be fun. We should work to make sure sex never becomes boring. We continually should explore new ways to play together.

The Song of Solomon also reflects the playfulness of marital sex. Not once does this book talk of sex as a means of procreation. It is an erotic book filled with sexual images. Eros, the Greek word for sexual love, means that a couple physically enjoys one another. In the Song of Solomon, it talks of the beloved going to his garden to the beds of spices.[593] In the same verse, Solomon talks of gathering lilies. There is fantasy and passion in lovemaking. Rosenau notes that "sex is the curious and excited exploration of each other's erogenous zones to create pleasure. It is creating stimulating atmospheres and frolicking in each other's garden, sharing choice fruit, and drinking till contented from the flowing water of your sexual relationship."[594]

Sexual Differences in the Genders

We have shown in several parts of this book that men and women are different. Society has, as stated before, tried to make the genders equal in all the wrong ways. Paul does write in both Galatians 3:28 and Colossians 3:5–13 that men and women are different but equal in Christ; however, this does not negate the fact that men and woman are not the same. The variations of the genders interact in a way that brings richness to personality, a meaning to relationships, and an awareness of and appreciation for these differences.

Married couples need to be aware of the things that distinguish the genders and be willing and ready to change accordingly for the benefit of their partner. There are differences that God wrote into our creation; there are others that society has established. For instance, I grew up believing that men don't cry, but Christ changed my thoughts. In John 11:35, Jesus wept.[595] Another common misconception is that men are not affectionate; again, the Bible disproved this one when, in John, we read about the male disciple who rested on Jesus' chest because he was comfortable with showing Jesus this kind of affection.[596] In regards to sex, there are stark differences between the genders that we should keep in mind.

Men

Probably the most obvious and, sadly, mocked difference between men and women is that men are more visual. They are affected by what they see. In the secular world, men can become trapped in this distinction. Peplau notes, "Men are more interested in visual sexual stimuli and more likely to spend money on such sexual products and activities as X-rated videos and visits to prostitutes."[597] Men tune in more visually to erotic sexual signals and can become aroused almost too easily if left to the stimulations of our over-sexed media.

Men are more physical than women in every way. Little boys rough house with their dads and with each other. Men show affection through punching shoulders and high-fiving and even chest-bumping. It is all part of their design, yet, as we live in a fallen world, this gloriously wild aspect of men becomes dangerous if not reined in by a committed and submitted life with Christ. Men are more aggressive in their sexual pursuits. They are protective of their penis and testes; seeing both as a sign of their manly prowess. Their need to express themselves physically makes them more permissive in regards to multiple sexual partners, and they will, more often than not, cross the physical boundaries of a relationship before women. When fantasying, men are not particular in the who; they emphasize the what—the body part, the act, and the result.

Men are often less able to express their feelings. They like to touch their women and can come across as shallow and obsessed with sex. Though it cannot be said that a woman desires an overly emotional male, men do need to learn to express their hearts to their wives. Men are more egotistical, but that is, again, a part of their fallen nature. Men desire respect more than love; it is how God designed them; and when twisted by the Fall, it can manifest as arrogance. The Men's Ministry in our church has worked hard to help the men in our congregation find the balance between physical and emotional while walking in true manhood found in God.

Men can struggle with monogamy because of their obsession with the physical. They see, and have been trained by the media to see, women as a one-dimensional being. Society has placed it in the minds of men that women must be a quintessential physical equal. If left unchecked, men can become far too focused on the body that they forget the soul, and if they find themselves happily situated in a monogamous relationship, they can begin to find flaws in their wives' bodies. It is best not to look for flaws in your wives, men, but if you find yourself stuck in that particular trap, it is important not to obsess. Do not tell her; it will hurt her. Remember that the image presented by the media is unrealistic and can never be attained no matter how much we fast, pray, or beg God. Instead, choose to submit to Him by appreciating the body of your wife. Love, accept, and enjoy her.

Women

Women are mental creatures. They are rarely aroused by sensual images nor do they allow the physical to be the sole deciding factor in their choice of a man. In this society where women are encouraged to be independent and equal to their male counterparts, women can and will seek out the "hot" guys because that is what they have been taught to do; however, it is the true and deep cry of a woman's heart to find a man who will be tender, loving, and strong for her. She longs "to be emotionally intimate and to express love for another person."[598] She wants a man who will be her knight, who will pursue her, and who will never let her go. This kind of hope is difficult for it makes her vulnerable; each time she is abandoned by yet another lover, her hope fades.

It is interesting to note that, in this society of rampant sexual encounters, it is the married woman that is most orgasmic.[599] Married women have found that ideal situation to reach their sexual peak. Women crave security. They want an environment of nurture and protection. Their sexual nature is emphasized in a committed relationship. Women want to be their men's one and only. They want to have the safety net of trust where she knows beyond a shadow of a doubt that the intimate moments shared with her husband are confidential; that he will not share their private jokes, love language, or secret moments.

Romance is important for a woman. It makes her feel desired and pursued. Women want to be chased. They crave to be a mystery to their men. They want their men to be their champions, to cover their modesty, and fight to win their hands. Shalit writes, "Modesty is a reflex, arising naturally to help a woman protect her hopes and guide their fulfillment—specifically, this hope for one man."[600] A man who can rise above the influence of the world and be that knight in shining armor for her will keep her for eternity.

Women are not immune to the physical. They are affected by it in a different way. For starters, women will look at a man on the whole before deciding to pursue. They may focus on the eyes to see how he looks at her; the stomach and buttocks; and his hands, for she will probably imagine him touching her.[601] Women do not prefer men who are crude or crass in their language or physical presentation. Clean bodies and minds are what they desire. Crude language especially can drive a woman away; even if, on the outside, she acts like it does not bother her, this type of treatment makes her believe that he only sees her as an object and not a person. In regards to the sexual experience, foreplay is important because women tend to shift and change on a regular basis regarding what they do and do not like.

Overall, men and women view sex very differently. While men are visual, the woman looks more at personality, intelligence, kindness, or a sense of humor. While the guy will notice a woman walking down a street, a woman will not discover the qualities for which she is looking in the same way that does a man. Women will less often find a naked picture of a man sexy; rather, mystery is sexier. Having sex isn't going to help her decide if he is one with whom she can have a future.[602] These differences are beautiful things that, when celebrated in a relationship, help both to have a more fulfilling sexual experience.

Communication

It is often easier to physically make love than to converse about it. Asking for what one wants in the sexual arena can be embarrassing and awkward. In this day and age, there is a seemingly unending list of slang used in regards to sex and sexual actions. These terms are degrading, suggestive, and disrespectful to the intimacy of sex. We need to take care with the use of these terms. As believers, to remember that God was our Creator and the inventor of sex helps us to monitor our vocabulary. The Bible uses a variety of vocabulary to describe sex. These terms are mysterious and enhance the act instead of being degrading to either sex. In the King James Version of the Bible, Isaac knew his wife Rebekah, and while I thought this an odd term for sexual intercourse, it takes on another meaning. We need to know the needs, likes, and dislikes of our spouses. Respect what appeals to each other. As written above, most women will not acknowledge their feelings regarding sexual terms. Women want to be romanticized, to be unique in the eyes of a man, and so, of course, crude sexual terms are degrading. If a word seems to repel the other, it should not be used.

It is vital for men to persist in understanding their wives. Being a great lover is often more about attitude than physically trying to arouse her. There is nothing appealing to a woman who feels she is a failure by not attaining an orgasm due to his comments. Attitude and words are possibly a greater threat to her arousal than any sexual position or technique. In the same regard, a woman needs to remain respectful of her husband. This will help him to become a great lover. Men are not born knowing all about sex, as many women believe; therefore, women need to be tolerant, loving, and respectful toward him. He will take time to discover her needs and likes.

Personal love languages built and developed in marriage enhance love and intimacy. Pet names for body parts and each other can be erotic and fun. Words that are a language just between a couple can be arousing and expressive. Sex means that we are to be playful and silly and invent our own terms of love. We should study the likes and dislikes of the other and remember these things, implementing them into our lovemaking.

Communication is the most crucial key for an intimate relationship. Without it, we cannot get to know the needs or understand another person. In communication, we need to abandon the desire to win. Listen when your spouse is talking. Focus on not being distracted. Be slow to answer or judge and ask more questions to clarify need and understanding, and, rather than being critical, validate the partner's feelings and content. Their values and desires should be important to you.

There will be times when one is disappointed with sexual encounters. Men experience premature ejaculation or moments of impotency. Women require extreme concentration to achieve orgasm and sometimes she does not reach this point. She can "be nearly there" but then "no she's not!" This can leave her feeling frustrated. For a man it takes concentration and focus to bring his wife to orgasm. These moments can cause irritation between a husband and wife as one of them may be left hanging! Orgasms for both sexes are muscle contractions and are reflexive responses. They are not an intentional act of the will.[603] They are the result of the accumulation of the physical, mental, and emotional stimulation as the mind focuses on the increasing sexual tension.[604] Our responses to these moments should be understanding and positive. Our comments should show our care and encouragement. Statements should not be aggressive, increase conflict, or allocate blame to the other. If you get angry, then learn to apologize. In marriage, we fight only about things that really matter; therefore, keep to the topic, negotiate solutions, and reconcile the relationship.

The Design of the Physical Body

Each person comes from a different background, and it is important to remember this when going into a marriage. Some come from arenas where sex was a forbidden topic while others have no inhibitions at all. Humans are created with a need for stimulation and variety. God has designed our bodies so that "our hormones, nerve endings, and minds can create sexual arousal. It is a cooperative process of hormones and the nervous system."[605] One reason for which I recommend exploring the other's body in marriage is that many of us are unaware of our sensuality. Those that have come from a highly legalistic and sheltered upbringing can take a while to realize the amazing sensitivity of their physical body and thus can have a difficult time relaxing into the sexual process.

Certain sexual acts are unnatural. We can make the body do certain things, but this is not good. The anus was designed to expel rather than to take in another object. The vagina, while designed to also expel, was designed to expand and take in.

> Anal sex may make a person more susceptible to bacterial infection around the anus and rectum. This is because the lining of the rectum is not as heavy as the lining of the vagina, so it is more susceptible to tears. If the anus or rectum does get torn, it does not heal as quickly. Because feces that pass through the rectum contain bacteria, any tear in the lining is at risk of getting infected. Lining tears may lead to other problems such as an anal abscess, which can make transmission of STIs and HIV more likely. This is why unprotected anal sex is often considered riskier than unprotected oral or vaginal sex.[606]

Overall, the Bible does not speak about anal sex between a husband and wife. Men typically hold a greater fascination for anal sex than do women. It is a decision to be made between each couple.

The anatomy of each sex is built to complete the other. While the woman's vagina is designed to receive, a man's penis is designed to fit the woman's vagina. As such, this fit is designed to also create and birth life through the woman's vagina. This is how God has made man and woman, "similar enough so that they can truly blend together, and yet different in such a way that each needs the other. In a sense, each is incomplete alone, and only finds completion in unity with the other."[607] Sometimes we wonder what it would be like to have sexual experiences with others apart from our spouse. One body, though, is similar to another. Despite our shape, size, and genitalia, sex is sex. Fantasy is thrilling, but another body is no different than the body of the partner to whom we have committed.

Areas of Sexual Sensitivity

Married couples need to explore each other's bodies to discover those areas that heighten the thrill of sex. These areas should be remembered for future use in intimate moments. Men's nipples are often sensitive to touch as are a woman's.[608] A man is proud of but protective of his penis. For a man, it is sensitive to touch, particularly the head. A husband should show his wife ways in which to treat this organ. He desires his wife to arouse and make love to it. The scrotum and testes are also enjoyable organs for a man as is the perineum, the area between the scrotum and anus.

For the woman, stimulation and foreplay tend to be more important. Her breasts and nipples are sensitive to touch. Her breasts tend to enlarge in sexual encounters while her nipples become erect.[609] Her labia, both the inner and outer lips, also respond to touch. The clitoris is the most sensitive part of her and is homologous to the penis.[610] Its sole purpose is for sexual pleasure, and stimulation of the clitoris is key to sexual tension, buildup, and climax.[611] Most women cannot achieve orgasm without direct stimulation of the clitoris.[612] The clitoral shaft is beneath the clitoral hood, mainly beneath the surface of the skin. The man's penis is a great tool to use in rubbing against a woman's labia and clitoris, but she is likely to have to show her husband how this is to be done.[613] The outer third of the woman's vagina is the more sensitive part of this area[614] as is her perineum, the area between her anus and vagina. The degree and type of touch vary according to her menstrual cycle. Husbands need to be aware of this as repeat performance regarding parts of her body will bring a different reaction.

Sex—Both Selfish and Unselfish

Rosenau notes that the sexual relationship is both selfish and unselfish.[615] It is unselfish in the sense that we are giving to another, but it is selfish in the sense that we cannot always suppress our sexual needs for the sake of another. Orgasm is a great example of selfishness and unselfishness. Our spouse does not experience our orgasm but helps us to achieve it. While we each focus on our sexual arousal, it climaxes in an orgasm. This brings a person immense personal pleasure. Our partner unselfishly focuses on providing us with this amazing moment, but they are also aroused by this moment. This actually creates a greater excitement, bonding, and intimacy.

In a way, these acts of selfishness and unselfishness need to be monitored. While women tend to be more compliant, that there is a balance of unselfishness and selfishness for both keeps the sexual act in marriage balanced. In heterosexual couples, one partner—most often the woman—complies when not feeling interested in intercourse. They tend to take their partner's welfare into account as their view of sex is about love and care. That one is always giving and not receiving becomes selfish and can destroy a marriage. Unselfishness means that we will care for the other's needs, including sexual needs. Part of our enjoyment is in seeing our spouse aroused and fulfilled.

What about Appearance?

When we think of Adam and Eve, we tend to think of them as the perfection of beauty. The image of what is perfection will differ in each person's mind as various attributes appeal to each of us. Maybe as a woman, one desires a smaller backside or larger breasts. As a guy, the desire may be for a bigger penis or a more muscular build. We are heavily influenced by pop culture that is constantly before us.

Our imaginations of Adam and Eve will be false as no one actually knows their appearance. We see many illustrations of artists' assumptions, but these are all products of imaginations. God does not describe what they looked like. He preferred that we know that He created a woman for a man. He wanted us to know that they liked what they saw in each other and that He described all creation as "very good."[616] God knew what was right for both Adam and Eve.

We do, though, have a responsibility to make the most of our appearance. Eating well, relaxation, and exercising the body mean that we live longer and can accomplish more in life. Part of this is a fulfilling of our marriage vows of loving the other. Apart from this, a healthy sex life is more easily fulfilled if one is physically healthy. I'll never forget a conversation with a couple in which they revealed that sex had become impossible because they were both excessively overweight. They had not had sex in years, and they were not even yet in their fifties.

Adam and Eve were probably physically healthy as their lifestyle and work involved bodily labor in tending to crops and livestock. Both were instructed to work in the garden and rule over the animals, to subdue the earth, and to grow the human race.[617] The author writes in Genesis 1:28, "God blessed them; and God said to them, 'Be fruitful and multiply, and fill the earth, and subdue it; and rule over the fish of the sea and over the birds of the sky, and over every living thing that moves on the earth.'"[618] Adam and Eve were instructed to rise and take dominion. The author also writes in Genesis 2:15, "Then the Lord God took the man and put him into the Garden of Eden to cultivate it and keep it."[619] My recent dissertation connects physical health to our wellbeing in every way. Maintaining our physical health will aid us in having great sex lives.

Part of our marriage vows means that we embrace the worst. None of us enjoy aging physically, but there is a sense of fun of doing this together. We learn to laugh with each other and support each other in this process. Illness can come, weight comes and goes, body shapes change, but we still love and support the other. There are the reminders that, despite the years, the other is still our one and only.

In Psalm 139, the famous words that each person is "fearfully and wonderfully made"[620] are written. God's definition of beauty is not the same as the one that we find in pop culture. He does not set us up for failure or disappointment like the media does when it parades the unrealistic images of supposed perfection in front of our eyes. God creates variety from which we choose a partner and then He instructs us to live with this partner through the good and the bad, in our youth and old age. In God's eyes, each of us is magnificent regardless of the world's standard of beauty. We need to remember that our chosen partner is one of God's wonderful ideas and, therefore, do nothing that could damage, dishonor, or disrespect our marriage vows. We experience dissatisfaction with our physical appearance, particularly as we age. God, though, wanted and designed both of us; therefore, each of us should dwell on our better attributes and also those of our spouse. To dwell on what we do not have or what our partner does not have only negatively impacts a marriage.

In the Know

Married couples need a huge sense of humor. The sex life develops and grows as does a marriage. Each needs to be forgiving of self and the other. Sex is not a neat and tidy affair, and bodies don't always look romantic as they are portrayed in the media. Bodies do create great sexual connection and bring a closeness and intimacy that is achieved in no other way. "Great sex, like a good marriage, allows an individual to strategically focus on personal pleasure as well as the mate's."[621]

Lovemaking is a cycle of emotional and physical arousal that involves a series of changes from excitement to plateau through to orgasm and then resolution.[622] Lovemaking for a woman is a process rather than just intercourse. She desires to be held closely often before and after sex. It is important for her that her husband not just roll over and fall asleep or depart for the bathroom after intercourse; though, to not go to sleep after the act for him can be difficult. Sex relaxes him. Men want a wife that is involved in the arousal part of sex and who will initiate sexual and seductive activity.[623] He prefers her to be spontaneous with few unbending expectations while he likes to mix intercourse through the process.

Concentration is needed by a man to not ejaculate. Ejaculation too quickly can leave a woman frustrated as she has not achieved orgasm. That a wife can concentrate during lovemaking is vital. Her orgasm requires immense concentration on her behalf, thus the couple should try to work together to avoid distractions and have any lingering conflicts resolved beforehand. Women are multi-orgasmic and take time to reach their peak; men do not have as much trouble but can usually only achieve release once. Each phase of the sexual cycle needs attention and care for the other.

Every man will struggle at times to maintain or achieve an erection. Despite commercials displaying this, men find this most embarrassing. His concentration on his wife or distraction means that at some time during intercourse his erection can soften. Medication, anxiety, alcohol, and tiredness can also affect his erection. It's important that a woman not take this personally. Concentration and stimulation, though, often mean that his erection returns. Since men attain orgasm more quickly than women, great sex means that a couple intersperse intercourse throughout the plateau phase as a husband sporadically stops and starts his thrusting which keeps his arousal on a plateau without peaking too soon.

Many people, particularly women, unrealistically romanticize sex and then are disappointed because of various happenings. Sex involves body fluids and the use of body parts that excrete wastes such as urine and feces. The body fluids from our mouth are not such an issue, but the body fluids from other areas can really be upsetting to some. If this is you, be discreet. Your offense can be taken personally by your spouse. If on the receiving end of the offense, don't get upset as all people have these same bodily fluids and reactions. Bodily fluids and secretions are a part of lovemaking. We never see the messy sheets or stains of semen and vaginal discharge in a movie, but, there again, the couple looks immaculate despite a night of sexual activity. Movies also lead us to believe that couples have sex all night. How sore would they be after so many hours of lovemaking? We need to adjust our thinking and make light of messy situations. Perhaps keep a towel or wipes close by. For the body to not produce lubrication would make sexual encounters rather painful and unpleasant. To make a big deal of the other's bodily fluids is only to make the other uncomfortable and less willing to perform. Messy sheets can be washed as can messy bodies.

Secondly, sex is not accompanied by beautiful music or the erotic sounds that we hear in movies. Media also does not provide the necessary dialogue either that is needed to develop a great sexual relationship. In movies, two people who virtually do not know each other, grope each other to the bed and perform magnificent sex. Be aware that bodies can make weird sounds over which we have no control. Air escapes from the vagina, or the penis causes sounds as it thrusts against a woman. This certainly detracts from the romance of the event, but again, we should know that it is normal.

Menstruation is a part of a woman's life, and, in marriage, it, therefore, becomes a part of a husband's life. Some couples enjoy sex during menstruation, but for others, it is dirty. Regarding the latter, it is important for the male to not be obvious about his thoughts regarding her cycle. If the man doesn't enjoy sex during menstruation, then let him be considerate to his wife and agree in advance about this normal female function. A woman's flow of blood in the Old Testament was considered a time of cleansing for her. The writing of the New Testament changed these rigid rules and so there is no sin in having intercourse during a woman's menstrual period. Couples need to sort out their thoughts regarding sex and menstruation for themselves. Some women, though, during menstruation are easily aroused.

Personal hygiene and timing are other issues for couples. The sweaty husband returns from yard work or a sporting event and wants to make love to his wife. All she sees is sweaty dirt and grime, and all she smells is body odor. Sex, though, is extremely intimate which means that she has to touch him. She is nice and clean. On the other hand, some people have no problem with these things. Each situation needs consideration. One has to get messed up or one needs to shower. Perhaps the promise of a great time later is sufficient.

Often husbands are aroused by their wives getting dressed. This can be frustrating for her as she is showered and dressing for work. In her mind she is not prepared for a sexual encounter. Her hair and makeup are done and she is ready for work. While we see women redress and return to work in movies, most women are thinking of the bodily secretions that are occurring during the day after a sexual encounter.

Another issue that is often unknown in early marriage is the self-consciousness regarding bouncing body parts during the act. Again, we rarely see this on a screen, but it is a reality. Sex rarely looks beautiful as most of us are everyday-looking people. We are not surgically enhanced, while the years age us. Bouncing body parts and positions that are physically awkward for some are all a normal part of sex. Most are shy or assume that conversation and direction are strange during intimacy. In early sexual encounters, conversation is embarrassing, but we need to push ourselves to talk, particularly regarding likes and dislikes; otherwise, we face great frustrations that can be resolved in one sentence.

Sex involves abandonment to one's inhibitions and being confident in your own self. Take care of your body and determine to not be self-conscious. This means that we can then focus on loving our partner as expressed in the Bible. Paul writes in 1 Corinthians 13:4–7 that we are to keep no record of wrongs and that we are to protect the other. To stay focused on the positives of the other, particularly physically, is essential; to point out his or her physical failings is cruel and only damages a relationship; and to allow preoccupation in thoughts regarding a partner's shortcomings is damaging to both man and wife. Any new sexual exploitation—whether technique, movement, or position—is awkward at first; a thing to remember though is practice makes things better.

Great sex does take honesty. To think that it is only about an orgasm is wrong. Women must not play manipulative sexual games in which she withholds sex. Men must commit to the belief that sex is much more than intercourse. Sexual happiness and enjoyment grow as the couple remains creative regarding their sexual encounters. This creativity applies to not just the act but in our everyday lives. We may not think of ourselves as creative, but each of us was made in the image of our Creator, and if we think of ourselves in this light, we will surprise ourselves.

Many question the rightness of oral sex. The Bible makes no specific mention of this. This is pleasuring your partner's genitals with your mouth. It is up to each couple regarding this. Some people are repulsed of the thought of bodily fluids in their mouth; to others, this is not a concern. Masturbation or genital pleasuring may also be stimulating between partners. Many women do not want to initiate lovemaking, but the more sexually demanding woman is arousing to most men.

The idea that the thrusting male is the greatest turn on is simply a myth.[624] Another myth is that a woman wants to be suddenly taken sexually and that she will be enthralled as his penis fills her vagina. While the thrust of the male into the female can be extremely pleasurable, it can cause unnecessary pain for a female if the male does not control himself and she is not prepared. Though it can be exciting for both spouses, varying the rate and depth of thrusting is a learned art that is determined by a loving male who watches and listens to his wife.

Most wives want husbands that are strong, caring, and confident lovers. They want their husbands to be a little spontaneous, romantic, and mysterious. She desires that her husband lead and be confident, but again, it is unfair of her to expect a husband to know and do it all. She needs to participate and overcome any intimidations. The husband should realize that she, as all women, is unpredictable. Hormones, because of her menstrual cycle, mean that at different times, her body will react in different ways. As previously mentioned, a woman does change in what is arousing to her. One time, a particular touch is exciting, but then next time it is irritating. She also often needs affirmation regarding her looks and body. Romance helps in this area. She needs romantic affirmation after making love; therefore, verbal appreciation and gestures regarding her form help her become a confident lover.

Don't expect her to achieve an orgasm through vaginal stimulation alone. This is similar to expecting a man to have an orgasm by playing with his testicles only. Women enjoy a variety of kisses and caresses over various parts of her body. Husbands, again, should watch and learn in their lovemaking.

Sex for a woman is less hormonal and more an emotional choice. "Women view sex as the physical expression of an intimate, tender, stable and committed relationship."[625] She will not necessarily want to jump into bed the moment vacation is commenced nor will she desire to commence a romantic evening in this way. She does love spontaneity, but she more appreciates being able to plan for sex. She is more easily distracted by the environment and attitudes during the sex act, and so, as a husband, look ahead for distractions and understand that her concerns are often real. Are the children safe? Can anyone see or hear? Wives particularly are embarrassed to have sexual encounters in a parents' home. The stories that I know of wrecked sexual encounters and embarrassing moments for both parents and children due to lack of preparation are many, so be prepared for all scenarios.

The primary way in which a husband feels connected to his wife is often through sex. He can view sex as tender and intimate, but he is also more able to "separate sex from the rest of the relationship"[626] and treat it as a physical event. This connection may be diminished by tiredness, anxiety or depression, conflict, or a fear of losing control. Anxiety and hurt can add to shutting him down emotionally and sexually. On the whole, though, desire is consistent due to testosterone production.

In the marriage relationship, women should be suggestive with their husbands. There is a place for this between a husband and wife in marriage. Christian women can become too conservative. There is, however, nothing conservative in the Song of Solomon. Women should exaggerate their movements and get his attention. Meet him naked and play hide and seek. Wait for him in bed in a suggestive pose. You may be older and not in the greatest shape, but this is not important. It is the confidence that you carry in yourself and the fact that you are sending a message of desire to him. Make it obvious to him that you want him even when you do not. Sexual intimacy is a decision that can start with your actions. If the plan is fun, then you will have fun.

Scripture tells us to be gentle, thoughtful, and non-offensive to the other. We are also told to not hurt another. Our bodies are temples of the Holy Spirit,[627] thus each one's body parts should be respected and not damaged. We entrust our body parts to our mates just as is written, "My own vineyard is mine to give."[628] Be caring and considerate in the exploration of your spouse's body.

The Quickie

The quickie is a spontaneous episode of sexual activity that brings one to orgasm with the act finishing in a brief amount of time. There is nothing wrong with quickly fulfilling the other as long as it does not replace the deep intimacy built through sexual encounters. It is usually the man that desires these quick sexual encounters. This means that the wife allows him his way so that he is fulfilled. She likely will not climax. It is important to remember that one member of the couple will desire more intimate sexual encounters that the other. Do not complain about your partner's sexual demands; instead, realize that you are desired! Get spontaneous and make the quickie fun. Sometimes quickies stir the other to action, and it becomes an intimate, fun and fulfilling occasion for both.

Fantasy

I have already discussed fantasy to some degree but not enough can be written about it. Some of us would be embarrassed to admit the degree to which we fantasize. Fantasy can be a very powerful enhancement to our marriage. Fantasy is perhaps eighty percent of the sex act.[629] The key is to keep fantasy centered on your marriage and your partner. Any sexual fantasies beyond this should be shut down. The minute that we allow our minds to sexually fantasize about another apart from our spouse, we wander toward adultery. We will only cause hurt and disappointment for ourselves and our spouse. We have control over our minds and need to exercise it.

Should we share all of our fantasies with our spouse? Probably not. At times we have wrong thoughts. While we need to shut them down, we do not necessarily need to share them with our spouses; especially if these fantasies are offensive or degrading. Paul writes in Philippians 4:8, "Whatever things are true, whatever things are noble, whatever things are just, whatever things are pure, whatever things are lovely, whatever things are of good report—meditate on these things."[630] We have the ability to control our thought life. If thoughts are difficult to control, this is an issue that needs to be talked over with a pastor or biblical counselor. Other fantasies are great to share with our spouse and even implement into our sex life and intimate moments. They can be arousing and enhance our love life. They can be fun to act out and spice up the love life.

We will all at times wonder about having sex with other people apart from our spouse. Some of us feel guilty about this while others are not concerned. Imaginations and fantasy are pleasurable. Our choice, though, must always be our spouse. The one you have chosen becomes your standard for physical desire. If you have chosen tall and lean, then this is the standard to which you conform; that is the standard that remains even as tall and lean ages. This chosen relationship becomes more precious with time; woven into this relationship is trust, security, and safety.

Keeping It Up

Sex needs to become and remain a priority in a marriage. Life gets busy and some seasons are more stressful and demanding than others. An undisciplined lifestyle, however, means infrequent sexual encounters; therefore, while spontaneity is great, organized sex is a necessity. Shift your nightly routine to help keep the intimacy alive. Do things such as going to bed together rather than one always remaining awake to watch a movie. This sends the message to the other that they are significant. Despite weariness, discipline yourself to make love. Mature sexual intercourse takes little time. In fact, "any reduction in the frequency of sex with age may be more than compensated for by increased skill and knowledge."[631]

When single or newly married, one cannot believe that another is not interested in sex, but it being forbidden and, therefore, enticing is not always the case. Couples can easily begin to take their significant other and their sexual encounters for granted. Family and work demands, stress, tiredness, and wrong priorities mean that marital sex can fall low on one's list of priorities. It's easy to believe that this doesn't matter and that love and commitment are enough. This is not true. If sex is not scheduled, couples can find themselves going months with no sexual activity. Sexual goals are a necessity for many couples. It is a qualitative goal to include intimacy as a part of life regardless of how tired one or the other is. Push past the tiredness for the sake of the other.

Mentally, we need to make the decision to have sex. In the early years of a marriage, sex rarely needs to be made a priority, but, as time passes, good sex is not always spontaneous. It frequently requires some effort to make it happen.[632] Choose to go with the moment rather than not. Fantasize about and imagine sex with your partner and past fun sexual moments. This helps to get us in the mood. Respond to the sexual cues of your mate. Constant rejection is cruel and degrading. Keep this vital component of marriage alive by responding to their invitations or initiating intimacy yourself.

Creating the mood keeps sex exciting. Lighting candles or dimming the lights brings a sense of romance and expectation. The husband can help to build expectation during the day by helping with children and housework; this is, in some ways, a part of foreplay for her. Hiding from each other or chasing each other through the house when children are not at home seems so childish, but these activities bring the fun back into the marriage. Sending each other playful text messages or leaving notes on desks or pillows for a spouse's eyes only sends a great message. These things bring a sense of life and levity into our most important earthly relationship.

It's important that we don't compare our "how often" with other couples. We can get anxious about our sex lives after reading a book about a couple's unrealistic sexual encounters or after chatting with friends about how often they do it. We start to panic that we are lazy, unattractive to our spouse, or that our marriage is failing. Keeping the sexual side of a marriage alive is important, but we don't need to compare ourselves to others. Age, jobs, family, and life's seasons among other things all affect us. Your sex life is your sex life. You will find your own comfortable rhythm as long as this includes the wants and needs of your spouse.

There is so much more to marital sex than is written here, but then, this book was not supposed to merely be regarding marital sex. While books and information are good, the best lessons learned concerning marital sex are through your spouse. Books tend to be theoretical and clinical; a spouse is not. A spouse can communicate their likes and dislikes, and that is more relevant to your relationship than any book.

Conclusion

Sexuality is a topic that is wrought with confusion. Sex was created by God to be fun within the confines of marriage, but it has been twisted and misunderstood. Many, including believers, fear to involve God in their sexuality because they think that He is against their happiness and welfare. People are deceived into believing that they can find joy without God's involvement. They lean on their own understanding and align their beliefs with trendy teachings that are more easily understood than the ways of God. We hear stories and information through the media, friends, schooling, and even churches that differ from the truths of God's Word and align ourselves with these beliefs. They are enticing and seem exciting and make the Bible seem, in comparison, limiting and unfair.

God asks that we risk our reputation for His. In fact, the truth is that all knowledge begins, as Proverbs 9:10 says, with the fear of the Lord.[633] We are to stand for what is right. Theology is the lens through which Christians should interpret research.[634] This does not mean that we bomb and placard abortion clinics nor should we parade down a street with signs. This does mean that we should not bow to the next trendy theory. At times, we need to do right even though we do not understand why it is right.

The Bible is very sexual and is easily understood if we bother to read and practice its teachings. It is far more sexual than most people realize. In Genesis, we read how God created man with a sexual nature and a desire to physically connect with the opposite sex. God did not cry out in amazement, shock, or woe when Adam and Eve consummated their relationship. He created each of us for such an act. He created a man and woman's bodies to fit together. Sex was a part of God's design and plan. Sex is not just for procreation; it is for pleasure.

After man's Fall in Genesis 3, we see many different scenarios that involve sexual events. These scenarios are both good and bad and have continued throughout time, all the way to today. The Fall was the moment we determined that we were wiser than God, could live our lives better without His direction, and thus became separated from Him. For example, there was King Solomon who was very wise, but he compromised God's standards by marrying many women. King David decided to commit adultery and then tried to hide it. The Samaritan woman in John 4 tried to hide from Jesus the fact that she had had five husbands and was now living with another man. In John 8, Jesus addressed and forgave a woman caught in adultery. The Bible is filled with many sexual scenarios. There is no new sexual idea that society can produce. Abuse, rape, pornography, adultery—it is all found in the Bible and it is all a result of the Fall of Man.

One of the greatest areas of attack in society is upon marriages. Sex was created for one man and one woman to share within the confines of marriage. This standard can seem limiting and harsh in our sexually free society. People are in fear because they see this as a standard to which they cannot conform. How can one man commit for life to one woman? How can a woman remain with one man? Won't this be boring? What if that one other is not faithful to me? Marriage is the opposite of these fears. Sexual fidelity to one person is liberating. The level of safety and security found in just one other is an overwhelming thrill. This freedom is found as long as a married couple continues to submit and trust. Commitment to one in marriage is comforting and brings an indescribable happiness.

In regards to homosexuality, the jury is still out as far as popular culture is concerned. Perhaps this type of relationship will be proven as genetic and natural. One thing we must understand, though, is that it will never be right in the eyes of God. Because a behavior feels right does not make it right. It feels natural to drink too much, or it feels normal to be mad and violent toward another. At times, we are sexually and emotionally attracted to one that is not our spouse, but the decision to act upon these things, whether through fantasies or sexual encounters, is not wise. Pornography and other such addictions feel nice and natural too for some people, but we don't say, "Go ahead."

Scientific proof will not make something, such as homosexuality, right. Genetics determine many things, both good and bad. Science is wonderful but is also fallible. This is because science is ever changing and is determined by a man's limited mind. Science and genetics have been used as the deciding factor by doctors to convince parents that they should abort a child that may be born with a deformity. Genetic science can attempt to determine if a person will become a homosexual, but genetics do not make that person choose to practice gayness. We are in a frightening predicament unless we return to God's standards.

The genetic argument is fraught with problems and unanswered questions. Genetics may be able to determine if one is predisposed to addiction or sexual issues. This cannot make anyone perform these issues. One cannot separate choice and responsibility from a person. These two things are the ingredients that actually make us unique as individuals and give us each a life that differs from those around us. Each of us faces dilemmas. We then can exercise our will to build what is good and conquer what is wrong. We must realize that, even though we know and love homosexual people, their lifestyle choices are a dead end. God repeatedly in Scripture speaks against the practice.

We must not overlook the consequences of homosexuality. The body is not designed for sex of this type nor does the body respond well. Humans have the capability to conform to these sexual acts; however, they often cause irreparable damage to the body. The homosexual community tries to suppress the statistical proof about rampant disease in their community, but that does not make the diseases any less real. Our embracing of, arguing for, and encouragement of homosexuals, because of our mercy and limited comprehension, does nothing more than lead people down a dangerous path. If we do not take a biblical stand now, there will only be more pain for friends and loved ones tomorrow.

I have numerous friends and acquaintances that are homosexual and bisexual. They are fun, intelligent, creative, and many are Christian. Can I condone what they do? No way! I see them as myself, though. We all have "stuff" with which we are dealing; this "stuff" can act as a barrier between us and God. A healthy and open relationship with God requires us to deal with our "stuff" each and every day. We submit, like the first story in this book advised us, to God's way of living on a day-to-day basis and trust Him to see us through.

As I have accountability for my life with other people, so each of us can be a friend and support to those who struggle with any sexual issue. Create an environment in which people can come forward for help. Realize, for a start, just how difficult it is to admit a struggle with any of the issues discussed in this book. Jesus did not treat people with sexual dysfunctions any differently than He treated other sinners. He didn't look down His nose in disgust or snicker with others behind closed doors. God's standards may seem black and white, but He has definitely created a world full of color as each of us walks out our life, our growth, and our healing.

The Bible is not a textbook from which we take rules for our lives. That would be so depressing. The Bible is an expression of an eternal and all-powerful God that loved each of us so much that He sacrificed His own Son on our behalf. The Bible describes not only how we are to do life but also ways in which we can know Him and draw near to Him so that we can have a great life—a life far better than any of us can envisage.

I would say then to any that are dealing with any of these challenges presented in these pages that you are, no matter what, created in God's image. You are no less than any other person. There are days when you feel that your life is too much to bear. Do not despair. There are those that have gone before you and have felt this same way. They survived and overcame, and they can help you do the same. The stories in this book are illustrations of this. Find great friends, share your dilemma, and get help. Find a church home, find Scriptures that encourage you in the knowledge that your life will get better, and start living by these Scriptures.

We should use the Bible as our guide in understanding what is happening in the society around us. What we don't understand, we should study so that we are not ignorant. God says so much and provides us with a wealth of information through His Word. To know His Word makes us stronger, and to live His Word means that we can speak and minister with wisdom. We all fight the battle of sexual sin in some form or fashion; therefore be merciful and gracious. Let's fight to live within the standards God put in place for each one of us.

Biography

Dr Jill Sweetman and her husband, Dean, are a part of the C3 Church based out of Australia. C3 was founded by Pastors Phil and Chris Pringle and currently is comprised of more than 300 churches from all around the world. In 1996, Dean and Jill moved from Sydney, Australia, to Lawrenceville, Georgia, USA to plant a church. She and Pastor Dean oversee more than thirty thriving C3 churches across both North and South America.

Jill has a unique prophetic gift that she uses to bring freedom, encouragement, and empowerment to God's people. She is a globally sought-after expert in the fields of marriage, family, and relationships. Her experiences brought forth great books like *Marriage: How to Remain Married Forever* and *Little Shakers: Parenting in the 21st Century*.

In 2007, she and Pastor Dean planted a church in North Hollywood. This church drew in many young adults who were struggling in many ways, including sexually. It was during this time that the dream of *God Sex* was born. Dr Jill's passion for outreach had already seen the building of a home for women in troubled situations and the creation of a thriving local charity at C3 Church Lawrenceville. Her experience in pastoring in North Hollywood and Lawrenceville in addition to her travels around the world is reflected within *God Sex*.

Dr Jill and her husband travel extensively for both work and pleasure. When she is home, she likes to decorate her home, shop for antiques, and spoil her little dog, Choo Choo. She loves to read and write and learn new things. Dr Jill has just completed her PhD in Biblical Counseling and is now working on her doctorate in Ministry and hopes to be awarded that honor in late 2013. She has two grown sons and two amazing daughters-in-law. Her eldest son, Barn, and his wife, Holly, are a part of the executive team at C3 Lawrenceville; Jake and his wife, Nicole, serve as the campus pastors for C3 Silverlake, the first church campus of C3 North Hollywood.

You can check out more of Dr Jill on her blog: jillsweetman.com.

You can also follow her on twitter: @jillsweetman.

Glossary

Abortion – The termination of a pregnancy after, accompanied by, resulting in, or closely followed by the death of the embryo or fetus.

Addiction – Compulsive need for and use of a habit-forming substance characterized by tolerance and by well-defined physiological symptoms upon withdrawal.

Adultery – Voluntary sexual intercourse between a married man and someone other than his wife or between a married woman and someone other than her husband.

Affair – A romantic or passionate attachment typically of limited duration.

Asexual – Little to no sexual attraction to others or interest in sexual activity. It may also be considered a lack of a sexual orientation.

Bestiality –Inolving sexual activity between human and non-human animals or a fixation on such practice.

Bisexual – Characterized by a tendency to direct sexual desire toward both sexes.

Climax – The highest point of tension during the act of sex.

Coitus interruptus – An act in which the penis is withdrawn prior to ejaculation to prevent the deposit of sperm into the vagina.

Disorder – To disturb the regular or normal functions of.

Ephebophilia – The primary or exclusive adult sexual interest in mid-to-late adolescents, generally ages 15 to 19.

Evolutionary Theory – Evolution is the change in the inherited characteristics of biological populations over successive generations. Evolutionary processes give rise to diversity at every level of biological organization, including species, individual organisms and molecules, such as DNA and proteins.

Hermaphrodite – Having, to some extent, both male and female reproductive organs.

Heterosexual – Characterized by a tendency to direct sexual desire toward the opposite sex.

Homosexual – Characterized by a tendency to direct sexual desire toward another of the same sex or involving sexual intercourse between persons of the same sex.

Hypersexuality – Extremely frequent or suddenly increased sexual urges or sexual activity.

Incest – Sexual intercourse between persons so closely related that they are forbidden by law to marry.

Infanticide – The killing of an infant.

Lesbian – Relating to homosexuality between females.

Monogamy – The state or custom of being married to one person at a time.

Nymphomania – Excessive sexual desire by a female.

Orgasm – An explosive discharge of neuromuscular tensions at the height of sexual arousal that is usually accompanied by the ejaculation of semen in the male and by vaginal contractions in the female.

Pedophilia – Sexual perversion in which children are the preferred sexual object.

Penis – The male sex reproductive organ. It functions as a means to urinate and releases an ejaculate during orgasm.

Pessary – A device worn in the vagina to support the uterus, remedy a malposition, or prevent conception.

Polygamy – One party in a marriage having two or more spouses of the opposite sex.

Pornography – Material (as books or a photograph) that depicts erotic behavior and is intended to cause sexual excitement.

Promiscuity – Not restricted to one sexual partner.

Psychiatry – A branch of medicine that deals with mental, emotional, or behavioral disorders.

Psychology – The study of mind and behavior in relation to a particular field of knowledge or activity.

Rape – To seize and take away by force, usually referring to a sexual context.

Sex Addiction – A progressive intimacy disorder characterized by compulsive sexual thoughts and acts.

Sexual Abuse – The forcing of unwanted sexual activity by one person on another, as by the use of threats or coercion.

Sexual Orientation – A person's sexual preference.

Sexting – Creation, sharing and forwarding of sexually suggestive nude or semi-nude images.

Theory – A belief, policy, or procedure proposed or followed as the basis of action.

Urethra – A tube connected to the urinary bladder that dispels urine from the body. In males the opening of the urethra is at the tip of the penis, carrying semen as well as urine. In women, the urethra is shorter and is located just above the vagina.

Vagina – The female sex reproductive organ. It serves two purposes, sexual intercourse and childbirth.

Virginity – The state of a person that has never engaged in sexual intercourse.

Abbreviations

AIDS: Acquired Immune Deficiency Syndrome

ADHD: Attention Deficit Hyperactivity Disorder

APA: American Psychological Association

ASAM: American Society of Addiction Medicine. This society improves the care and treatment of people with addiction and advances the practice of Addiction Medicine.

CDC: Center for Disease Control and Prevention

CMI: Creation Ministries International

CSA: Child Sexual Abuse

CSI: Crime Scene Investigation (a television show)

DSM-IV-TR: The Diagnostic and Statistical Manual of Mental Disorders, Version Four Text Revision

DTS: Discipleship Training School

EEOC: Equal Employment Opportunity Commission. The agency of the United States Government that enforces the federal employment discrimination laws.

et al: Latin for "and others."

HIV: Human Immunodeficiency Virus.

IVF: In Vitro Fertilization

M.D.: Medical Doctor

NARTH: National Association for Research & Therapy of Homosexuality

NC-17: No Children Under 17

PhD.: Doctor of Philosophy

P&S Syphilis: Primary and Second Stage Syphilis

STD: Sexually Transmitted Disease

STI: Sexually Transmitted Infection

USCCB: United States Conference of Catholic Bishops. A group of members of the Catholic Church whose goal is to promote the greater good which the Church offers humankind, especially through forms and programs of the apostolate fittingly adapted to the circumstances of time and place.

YWAM: Youth With A Mission

Bibliography

"132 Bible Verses about Pedophiles." Crossway Bibles.http://www.openbible.info/topics/ pedophiles (accessed November 1, 2012).

"2012: The Year of the Inane Political Fatwa." The Voices of the Middle East. http://mideastposts.com/ category/ region/ (accessed January 1, 2013).

"About, Gunter Dorner." http://translate.google. com/ translate?hl=en&sl=de&u=http ://de.wikipedia.org/wiki/G%25C3%25BCnter_D%25C3 %25B6rner&prev=/search%3Fq%3DGunter%2BDorner, %2Ba%2Bneuroendocrinologist%26hl%3Den%26client% 3Dsafari%26rls%3Den%26biw%3D1423%26bih%3D764 &sa=X&ei=RDJTUbSkIJDc8AS_3YGACw&ved=0CEw Q7gEwAw (accessed March 27, 2013).

"About Narth." http://narth.com/menus/mission. html (accessed March 27, 2013).

"About Us." http://www.mygenes.co.nz/ About%20Us.htm (accessed March 27, 2013).

Abowitz, Richard. "Porn Film Biz Rocked by Syphilis Scare." The Daily Beast. http://www.thedailybeast.com/articles/2012/08/20/porn o-film-business-rocked-by-syphilis-scare.html (accessed November 10, 2012).

Ackland, Donald F. *Studies in Deuteronomy*. Nashville, TN: Convention Press, 1964.

Adams, Jay E. *The Christian Counselor's Manual*. Eugene, OR: Harvest House, 1986.

Adler, Seymour. "Maslow's Need Hierarchy and the Adjustment of Immigrants." *International Migration Review* 11, no. 4 (Winter, 1977): 333–345. http://www.jstor.org.libproxy. ggc.edu/stable/pdfplus/2545398.pdf?acceptTC=true (accessed March 12, 2013).

Alexander, David and Pat Alexander. *The Lion Handbook to the Bible.* Icknield Way, England: Lion Publishing, 1973.

"Archive Exposing the Myth of Evolution." The True Origin. http://www.trueorigin. org/gaygene01.asp (accessed March 12, 2013).

Arsove, Pamela, MD, FACEP. "Lymphogranuloma Venereum." http://emedicine.medscape.com/article/220869-overview (accessed March 12, 2013).

"Article: John Boswell." http://en.wikipedia.org/wiki/John_Boswell (accessed March 25, 2013).

"Author George Bush." http://en.wikisource.org/ wiki/Author:George_Bush (1796–1859) (accessed March 26, 2013).

Bell, Robert. *Sex God: Exploring the Endless Connections Between Sexuality and Spirituality.* (2007), New York, NY: Harper One, 2012.

Benware, Paul N. *Survey of the New Testament.* Chicago, IL: Moody Publishers, 2003.

———. *Survey of the Old Testament Revised.* Chicago, IL: Moody Press, 1993.

Blanchard, Ray. "Fraternal Birth Order, Maternal Immune Reactions, and Homosexuality in Men." *Politics and the Life Sciences* 19, no. 2 (September 2000): 157–159. http://www.jstor.org/stable/4236585 (accessed September 26, 2012).

Boehmer, Ulrike, Deborah Bowen & Greta Bauer. "Overweight and Obesity in Sexual-Minority Women: Evidence From Population-Based Data," http://www.ncbi.nlm.nih.gov/ pmc/articles/PMC1874217/ (accessed March 16, 2013).

Bogaert, Anthony F. "Biological versus nonbiological older brothers and men's sexual orientation." *Proceedings of the National Academy of Sciences of the United States of America* 103, no. 28 (June 2006): 10771–10774. http://www.pnas.org/search?author1= Anthony+F.+ Bogaert&sortspec=date&submit=Submit (accessed March 27, 2013).

Book Description. The Marketing of Evil. http://www.amazon.com/dp/1581824599/?tag=googhydr20&hvadid=9618339261&hvpos=1t1&hvexid=&hvnetw=g&hvrand=12323796415594788 57&hvpone=&hvptwo=&hvqmt=b&ref=pd_sl_5kqpdwiw41_b (accessed March 16, 2013).

"Born or Bred?" The Daily Beast. http://www.thedailybeast.com/newsweek/1992/02/23/born-or-bred.html (accessed March 11, 2013).

Both, Stephanie, Mark Spiering, Walter Everaerd & Ellen Laan. "Sexual Behavior and Responsiveness to Sexual Stimuli following Labatory-Induced Sexual Arousal." *The Journal of Sex Research* 41, no.3 (August 2004): 242-258. http://www.jstor.org/ stable/4423782 (accessed December 21, 2012).

Bott, Michael and Jonathan Sarfati. "What's Wrong With (Former) Bishop Spong?" UK Apologetics. http://www. ukapologetics.net/08/spongwrong2.htm (accessed March 25, 2013).

"Boundless Homosexuality in Animals." https://www.boundless.com/psychology/gender-development-and-sexuality/sexual-orientation/homosexuality-in-animals/ (accessed March 12, 2013).

Bowater, Donna. "Pornography is replacing sex education." http://www.telegraph.co.uk/ education/educationnews/8961010/Pornography-is-replacing-sex-education.html (accessed October 27, 2013).

Brempah, Abigail. "Know the man: John Wyatt." *Easter* (2010). http://www.cmf. org. uk/ publications/content.asp?context=article&id=25497 (accessed March 27, 2013).

Bruce, F.F. *Paul Apostle of the Heart Set Free.* Grand Rapids, MI: Eerdmans Publishing, 1977.

Buckley, Cara. "Spreading the Word (and Pictures) or 'Real' Sex." The New York Times., http://www.nytimes.com/2012/ 09/09/fashion/cindy-gallops-online-effort-to-promote-real-not-porn-fed-sex.html?_r=0 (accessed November 4, 2012).

Bush, George. *Notes, Critical and Practical, on the Book of Leviticus*. Minneapolis, MI: James Family Christian Publishers, 1979.

Byne, M. and B. Parsons. "Human sexual orientation. The biologic theories reappraised." *Arch Gen Psychiatry* 50, no. 3 (March 1993): 228–39. http://www.ncbi.nlm.nih.gov/pubmed/8439245 (accessed March 12, 2013).

Byrd, Dean A. Ph.D., Shirley E. Cos DSW, & Jeffery W. Robinson Ph.D. "The Innate-Immutable Argument Finds No Basis in Science" http://www.narth.com/docs/innate.html (accessed February 2, 2013).

Caballos, Dr. Antonio Pardo. http://www.unav.es/humbiomedicas/apardo/ (accessed March 27, 2013).

"California Senate Approves Counseling Ban." Narth. http://narth.com/2012/05/ california-senate-approves-counseling-ban/ (accessed December 12, 2012).

Campbell, Ken. *Marriage and Family in the Biblical World*. Downers Grove IL: Inter Varsity Press, 2003.

"Canadian Community Health Survey." The Daily. http://www.statcan.gc.ca/dailyquotidien/040615/dq040615b-eng.htm (accessed March 16, 2013).

Carey, Greg. "Rob Bell Comes Out for Marriage Equality." http://www.huffingtonpost. com/mobileweb/greg-carey/rob-bell-comes-gaymarriage_b_2898394. html?utm_hp_ref=fb&src=sp&comm_ref=false (accessed March 28, 2013).

Carmelia, Ray. "How to have an affair without getting caught [expert]." www.yourtango.com/ experts/carmelia-ray/how-to-have-an-affair-without-getting-caught (accessed March 10, 2013).

"Causes of Homosexuality Environment." http://www.conservapedia.com/Causes_of_ Homosexuality#Nature_of_ man_and_causes_of_homosexuality (accessed March 12, 2013).

"Causes of Homosexuality, Sexual Abuse." Conservapedia. http://www. conservapedia.com/ homosexuality (accessed October 2, 2012).

"Cell Guidance Systems." http://www.pnas.org/search?author1=Anthony+F.+Bogaert&sortspec=date&submit=Submit (accessed March 27, 2013).

Chambers, Alan, Julie Hamilton, Mike Ensley, Christine Sneeringer & Jack Harren. Homosexuality 101. DVD. Exodus International (2006).

"Christopher Nolan, Irish novelist, dies at 43." Today Book News, http://www. today.com/id/ 29319433/ns/today-todaybooks#.UUth7aVhB8g (accessed March 21, 2013).

Church of St. John the Baptist. "Homosexuality." http://www.catholic.com/tracts/homosexuality (accessed January 2, 2013).

Citalu, Ron. "Healing the True Masculine." Desert Streams Ministries. Grandview, MO: Desert Stream Press, CD.

Cochran, Susan D. and Vickie M. Mays. "Physical Health Complaints Among Lesbians, Gay Men and Bisexual and Homosexually Experienced Heterosexual Individuals: Results from the California Quality of Life Survey." *American Journal of Public Health* 97, no. 11 (November 2007): 11–12. http://ajph.aphapublications.org/doi/pdf/10.2105/AJPH.2006.087254 (accessed March 14, 2013).

Colapinto, John. *As Nature Made Him: The Boy Who Was Raised as a Girl.* Harper Collins Publishers, USA, 2000.

Coleman, Lyman. *1 Corinthians Taking on the Tough Issues*. Australia: Globe Press Pty Ltd, 1989.

Collins, Nick. "Premature baby survives after doctors advised abortion." The Telegraph, http://www.telegraph.co.uk/health/healthnews/8660450/Premature-baby-survivesafterdoctors-advised-abortion.html (accessed March 13, 2013).

Comiskey, Andrew. *Pursuing Sexual Wholeness Workbook*. Anaheim, CA: Desert Stream Ministries, 1988.

———. "Tell the Truth." Desert Streams Ministries. http://desertstream. org/Groups/1000040181/Desert_Stream_Ministries/Looking_For_Help/Free_Resources/Free_Resources.aspx (accessed October 3, 2012).

Comiskey, Andy and Annette Comiskey. "Understanding for Family and Friends; The Father's Way for Our Sexuality; Help for the Families and Friends of the Sexually Broke." Desert Stream Ministries. Grandview, MO: Desert Stream Press, CD

Comiskey, Annette. "Healing the Mother Wound." Desert Streams Ministries. Grandview, MO: Desert Stream Press, CD.

———. "Help! I'm Married to a Sex Addict." Desert Streams Ministries. Grandview, MO: Desert Stream Press, CD.

"Cost of Abortion," National Abortion Federation, http://www.prochoice.org/ aboutabortion/facts/ economics.html (accessed March 29, 2013).

Cotton, Wayne L. "Social and Sexual Relationships of Lesbians." *The Journal of Sex Research* 11, no. 2 (May 1975): 139–148. (accessed October 3, 2012).

Dailey, Timothy J. Ph. D. and Peter Sprigg. "Getting It Straight: What the Research Shows About Homosexuality." http://www.dennisrichardson.org/pdf/homosexualcausati on.pdf (accessed October 2, 2013).

"Dean Hamer," http://en.wikipedia.org/ wiki/Dean_Hamer (accessed March 27, 2013).

"Definition of Addiction." American Society of Addiction Medicine/ http://www.asam. org/for-the-public/definition-of-addiction (accessed September 21, 2012).

Denov, M. S. "The Myth of Innocence: Sexual Scripts and the Recognition of Child Sexual Abuse by Female Perpetrators." *The Journal of Sex Research.* www.jstor.org.libproxy. ggc.edu/stable/ 3813326, 40, no. 3 (August 2003): 303–314. (accessed September 25, 2012).

DePaulo Jr., J. Raymond. *Understanding Depression: What We Know and What You Can Do About It.* Hoboken, NJ: John Wiley & Sons, 2002.

Douglas, J. D. *The New Bible Dictionary.* Leicester, England: Inter-Varsity Press, 1962.

"DSM-II (1968)." http://en.wikipedia.org/wiki/ Diagnostic_and_Statistical_Manual_of_ Mental_Disorders (accessed March 27, 2013).

Driscoll, Mark. and Grace Driscoll. *Real Marriage, The Truth About Sex, Friendship & Life Together*. Nashville, TN: Thomas Nelson, Inc., 2012.

Eckholm, Erik. "California is First State to Ban Gay 'Cure' for Minors." The New York Times. http://www.nytimes.com/ 2012/10/01/us/california-bans-therapies-to-cure-gay-minors.html?_r=0 (accessed September 30, 2012).

Evans, John. "Polarization in Abortion Attitudes in U. S. Religious Traditions, Sociological Forum," *Sociological Forum* 17, 3 (September 2002): 397–422 (accessed September 20, 2012).

"Everyone Needs Vaccinations!" Immunization Action Coalition. http://www.immunize. org/catg.d/p4115.pdf (accessed March 14, 2013).

"Facts and Figures Relating to the Frequency of Abortion in the United States." http://www. abort73.com/abortion_facts /us_abortion_statistics/ (accessed March 12, 2013).

"Family Violence in Canada: A Statistical Profile." Canadian Centre for Justice Statistics, Ontario, Canada: Minister of Industry (2011), www.statcan.gc.ca/ pub/85-224-x/85-224-x2010000-end.pdf (accessed January 5, 2013).

"Female Genital Mutilation: Still Major Issue in Oman." Mideastposts. http:// mideastposts.com/category/region/ (accessed January 2, 2012).

Furtick, Steven. "The New Rules of Resolution." Elevation Church Podcast. https://itunes. apple.com/us/podcast/elevation-church-charlotte/id216015753 (accessed February 8, 2013).

Geisler, Norman L. *Christian Ethics Options and Issues*. Grand Rapids, MI: Baker Academic, 1989.

Glickman, S. Craig. *A Song for Lovers*. Downers Grove, IL: Intervarsity Press, 1976.

Gundry, Robert H. *A Survey of the New Testament*. Grand Rapids, MI: Zondervan Publishing House, 1994.

Hamer, Dean. http://en.wikipedia.org/wiki/ Dean_Hamer (accessed March 27, 2013).

Hamilton, Julie PhD. "Homosexuality 101: Where Does It Come From, Is Change Possible, and How Should Christians Respond?" Exodus International, 2006. DVD.

Harley, Willard F. Jr. *His Needs Her Needs Building an Affair-Proof Marriage.* Grand Rapids, MI: Baker Book House Company, 2002.

Harren, Julie PhD. "Homosexuality 101: What Every Therapist, Parent, and Homosexual Should Know." http://www.narth.com/docs/hom101.html (accessed March 11, 2013).

Harrub, Brad Ph.D., Bert Thomas Ph.D., and Dave Miller Ph.D. "'This Is The Way God Made Me' A Scientific Examination of Homosexuality and the 'Gay Gene,'" The True Origin, http://www.trueorigin.org/gaygene01.asp (accessed March 12, 2013).

Hendin, Herbert MD. http://euthanasia.procon.org/view.source.php?sourceID=000493 (accessed March 27, 2013).

Highley, Ron & Joanne Highley. "Come Let Us Reason Together Part 1" Living In Freedom Eternally. http://www.lifeministry.org/come-let-us-reason-together-part-1 (accessed March 1, 2013).

Hill, John L. *From Joshua to David.* Nashville, TN: Convention Press, 1959.

"Homosexuality and Choice," Conservapedia, http://www.conservapedia.com/ Homosexuality_and_choice (accessed February 12, 2013).

"Homosexuality and Genetics." http://www.conservapedia.com/Homosexuality_and_Genetics (accessed March 1, 2013).

"Homosexuality in Animals." https://www.boundless.com/psychology/gender-development-and-sexuality/sexual-orientation/homosexuality-in-animals/ (accessed March 12, 2013).

"Homosexuality in Animals a Myth." Conservapedia. http://www.conservapedia.com/Homosexuality _in_animals_myth (accessed December 9, 2012).

"Homosexuality Statistics." Conservapedia. http://www.conservapedia.com/HomosexualityStatistics (accessed February 12, 2013).

"How can we Stop Pedophiles?" http://www.slate.com/articles/health_and_science/medical_examiner/2012/09/stop_childhood_sexual_abuse_how_to_treat_pedophilia_.html (accessed March 22, 2013).

"Hupatasso." BibleStudyTools.com, http://www.biblestudytools.com/lexicons/greek/kjv/hupotasso.html (accessed March 24, 2013).

"If bigamy is a sin, why did King Solomon have so many wives?" Christian Answers. www. christiananswers.net/q-eden/rfsm-solomon.html (accessed December 12, 2012).

"Improving Communities: Diseases, Disorders—HIV/AIDS." The Community Foundation for Greater Atlanta. http://www.cfgreateratlanta. org/issues/diseases-disorders-hivaids.aspx (accessed December 21, 2012).

Instone-Brewer, David. *Divorce and Remarriage in the Church: Biblical Solutions for Pastoral Realities*. Downers Grove, IL: IVP Books, 2003.

James, E. L. *Fifty Shades Freed*. New York, NY: Random House, 2011.

———. *Fifty Shades of Grey*. New York, NY: Random House, 2011.

James, Susan Donaldson. "Gay Americans Make Up 4 Percent of Population." ABC World News. http://abcnews.go.com/Health/williams-institute-report-reveals-million-gay-bisexual-transgender/ story?id=13320565#.UIx7-UKi5ek (accessed January 15, 2013).

Jefferson, Judykay. "Polgamy: A Practical Solution for 21st Century Problem." Yahoo! Voices. http://voices. yahoo.com/polygamy-practical-solution-21st-century-problem-173691.html (accessed November 5, 2012).

John, J. *Marriage Works: The Ultimate Guide to Marriage*. Colorado Spring, CO: Authentic Media, 2008.

Kalichman, Seth. C., Eric Benotsch, David Rompa, Cheryl Gore-Felton, James Austin, Webster Luke, Kari Buckles, Jeff Buckles, Florence Kyomugisha & Dolores Simpson. "Unwanted Sexual Experiences and Sexual Risks in Gay and Bisexual Men: Associations among Revictimization, Substance Use, and Psychiatric Symptoms." *The Journal of Sex Research* 38, no.1 (February 2001): 1–9. http://www.jstor.org/stable /3813257 (accessed September 9, 2012).

Kane, Michael N. "Research Note: Sexual Misconduct, Non-Sexual Touch, and Dual Relationships: Risks for Priests in Light of the Code of Pastoral Conduct." *Review of Religious Research* 48, no.1 (September 2006): 105–110. www.jstor.org.libproxy.ggc.edu /stable/20058121 (accessed September 25, 2012).

Karimi, Faith. "South African Doctor Invents Female Condoms with 'teeth' to fight rape." Cnnworld. http://www.cnn.com/2010/world/africa/06/20/south.africa.female.condom/index.html (accessed December 12, 2012).

Keller, Timothy. *Counterfeit Gods: The Empty Promises of Money, Sex and Power, and the Only Hope that Matters*. New York, NY: Penguin Group, 2009.

Kinsey, Alfred. *Sexual Behavior in the Human Male*. Bloomington, IL: Indiana University Press, 1998.

Koukl, Greg. "Paul, Romans and Homosexuality." Stand to Reason. http://www.str.org/site/News2?page=NewsArticle&id=6289 (accessed January 2, 2013).

Kronemeyer, Robert. *Overcoming Homosexuality*. Macmillan Pub Co, 1980.

Kupelian, David. WND Archives. http://www.wnd.com/author/dkupelian/ (accessed March 27, 2013).

Leff, Lisa. "Gay Population in U.S. Estimated at 4 million, Gary Gates says." Huffpost Healthy Living, http://www.huffingtonpost.com/2011/04/07/gay-population-us-estimate_n_846348.html (accessed January 10, 2013).

LeVay, Simon. "A Difference in Hypothalamic Structure Between Heterosexual and Homosexual Men." *Science* 253 (1991):1034–37 (accessed January 20, 2013).

———. http://en.wikipedia.org/wiki/Simon_LeVay (accessed March 27, 2013).

Levs, Josh. "California governor OKs ban on gay conversion therapy, calling it 'quackery." Cnn U.S. http://www.cnn.com/2012/10/01/us/california-gay-therapy-ban/index.html (accessed January 2, 2013).

"Limbaugh: Gay Marriage Is 'Inevitable.'" ABC News. http://abcnews.go.com/m/blogEntry?id=18835812 (accessed March 29, 2013).

Mahoney, Kelli. "What the Bible Says About… Homosexuality." About.com Christian Teens. http://christianteens.about.com/od/whatthebiblesaysabout/f/homosexuality.htm (accessed October 2, 2012).

Mainwaring, Doug. "I'm gay and I oppose gay marriage." http://www.lifesitenews.com/ news/im-gay-and-i-oppose-gay-marriage (accessed March 28, 2013).

Marcus, Ivan G. "The Jewish Life Cycle: Rites of Passage from Biblical to Modern Times." *AJS Review* 30, no. 1 (April 2006): 189–191. http://www.jstor.org.libproxy.ggc.edu/stable/4131644 (accessed December 12, 2012).

"Masturbation." Merriam-Webster. http://www.merriam-webster.com/ dictionary/masturbation (accessed December 18, 2012).

McKnight, Jim. *Straight Science? Homosexuality, Evolution and Adaptation.* New York, NY: Routledge, 1997.

McQueeney, Krista. "We are God's Children, Y'All: Race, Gender, and Sexuality in Lesbian-and Gay-Affirming Congregations." *Social Problems* 56, no. 1 (February 2009): 151–173. http://www.jstor.org/stable/10.1525/sp.2009.56.1.151 (accessed November 10, 2012).

Mielziner, Moss. "The Jewish Law of Marriage and Divorce in Ancient and Modern Times." *The Old Testament Student* 4, no. 5 (January 1885): 234–236. http://www.jstor.org.libproxy.ggc. edu/stable/3156404 (accessed December 17, 2012).

Miller, Barbara D. "Female-Selective Abortion in Asia: Patterns, Policies, and Debates." *American Anthropologist* 103, no. 4 (December 2001): 1083–1095. http://www.jstor.org.libproxy. ggc.edu/stable/684130 (accessed November 19, 2012).

"Misinformation Rampant in the Mental Health Field." Narth. http://narth.com/2012/05/ misinformation-rampant-in-the-mental-health-field/ (accessed Dec 2, 2012).

"Mission and Doctrine." Exodus International. http://exodusinternational.org/about-us/mission-doctrine/ (accessed March 27, 2013).

"Museum of American Culture." http://www.museum-of-american-culture.us/ samegendercivilaffiliations003.htm (accessed March 3, 2013).

"Natural Law and Homosexuality Made Simple." The Black Cordelias. http://theblackcordelias. wordpress.com/2008/05/24/natural-law-and-homosexuality-made-simple/ (accessed May 25, 2012).

"New Testament Scriptures on Homosexuality." Witness Freedom Ministries. http://www. witnessfortheworld. org/homont.html (accessed January 10, 2013).

"No Person is Born Gay." PFOX Parents and Friends of ExGays and Gays. http://pfox.org /No-one-is-born-gay.html (accessed March 13, 2013).

Odyssey Networks. "Interview: Why Rob Bell Supports Gay Marriage." YouTube, 02:48. http://www.huffingtonpost. com/greg-carey/rob-bell-comes-gay marriage_b_2898394. html?utm_hp_ ref=fb&src=sp&comm_ref=false (accessed March 28, 2013).

Okami, Paul and Amy Goldberg. "Personality Correlates of Pedophilia: Are They Reliable Indicators?" *The Journal of Sex Research* 29, no. 3 (January 2010): 297–328. http://www.jstor.org.libproxy. ggc.edu/stable/3812935 (accessed November 21, 2012).

"Old Testament Scriptures on Homosexuality." Witness Freedom Ministries. http://www.witnessfortheworld.org/homont.html (accessed January 10, 2013).

"Parental Consent and Notification Laws." Planned Parenthood. http://www.plannedparenthood.org/ health-topics/abortion/parental-consent-notification-laws-25268.htm (accessed February 21, 2013).

"Parents and Friends of Exgays and Gays." PFOX. http://pfox.org/No-one-is-born-gay.html (accessed March 13, 2013).

Pearce, Richard, et al. *1 Corinthians: Taking on the Tough Issues* (Littleton, CO: Serendipity House, 1988), 23.

Peplau, Letitia Anne. "Human Sexuality: How do Men and Women Differ?" *Current Directions in Psychological Science.* 12, no. 2 (April 2003): 37–40. http://www. jstor.org/stable/20182831 (accessed November 9, 2012).

Polhill, John B. *Paul and His Letters.* Nashville, TN: Broadman and Holman Publishers, 1999.

Powers, Ward B. "Biographical data." http://www.wardpowers.info. (accessed March 27, 2013).

———. http://www.bhpublishinggroup. com/authors/authors.asp?a=Powers B.%20Ward (accessed March 9, 2013)

———. *Marriage and Divorce: The New Testament Teaching.* Jordan Books, Australia, 1987.

"Ray Blanchard." http://en.wikipedia.org/wiki/ Ray_Blanchard (accessed March 27, 2013).

Ray, Carmelia. "How to have an affair without getting caught [expert]." www. yourtango.com/experts/carmelia-ray/how-to-have-an-affair-without-getting-caught (accessed March 10, 2013).

Regnerus, Mark. "How different are the adult children of parents who have same-sex relationships? Findings from the New Family Structures Study." *Social Science Research* 41, no. 4 (July 2012): 752–770. www.sciencedirect.com/ science/article/pii/s0049089x12000610 (accessed March 10, 2013).

"Regnerus Study on Homosexual Parenting." Narth, http://narth.com/2012/06/ regenerus-study-on-homosexual-parenting/ (accessed December 12, 2012).
"Religious Upbringing and Culture Affects Rates of Homosexuality." Conservapedia. http://www.conservapedia.com/Religious_Upbringing_and_Culture_Affects_Rates_of_Homosexuality (accessed March 11, 2013).
"Resource List: Homosexuality Resource." Focus on the family. http:// www.focusonthefamily.com/topicinfo/Homosexuality_Resources.pdf (accessed September 8, 2012).
Revised Standard Version (RSV) of the Bible, © 1946, 1952, and 1971 by the Division of Christian Education of the National Council of the Churches of Christ in the U.S.A.
"Risks of anal sex, other than STIs?" Go Ask Alice. http://goaskalice.columbia. edu/risks-anal-sex-other-stis (accessed March 27, 2013).
Robinson, B. A. "U.S. Laws and Senate hearings on polygamy." ReligiousTolerance. http://www.religioustolerance.org/polylaw.htm (accessed November 15, 2012).
Rogers, Sy. *One of the Boys Remix: The Sy Rogers Story*. Worthy Creations, 2005. DVD.
Rosenau, Douglas E. *A Celebration of Sex*. Nashville, TN: Thomas Nelson Publishers, 1994.
Rosenblatt, R. "More Gay Men Using Meth, Study Finds." *Los Angeles Times*, April 11, 2007, p. B6.
"Same Gender Civil Affiliations." Museum of American Culture. http://www.museum-of-american-culture.us/samegendercivilaffiliations003.htm (accessed March 7, 2013).
Savin-Williams, Ritch C. "Who's Gay? Does It Matter?" *Current Directions in Psychological Science* 15, no. 1 (February 2006): 40–44. http://www.jstor.org.libproxy.ggc.edu/stable/20183070 (accessed December 21, 2012).
Schlafly, Phyllis. "Obama Makes Polygamy a 21st Century Issue." http://www.canadafreepress.com/index.php/article/16588 (accessed January 1, 2013)

"Science Daily." Homosexuality. http://www.sciencedaily.com/articles/h/homosexuality.htm (accessed March 10, 2013).

Scroggs, Robin. "Summary of 'The New Testament and Homosexuality." http://www. lionking.org /~kovu/bible/section09.html (accessed March 12, 2013).

Sedgh, Gilda, Stanley K. Henshaw, Sushella Sinhg, Akinrinola Bankole & Joanna Drescher. "Legal Abortion Worldwide: Incidence and Recent Trends." *Perspectives on Sexual and Reproductive Health* 39 no. 4 (December 2007): 216–225. http://www.stor.org.libproxy.ggc.edu/ stable/30042979 (accessed November 19, 2012).

Seiss, Joseph A. *Gospel in Leviticus.* Grand Rapids, MI: Kregel Publications, 1981.

"Sexual Orientation and Homosexuality." American Psychological Association. http://www.apa.org/ helpcenter/sexual-orientation.aspx (accessed September 5, 2012).

Shalit, Wendy. *A Return to Modesty.* New York, NY: Simon & Schuster, 1999.

"Simon LeVay." http://en.wikipedia.org/ wiki/Simon_LeVay (accessed March 27, 2013).

Sion, Avi. "Logical and Spiritual Reflections." The Logican. http://www.thelogician.net/6_reflect/6_Book_6/6f_chapter_14.htm (accessed December 30, 2012).

Solimeo, Luiz Sérgio. "The Animal Homosexuality Myth." http://www.narth.com/docs/ animalmyth.html (accessed March 12, 2013).

Spong, John. "I was Given a Thorn in My Flesh: Paul and Homosexuality." Revelife. http://www.revelife.com/754851828/i-was-given-a-thorn-in-my-flesh-paul-and-homosexuality/ (accessed February 12, 2013).

———. "In the Modernity Ward." http://www.touchstonemag.com/archives/print.php?id=03-04-009-f (accessed March 13, 2013).

Sprigg, Peter. "New Study on Homosexual Parents Tops All Previous Research," Family Research Council. http://www.frc.org/issuebrief/new-study-on-homosexual-parents-tops-all-previous- research (accessed January 2, 2013).

Stafford, Tim. *Love, Sex & the Whole Person*. Grand Rapids, MI: Zondervan Publishing House, 1991.

Stefanelli, Al. "A Voice of Reason in an Unreasonable World: Homophobia – The Fear Behind The Hatred." https://alstefanelli.wordpress.com/2010/02/28/homophobia-the-fear-behind-the-hatred/ (accessed March 16, 2013).

"Success and failure among polygamous families: the experience of wives, husbands, and children." Pubmed, http://www.ncbi.nlm.nih.gov/m/pubmed/16984073/ (accessed December 19, 2012).

Sweetman, Dean. *MOVE: You Move…God Moves*. USA, 2007.

Sweetman, Jill. *Marriage: How to Stay Married Forever*. The C3 Church Atlanta, Instantpublisher.com.

"Syphilis Definition." Mayo Clinic Staff. http://www.mayoclinic.com/health/syphilis/DS00374 (accessed November 4, 2012).

"Talk: Homosexuality Statistics." http:/ /www.conservapedia.com/Talk: Homosexuality Statistics (accessed March 21, 2013).

"The biologic theories reappraised Human sexual orientation." Pub Med.gov. http://www.ncbi.nlm.nih.gov/pubmed/8439245 (accessed March 12, 2013).

"The Black Cordelias Natural Law and Homosexuality made simple." http://theblackcordelias. wordpress.com/2008/05/24/natural-law-and-homosexuality-made-simple/ (accessed May 25, 2012).

"The Cost of Abortion." National Abortion Federation. http://www.prochoice. org/about_abortion/facts/economics.html (accessed March 29, 2013).

"The Daily Canadian Community Health Survey." Canadian. http://www.statcan. gc.ca/daily-quotidien/040615/ dq040615b-eng.htm (accessed March 16, 2013).

The Holy Bible, English Standard Version (ESV) is adapted from the Revised Standard Version of the Bible, by copyright Division of Christian Education of the National Council of the Churches of Christ in the U.S.A., 2001.

The Holy Bible, King James Version (KJV), © 1611, 1987, public domain.

The Holy Bible, New International Version® (NIV®), © 1973, 1978, 1984, 2011 by Biblica, Inc.™

The Holy Bible, New Living Translation (NLT) © 1996, 2004, 2007 by Tyndale House Foundation, used by permission of Tyndale House Publishers Inc., Carol Stream, Illinois 60188.

"The Many Wives of David in the Bible." http://ancienthistory.about.com/od/biblepeople/a/020811-CW-King-Davids-Wives.htm (accessed December 22, 2012).

"The Marketing of Evil: How Radicals, Elitists, and Pseudo-Experts Sell Us Corruption Disguised As Freedom." Amazon. http://www.amazon.com/dp/1581824599/?tag=googhydr20&hvadid=9618339261&hvpos=1t1&hvexid=&hvnetw=g&hvrand=12323796415594788577&hvpone=&hvptwo=&hvqmt=b&ref=pd_sl_5kqpdwiw41_b (accessed March 16, 2013).

The Message (MSG). Copyright © 1993, 1994, 1995, 1996, 2000, 2001, 2002 by NavPress Publishing Group.

NET Bible® copyright ©1996-2006 by Biblical Studies Press, L.L.C.

New American Standard Bible® (NASB), © 1960,1962,1963,1968,1971,1972,1973,1975, 1977,1995 by The Lockman Foundation.

The New Bible Dictionary. Leicester, England: Inter-Varsity Press, 1003.

New King James Version® (NKJV), © 1982 by Thomas Nelson, Inc.

"Unborn Babies Can Feel Pain." Minnesota Citizens Concerned for Life. http://www.mccl.org/unborn-babies-can-feel-pain.html (accessed March 11, 2013).

Uria, Marian and Carmen Mosquera. "Legal Abortion in Asturias (Spain) after the 1985 Law: Sociodemographic Characteristics of Women Appling for Abortion." *European Journal of Epidemiology* 15, no. 1 (January 1999): 59–64. http://www.jstor.org.libproxy. ggc.edu/ stable/3581801 (accessed November 19, 2012).

Vitz, Paul C. *Psychology as a Religion: The Cult of Self-Worship 2nd ed.* Grand Rapids, MI: William B. Eerdmans Publishing Company, 1994.

Welch, Edward T. *Blame it on the Brain.* Phillipsburg, NJ: P & R, 1998.

Welch, Kelly. *Think Human Sexuality*. Boston, MA: Pearson Education, Inc., 2011.

"What does the Bible say about pedophelia?" Got Questions Ministries. http://www.gotquestions.org/pedophilia.html (accessed November 1, 2012).

"What was the Relationship Between David and Jonathan?" http://www.gotquestions. org/David-and-Jonathan.html (accessed January 20, 2013).

Whitbeck, Les B., Xiaojin Chen, Dan R. Hoyt, Kimberly A. Tyler & Kurt D. Johnson. "Mental Disorder, Subsistence Strategies, and Victimization among Gay, Lesbian, and Bisexual Homeless and Runaway Adolescents." *The Journal of Sex Research* 41 no. 1 (November 2004): 329–342. http://www.jstor.org/stable/3813541 (accessed November 19, 2012).

"Why are Abortions Performed?" About73.com. http://www.abort73.com/abortionfacts/us_abortion _statistics/ (accessed March 12, 2013).

Williams, Sarah. *The Shaming of the Strong.* Eastbourne, England: Kingsway Communications, 2005.

Wilson, Glenn and Qazi Rahman. *Born Gay: The Psychobiology of Sex Orientation.* 2005.

———. "Born Gay: The Psychobiology of Sex Orientation." http://queeressays. wordpress.com/the-prenatal-androgen-theory-searching-for-the-cause-of-exclusive-homosexuality-in-human-males-and-females/ (accessed February 13, 2013), 27.

Wink, Walter. "Homosexuality and the Bible." http://www.bridges-across. org/ba/winkhombib.htm (accessed November 19, 2012).

———. http://en.wikipedia.org/wiki/ Walter_Wink (accessed March 27, 2013).

"Witness Freedom Ministries." http://www.witnessfortheworld.org/homont.html (accessed March 20, 2013).

Wolkomir, Michelle. "Giving it up to God." *Gender and Society* 18, no. 6 (December 2004) 735–755. http://www.jstore.org/stable/4149392 (accessed September 26, 2012).

Woods, Ramona & Ron Fisher. "*Ministry to the Sexually Abused.*" Desert Streams Ministries. CD.

Wyatt, John. *Matters of Life and Death: Human Dilemmas in the Light of the Christian Faith.* Nottingham, England. Inter-Varsity Press, 2009.

Zapka, J., Stephanie Lemon, Laura Peterson, Heather Palmer & Marlene Goldman. "The Silent Consumer Women's Reports and Ratings of Abortion Services." *Medical Care* 39 no. 1 (February 2000): 50–60. http://www.jstor.org.libproxy.ggc.edu/stable/3767699 (accessed November 9, 2012).

End Notes

[1] "Sexual Orientation and Homosexuality," American Psychological Association, http://www.apa.org/helpcenter/sexual-orientation.aspx (accessed September 5, 2012).
[2] Walter Wink, "Homosexuality and the Bible," Bridges Across, http://www.bridges-across.org/ba/winkhombib.htm (accessed November 19, 2012), 1.
[3] Wink, "Homosexuality and the Bible," 1.
[4] "Resource List: Homosexuality Resource," Focus on the Family, http://www.focusonthefamily.com/topicinfo/Homosexuality_Resources.pdf (accessed September 18, 2012), 1.
[5] Isaiah 40:8 (NASB).
[6] Ibid.
[7] Lamentations 3:22–23 (NIV).
[8] 2 Corinthians 12:9 (NIV).
[9] 1 Corinthians 10:13 (NIV).
[10] Isaiah 42:16 (NIV).
[11] 2 Corinthians 12:9 (NIV).
[12] Romans 12:2 (NIV).
[13] Matthew 18:20 (NIV).
[14] Kelly Welch, *Think Human Sexuality* (Boston, MA: Pearson Education, Inc, 2011), 218.
[15] K. Welch, *Think Human Sexuality*, 219.
[16] Rosenau, *A Celebration of Sex* (Nashville, TN: Thomas Nelson, Inc.), 181.
[17] Timothy Keller, *Counterfeit Gods: The Empty Promises of Money, Sex, and Power* (New York, NY: Penguin Group, 2009), 39.
[18] 1 Corinthians 6:19 (NIV).
[19] Wendy Shalit, *A Return to Modesty* (New York, NY: Simon & Schuster, 1999), 12.
[20] Shalit, *A Return to Modesty*, 56.
[21] John 14:15 (NASB).
[22] Colossians 3:2 (NIV).
[23] 2 Corinthians 6:14 (NIV).
[24] Proverbs 4:23 (NIV).
[25] Shalit, *A Return to Modesty*, Back Cover.
[26] Ibid., 212.
[27] Ibid., 54.
[28] Song of Solomon 2:7 (NLT).
[29] Robert Bell, *Sex God* (New York, NY: Harper One, 2012), Back Cover.
[30] Bell, *Sex God*, 135.
[31] Ibid., 153.
[32] Matthew 6:12 (NLT).
[33] Matthew 6:14–15 (MSG).
[34] 2 Corinthians 10:5 (KJV).
[35] Romans 12:3 (NLT).
[36] 1 Samuel 16:7b (NLT).
[37] Isaiah 53:6 (KJV).
[38] K. Welch, *Think Human Sexuality*, 285.
[39] Norman L. Geisler, *Christian Ethics Options and Issues* (Grand Rapids, MI: Baker Academic, 2007), 135.

[40] Ibid.
[41] Ibid., 285.
[42] J. Zapka, Stephanie Lemon, Laura Peterson, Heather Palmer and Marlene Goldman, "The Silent Consumer Women's Reports and Ratings of Abortion Services," *Medical Care (*February 2000): 50–60, http://www.jstor.org.libproxy.ggc.edu/stable /3767699 (accessed November 9, 2012), 50.
[43] K. Welch, *Think Human Sexuality*, 285.
[44] Gilda Sedgh, Stanley K. Henshaw, Sushella Sinhg, Akinrinola Bankole and Joanna Drescher, "Legal Abortion Worldwide: Incidence and Recent Trends," *Perspectives on Sexual and Reproductive Health (*December 2007): 216–225, http://www.jstor.org.libproxy.ggc.edu/ stable/30042979 (accessed November 19, 2012), 218.
[45] Barbara D. Miller, "Female-Selective Abortion in Asia: Patterns, Policies, and Debates," *American Anthropologist,* http://www.jstor.org.libproxy.ggc.edu/stable/684130, 103, no. 4 (December 2001): 1083–1095 (accessed November 19, 2013).
[46] Sedgh, "Legal Abortion Worldwide," 218.
[47] Ibid.
[48] Ibid.
[49] "Why are Abortions Performed?" About73.co, http://www.abort73.com/abortion_ facts/us_abortion _statistics/ (accessed March 12, 2013).
[50] Ibid., 222.
[51] Ibid., 223.
[52] "Parental Consent and Notification Laws," Planned Parenthood, http://www.planned parenthood .org /health-topics/abortion/parental-consent-notification-laws-25268.htm (accessed February 21, 2013).
[53] "Cost of Abortion," National Abortion Federation, http://www.prochoice.org/about_ abortion/facts/economics.html (accessed March 29, 2013).
[54] Ibid., 59.
[55] Zapka, "The Silent Consumer," 58.
[56] K. Welch, *Think Human Sexuality,* 287.
[57] John Wyatt, *Matters of Life and Death: Human Dilemmas in the Light of the Christian Faith* (Nottingham, England: Inter-Varsity Press, 2009), 147.
[58] Wyatt, *Matters of Life and Death*, 147.
[59] Geisler, *Christian Ethics*, Back Cover.
[60] Ibid., 140.
[61] "Unborn Babies Can Feel Pain," Minnesota Citizens Concerned for Life, http://www.mccl.org /unborn-babies-can-feel-pain.html (accessed February 12, 2013).
[62] "Unborn Babies Can Feel Pain."
[63] Lamentations 3:22–23 (MSG).
[64] Luke 6:31 (NKJV).
[65] Exodus 20:13 (KJV).
[66] Geisler, *Christian Ethics*, 140.
[67] Wyatt, *Matters of Life and Death*, 135.
[68] Ibid.,136.
[69] Ibid.
[70] Ibid., 139.
[71] Ibid., 140.
[72] Matthew 22:37–40 (NIV).
[73] Psalm 127:3 (NASB).
[74] Psalm 127:4 (NASB).
[75] Psalm 139:13–16 (NIV).

[76] Abigail Brempah, "Know the man: John Wyatt," *Easter* (2010), http://www.cmf.org.uk/ publications/content.asp?context=article&id=25497 (accessed March 27, 2013).
[77] Sarah Williams, *The Shaming of the Strong* (Eastbourne, England: Kingsway Communications, 2005), 49.
[78] Nick Collins, "Premature baby survives after doctors advise abortion," The Telegraph, http://www.telegraph.co.uk/health/healthnews/8660450/Premature-baby-survives-after-doctors-advised-abortion.html (accessed October 27, 2013).
[79] 2 Samuel 9:1–13 (NIV).
[80] Luke 18:15–16 (NIV).
[81] Mark 2:1–12 (NIV).
[82] John 9:1–6 (NIV).
[83] Mark 5:1–13 (NLT).
[84] "Christopher Nolan, Irish novelist, dies at 43," Today Book News, http://www.today.com/id/ 29319433/ns/today-todaybooks#.UUth7aVhB8g (accessed March 21, 2013).
[85] Geisler, *Christian Ethics*, 137.
[86] Job 34:14–15 (NIV).
[87] Isaiah 57:16 (NASB).
[88] Geisler, *Christian Ethics*, 137.
[89] Luke 1:44 (NIV).
[90] Ecclesiastes 6:3–5 (NIV).
[91] Geisler, *Christian Ethics*, 139.
[92] John Evans, "Polarization in Abortion Attitudes in U. S. Religious Traditions," *Sociological Forum* 17/3 (2002): 418, http://www.jstor.org/stable/3070348 (accessed September 20, 2012).
[93] Hebrews 11:31 (NIV).
[94] Ward B. Powers, *Marriage and Divorce The New Testament Teaching* (Jordan Books, Australia. 1987), 347.
[95] B. A. Robinson, "U.S. Laws and Senate hearings on polygamy." Religious Tolerance, http://www.religioustolerance.org/polylaw.htm (accessed January 1, 2013).
[96] Judykay Jefferson, "Polygamy: A Practical Solution for 21st Century Problem." Yahoo! Voices, http://voices.yahoo.com/polygamy-practical-solution-21st-century-problem-173691.html (accessed November 5, 2012).
[97] "2012: The Year of the Inane Political Fatwa," The Voices of the Middle East, http://mideastposts.com/category/region/ (accessed January 1, 2013).
[98] "Success and failure among polygamous families: the experience of wives, husbands, and children," Pubmed, http://www.ncbi.nlm.nih.gov/m/pubmed/16984073/ (accessed December 19, 2012).
[99] Powers, *Marriage and Divorce*, 351.
[100] Acts 13:22 (NIV).
[101] "The Many Wives of David in the Bible," http://ancienthistory.about.com/od/ biblepeople/a/020811-CW-King-Davids-Wives.htm (accessed December 22, 2012).
[102] Deuteronomy 17:16–17 (NLT).
[103] "If bigamy is a sin, why did King Solomon have so many wives?" Christian Answers, www.christiananswers.net/q-eden/rfsm-solomon.html (accessed December 12, 2012).
[104] Genesis 16:2 (NIV).
[105] Genesis 16:6 (NIV).
[106] 1 Samuel 1:6 (NIV).
[107] Genesis 30:1 (NIV).
[108] Genesis 29:25 (NET).
[109] Genesis 29:25-30 (NIV).

[110] Phyllis Schlafly, "Obama Makes Polygamy a 21st Century Issue," http://www.canada freepress.com /index.php/article/16588 (accessed January 1, 2013).
[111] Powers, *Marriage and Divorce,* 349.
[112] E. L. James, *Fifty Shades Freed* (New York, Vintage Books, 2011), Back cover.
[113] Ibid., Back cover.
[114] Proverbs 28:26 (NASB).
[115] Paul C. Vitz, *Psychology as a Religion: The Cult of Self-Worship 2nd ed. (*Grand Rapids, MI: Eerdmans, 1977), Back Cover.
[116] Vitz, *Psychology as a Religion*, 19.
[117] Ibid.
[118] Mark 12:31 (NASB).
[119] Mark 12:30–31 (NASB).
[120] Isaiah 43:1b (NLT).
[121] Genesis 2:18 (NLT).
[122] "Misinformation Rampant in Mental Health Field," Narth, http://narth.com/2012/05/ misinformation-rampant-in-the-mental-health-field/ (accessed Dec 2, 2012).
[123] Shalit, *A Return to Modesty*, 7.
[124] Ibid.
[125] Josh Levs, "California governor OKs ban on gay conversion therapy, calling it 'quackery'," Cnn U.S, http://www.cnn.com/2012/10/01/us/california-gay-therapy-ban/index.html (accessed January 2, 2013).
[126] "Misinformation Rampant in Mental Health Field."
[127] Matthew 19:26 (NIV).
[128] John Colapinto, *As Nature Made Him: The Boy Who Was Raised as a Girl* (Harper Collins Publishers, USA, 2000), 239.
[129] Jeremiah 29:11 (NLT).
[130] Dean Sweetman, *MOVE: You Move... God Moves (*USA, 2007), 59.
[131] Ibid., 61.
[132] Nehemiah 8:10 (NIV).
[133] Psalm 37:4 (NKJV).
[134] Bell, *Sex God*, Front cover.
[135] Genesis 2:23 (NIV).
[136] Genesis 2:24 (NASB).
[137] Genesis 2:25 (NIV).
[138] Genesis 38:9 (NLT).
[139] Ibid., 12-26 (NLT).
[140] Matthew 5:17 (NIV).
[141] Hebrews 11:31 (NIV).
[142] 2 Samuel 11:2 (NLT).
[143] S. Craig Glickman, *A Song for Lovers* (Downers Grove, IL: Intervarsity Press, 1976), 13.
[144] Glickman, *A Song for Lovers*, 13.
[145] Proverbs 2; Proverbs 5:18 (NLT).
[146] Malachi 3:10b (NIV).
[147] Mark and Grace Driscoll, *Real Marriage, The Truth About Sex, Friendship & Life Together (*Nashville, TN: Thomas Nelson, Inc., 2012), 109.
[148] Steven Furtick, "The New Rules of Resolution," Elevation Church Podcast, https://itunes. apple.com/us/podcast/elevation-church-charlotte/id216015753 (accessed February 8, 2013).
[149] Jill Sweetman, *Marriage: How to Stay Married Forever* (The C3 Atlanta: instantpublisher.com), 106.
[150] 1 Corinthians 6:14–15 (MSG).

[151] Sweetman, *Marriage,* 106.
[152] 1 Corinthians 12:27 (NIV).
[153] 1 Corinthians 6:16–20 (MSG).
[154] Sweetman, *Marriage*, 106.
[155] Bell, *Sex God*, 31.
[156] Shalit, *A Return to Modesty*, 36.
[157] Ibid., 90.
[158] Ibid., 120.
[159] Ibid., 66.
[160] Ibid.
[161] Welch, *Think Human Sexuality,* 383.
[162] Ibid.
[163] Shalit, *A Return to Modesty*, 66.
[164] Hebrews 4:14–15 (NLT).
[165] 1 Corinthians 6:19–20 (NIV).
[166] Bell, *Sex God*, 41.
[167] Romans 12:1 (NIV).
[168] Driscoll, *Real Marriage*, 113.
[169] Shalit, *A Return to Modesty*, 49.
[170] Ibid., 51.
[171] Driscoll, *Real Marriage*, 113.
[172] Comiskey, *Pursuing Sexual Wholeness Workbook* (Anaheim, CA: Desert Stream Ministries, 1988), 115.
[173] Driscoll, *Real Marriage*, 109.
[174] Collins. "Premature baby survives advised abortion,"
[175] Rosenau, *A Celebration of Sex*, 337.
[176] Bell, *Sex God*, 7.
[177] Richard Abowitz. "Porn Film Biz Rocked by Syphilis Scare," The Daily Beast, http://www.thedailybeast.com/articles/2012/08/20/porno-film-business-rocked-by-syphilis-scare.html (accessed November 10, 2012).
[178] "Syphilis Definition," Mayo Clinic Staff, http://www.mayoclinic.com/health/syphilis /DS00374 (accessed November 4, 2012).
[179] Comiskey, *Pursuing Sexual Wholeness,* 114.
[180] Matthew 6:22–23 (NIV).
[181] K. Welch, *Think Human Sexuality*, 224.
[182] Jay E. Adams, *The Christian Counselor's Manual* (Eugene, OR: Harvest House, 1986), 399.
[183] "Masturbation," Merriam-Webster, http://www.merriam webster.com/dictionary/ masturbation (accessed December 18, 2012).
[184] Letitia Anne Peplau. "Human Sexuality: How do Men and Women Differ?" *Current Directions in Psychological Science* 12/2: 2003, http://www.jstor.org/stable/20182831 (accessed November 9, 2012), 37.
[185] K, Welch, *Think Human Sexuality*, 226.
[186] Ibid., 228.
[187] Comiskey, *Pursuing Sexual Wholeness,* 115.
[188] Ibid., 116.
[189] Adams, *Counselor's Manual*, 400.
[190] 1 Corinthians 7:5 (NASB).
[191] 1 Corinthians 6:12 (NASB).
[192] Adams, *Counselor's Manual*, 400.
[193] Proverbs 28:13 (NIV).
[194] 1 Corinthians 7:9 (NIV).

[195] Lamentations 3:23 (NKJV).
[196] Ray Carmelia, "How to have an affair without getting caught [expert]," www.yourtango.com/ experts/carmelia-ray/how-to-have-an-affair-without-getting-caught (accessed March 10, 2013).
[197] Shalit, *A Return to Modesty*, 73.
[198] Genesis 2:16–17 (NIV).
[199] Rosenau, *A Celebration of Sex,* 95.
[200] Matthew 5:28 (ESV).
[201] Adams, *Counselor's Manual*, 400.
[202] 2 Corinthians 10:5 (ESV).
[203] Rosenau, *A Celebration of Sex*, Back Cover.
[204] Ibid., 87.
[205] Romans 13:10 (NLT).
[206] 1 Corinthians 13:4–7 (NIV).
[207] Philippians 4:8 (NIV).
[208] Romans 12:2 (NIV).
[209] 2 Timothy 2:22 (NASB).
[210] Romans 8:28 (NIV).
[211] Annette Comiskey, "Help! I'm Married to a Sex Addict." Desert Streams Ministries CD (Desert Stream Press: Grandview, MO).
[212] "Definition of Addiction," American Society of Addiction Medicine, http://www.asam. org/for-the-public/definition-of-addiction (accessed September 21, 2012).
[213] Comiskey, "Help!" CD.
[214] Ibid.
[215] Psalm 23:3 (NASB).
[216] K. Welch, *Think Human Sexuality*, 326.
[217] Ibid.
[218] Ibid.
[219] Comiskey, *Pursuing Sexual Wholeness*, 111.
[220] Ibid.
[221] Ibid.
[222] Ibid.
[223] Rosenau, *A Celebration of Sex*, 339.
[224] Ibid.
[225] Bell, *Sex God,* 67.
[226] Ephesians 4:19 (NIV).
[227] Bell, *Sex God,* 69.
[228] 2 Samuel 13:15 (NIV).
[229] 1 Corinthians 6:12 (NIV).
[230] 1 Corinthians 6:13 (NIV).
[231] Comiskey, "Help!" CD.
[232] Ibid.
[233] Ibid.
[234] Ibid.
[235] Ibid.
[236] Ibid.
[237] Ibid.
[238] Ephesians 4:28 (NIV).
[239] Bell, *Sex God,* 73.
[240] Rosenau, *A Celebration of Sex,* 317.
[241] Welch, *Think Human Sexuality,* 371.

[242] Michael N. Kane, "Research Note: Sexual Misconduct, Non-Sexual Touch, and Dual Relationships: Risks for Priests in Light of the Code of Pastoral Conduct," *Review of Religious Research* 48/1 (2006): 108, www.jstor.org.libproxy.ggc.edu /stable/20058121 (accessed September 25, 2012).
[243] Myram S. Denov, "The Myth of Innocence: Sexual Scripts and the Recognition of Child Sexual Abuse by Female Perpetrators," *The Journal of Sex Research* 40/3 (2003): 303, www.jstor.org.libproxy.ggc.edu/stable/3813326 (accessed September 25, 2012).
[244] Ibid., 308.
[245] Ibid., 313.
[246] Ibid., 307.
[247] K. Welch, *Think Human Sexuality*, 371.
[248] Ramona Woods and Ron Fisher, "*Ministry to the Sexually Abused*," Desert Streams Ministries CD.
[249] Seymour Adler, "Maslow's Need Hierarchy and the Adjustment of Immigrants," *International Migration Review* 11/4 (1977): 444 (accessed March 20, 2013).
[250] 2 Corinthians 10:5 (KJV).
[251] "Causes of Homosexuality, Sexual Abuse," Conservapedia, http://www.conservapedia. com/homosexuality (accessed October 2, 2012).
[252] Jeremiah 32:27 (NIV).
[253] Psalm 103:3 (NIV).
[254] Rosenau, *A Celebration of Sex*, 319.
[255] John 11:25 (NASB).
[256] Woods, "*Ministry,*" CD.
[257] Deuteronomy 31:6 (NIV).
[258] Isaiah 55:8–9 (NIV).
[259] Psalm 27:10 (NKJV).
[260] Psalm 136:1 (NIV).
[261] Romans 8:28 (NIV).
[262] Proverbs 3:5 (NIV).
[263] 2 Corinthians 5:17 (NIV).
[264] Psalm 139:14 (NIV).
[265] Rosenau, *A Celebration of Sex*, 325.
[266] Ibid.
[267] K. Welch, *Think Human Sexuality*, 357.
[268] Seth. C. Kalichman, et al., "Unwanted Sexual Experiences and Sexual Risks in Gay and Bisexual Men: Associations among Revictimization, Substance Use, and Psychiatric Symptoms," *The Journal of Sex Research* 38/1 (2001): 1, http://www.jstor.org/stable/3813257 (accessed September 9, 2012).
[269] K. Welch, *Think Human Sexuality*, 372.
[270] Ibid., 372.
[271] Ibid., 361.
[272] 2 Samuel 13:2 (NLT).
[273] 2 Samuel 13:15 (NIV).
[274] Bell, *Sex God*, 59.
[275] Peplau, "Human Sexuality," 38.
[276] Ibid.
[277] Kalichman, "Unwanted Sexual Experiences," 1.
[278] Ibid.. 4.
[279] Ibid., 8.
[280] Faith Karimi, "South African Doctor Invents Female Condoms with 'teeth' to fight rape," Cnnworld,

http://www.cnn.com/2010/world/africa/06/20/south.africa.female.condom/index.html (accessed December 12, 2012).
[281] Shalit, *A Return to Modesty*, 41.
[282] "How can we Stop Pedophiles?"
http://www.slate.com/articles/health_and_science/medical _examiner/2012/09/stop_childhood_sexual_abuse_how_to_treat_pedophilia_.html (accessed March 22, 2013).
[283] Paul Okami and Amy Goldberg, "Personality Correlates of Pedophilia: Are They Reliable Indicators?" *The Journal of Sex Research* 29/3 (2010): 300, http://www.jstor.org.libproxy._ggc.edu/stable/3812935 (accessed November 21, 2012).
[284] Okami, "Personality Correlates of Pedophilia," 302.
[285] Ibid.
[286] Kane, "Research Note: Sexual Misconduct," 106.
[287] Ibid., 105.
[288] Ibid.
[289] Okami, "Personality Correlates of Pedophilia," 303.
[290] K. Welch, *Think Human Sexuality*, 323.
[291] Okami, "Personality Correlates of Pedophilia," 305.
[292] "What does the bible say about pedophilia?" Got Questions Ministries, http://www.gotquestions.org/pedophilia.html (accessed November 1, 2012).
[293] Matthew 18:6 (KJV).
[294] "What does bible say about pedophilia?"
[295] Jim McKnight, *Straight Science? Homosexuality, Evolution and Adaptation* (New York, NY: Routledge), 1997, 2.
[296] McKnight, *Straight Science?* Preface.
[297] Ibid., 5.
[298] Ibid.
[299] "Sexual Orientation and Homosexuality."
[300] Alan Chambers, Julie Hamilton, Mike Ensley, Christine Sneeringer, & Jack Harren, *Homosexuality 101 DVD* (Exodus International, 2006).
[301] "Sexual Orientation and Homosexuality."
[302] Ibid.
[303] Powers, "Biographical data," http://www.wardpowers.info (accessed March 27, 2013).
[304] Powers, *Marriage and Divorce*, 51.
[305] "Sexual Orientation and Homosexuality."
[306] Rosenau, *A Celebration of Sex*, 345.
[307] "Mission and Doctorine," Exodus International, http://exodusinternational.org/about-us/mission-doctrine/ (accessed March 27, 2013).
[308] Chambers, "Homosexuality 101" DVD.
[309] "Sexual Orientation and Homosexuality."
[310] McKnight, *Straight Science?* 13.
[311] "DSM-II (1968)," http://en.wikipedia.org/wiki/Diagnostic_and_Statistical_ Manual_of_Mental_Disorders (accessed March 27, 2013).
[312] "Sexual Orientation and Homosexuality."
[313] "Regnerus Study on Homosexual Parenting," Narth, http://narth.com/2012/06/regenerus-study-on-homosexual-parenting/ (accessed December 12, 2012).
[314] Mark Regnerus, "How different are the adult children of parents who have same-sex relationships? Findings from the New Family Structures Study," *Social Science Research* 41/4 (2012): 752–770. www.sciencedirect.com/science/article/pii/s0049089x12000610 (accessed March 10, 2013).
[315] Ibid.

[316] Geisler, *Christian Ethics*, 267.
[317] Dr. Antonio Pardo Caballos, http://www.unav.es/humbiomedicas/apardo/ (accessed March 27, 2013).
[318] Luiz Sérgio Solimeo, "The Animal Homosexuality Myth," http://www.narth.com/docs/animalmyth.html (accessed March 12, 2013).
[319] "About Narth," http://narth.com/menus/mission.html (accessed March 27, 2013).
[320] "Simon LeVay," http://en.wikipedia.org/wiki/Simon_LeVay (accessed March 27, 2013).
[321] "Boundless Homosexuality in Animals," https://www.boundless.com/psychology/gender-development-and-sexuality/sexual-orientation/homosexuality-in-animals/ (accessed March 12, 2013).
[322] "The Black Cordelias Natural Law and Homosexuality made simple," http://theblackcordelias.wordpress.com/2008/05/24/natural-law-and-homosexuality-made-simple/ (accessed May 25, 2012).
[323] Ibid., 158–159.
[324] Edward T. Welch, *Blame it on the Brain* (Phillipsburg, NJ: P & R), 1998, 157.
[325] "Homosexuality and Genetics," http://www.conservapedia.com/Homosexuality_and_Genetics (accessed March 1, 2013).
[326] K. Welch, *Blame the Brain,* 160.
[327] Ibid., 161.
[328] Ibid.
[329] McKnight, *Straight Science,* 22.
[330] "Born or Bred?" The Daily Beast, http://www.thedailybeast.com/newsweek/1992/02/23/ born-or-bred.html (accessed March 11, 2013).
[331] Simon LeVay, "A Difference in Hypothalamic Structure Between Heterosexual and Homosexual Men," *Science* 253 (1991):1043 (accessed January 20, 2013).
[332] Brad Harrub, Ph.D. , Bert Thompson, Ph.D. and Dave Miller, Ph.D., "'This Is The Way God Made Me' A Scientific Examination of Homosexuality and the 'Gay Gene,'" The True Origin, http://www.trueorigin.org/gaygene01.asp (accessed March 12, 2013).
[333] "About Us," http://www.mygenes.co.nz/About%20Us.htm (accessed March 27, 2013).
[334] "Regnerus Study on Homosexual Parenting."
[335] "Religious Upbringing and Culture Affects Rates of Homosexuality," Conservapedia, http://www.conservapedia.com/Religious_Upbringing_and_Culture_Affects_Rates_of_Homosexuality (accessed, February 20, 2013).
[336] "Religious Upbringing."
[337] Ibid.
[338] "Herbert Hendin, MD," http://euthanasia.procon.org/view.source.php?sourceID=000493 (accessed March 27, 2013).
[339] "Religious Upbringing."
[340] "Dean Hamer," http://en.wikipedia.org/wiki/Dean_Hamer (accessed March 27, 2013).
[341] "Archive Exposing the Myth of Evolution," The True Origin, http://www.trueorigin.org/gaygene01.asp (accessed March 12, 2013).
[342] Welch, *Blame the Brain,* 167.
[343] Ibid., 168.
[344] Julie Harren, PhD, "Homosexuality 101: What Every Therapist, Parent and Homosexual Should Know," http://www.narth.com/docs/hom101.html (accessed March 11, 2013).
[345] "Science Daily," Homosexuality, http://www.sciencedaily.com/articles/h/homosexuality.htm (accessed March 10, 2013).

[346] "Parents and Friends of Exgays and Gays," PFOX, http://pfox.org/No-one-is-born-gay.html (accessed March 13, 2013).
[347] "The biologic theories reappraised Human sexual orientation," Pub Med.gov, http://www.ncbi.nlm.nih.gov/pubmed/8439245 (accessed March 12, 2013).
[348] "Causes of Homosexuality."
[349] Welch, *Blame the Brain*, 170.
[350] "Causes of Homosexuality."
[351] Ibid.
[352] LeVay, *A Difference in Hypothalamic Structure*, 1034.
[353] Welch, *Blame the Brain*, 167.
[354] "Causes of Homosexuality."
[355] Alfred Kinsey, *Sexual Behavior in the Human Male*, Bloomington, IL: Indiana University Press, 1998.
[356] Susan Donaldson James, "Gay Americans Make Up 4 Percent of Population," ABC World News, http://abcnews.go.com/Health/williams-institute-report-reveals-million-gay-bisexual-transgender/story?id=13320565#.UIx7-UKi5ek (accessed January 15, 2013).
[357] Lisa Leff, "Gay Population In U.S. Estimated at 4 Million, Gary Gates Says," Huffpost Healthy Living, http://www.huffingtonpost.com/2011/04/07/gay-population-us-estimate_n_846348.html (accessed January 10, 2013).
[358] McKnight, *Straight Science,* 6.
[359] Ibid.
[360] Ray Blanchard, "Fraternal Birth Order, Maternal Immune Reactions, and Homosexuality in Men," *Politics and the Life Sciences* 19/2 (2000): 157, http://www.jstor.org/stable/4236585 (accessed September 26, 2012).
[361] Blanchard, "Fraternal Birth Order," 157.
[362] "Ray Blanchard," http://en.wikipedia.org/wiki/Ray_Blanchard (accessed March 27, 2013).
[363] "Cell Guidance Systems," http://www.pnas.org/search?author1=Anthony+F.+Bogaert&sortspec=date&submit=Submit (accessed March 27, 2013).
[364] Blanchard, "Fraternal Birth Order," 158.
[365] Timothy J. Dailey Ph. D. and Peter Sprigg, "Getting It Straight: What the Research Shows About Homosexuality," http://www.dennisrichardson.org/pdf/homosexualcausation.pdf (accessed October 2, 2012).
[366] McKnight, *Straight Science,* 134.
[367] Ibid., 116.
[368] Ibid.
[369] Ibid., 117.
[370] Ibid., 145.
[371] Ibid., 8.
[372] Ibid., 2.
[373] "About, Gunter Dorner," http://translate.google.com/translate?hl=en&sl=de&u=http://de.wikipedia.org/wiki/G%25C3%25BCnter_D%25C3%25B6rner&prev=/search%3Fq%3DGunter%2BDorner,%2Ba%2Bneuroendocrinologist%26hl%3Den%26client%3Dsafari%26rls%3Den%26biw%3D1423%26bih%3D764&sa=X&ei=RDJTUbSkIJDc8AS_3YGACw&ved=0CEwQ7gEwAw (accessed March 27, 2013).
[374] Glenn Wilson and Qazi Rahman, "Born Gay: The Psychobiology of Sex Orientation," http://queeressays.wordpress.com/the-prenatal-androgen-theory-searching-for-the-cause-of-exclusive-homosexuality-in-human-males-and-females/ (accessed February 13, 2013), 27.
[375] Wilson, "Born Gay," 28.

[376] McKnight, *Straight Science*, 30.
[377] Ibid., 31.
[378] Ibid.
[379] McKnight, *Straight Science*, 7.
[380] Ibid.
[381] Peplau, "Human Sexuality," 38.
[382] Ibid., 39.
[383] McKnight, *Straight Science*, Preface.
[384] "Causes of Homosexuality."
[385] Chambers, Homosexuality 101, DVD.
[386] Proverbs 27:7 (NKJV).
[387] Chambers, Homosexuality 101, DVD.
[388] Ibid.
[389] Ibid.
[390] Ibid.
[391] Ibid.
[392] Ibid.
[393] Ibid.
[394] K. Welch, *Think Human Sexuality*, 107.
[395] Chambers, Homosexuality 101, DVD.
[396] Ibid.
[397] Ibid.
[398] Ibid.
[399] Ibid.
[400] Ibid.
[401] Ibid.
[402] "Sexual Orientation and Homosexuality," 1.
[403] Chambers, Homosexuality 101, DVD.
[404] Peplau, "Human Sexuality," 38.
[405] Chambers, Homosexuality 101, DVD.
[406] Ibid.
[407] Ibid.
[408] Ibid.
[409] Ibid.
[410] Ibid.
[411] "Sexual Orientation and Homosexuality."
[412] Ibid.
[413] Romans 1:26–27 (NIV).
[414] "Museum of American Culture," http://www.museum-of-american-culture.us/samegendercivilaffiliations003.htm. (accessed March 3, 2013).
[415] "Causes of Homosexuality."
[416] Avi Sion, "Logical and Spiritual Reflections," The Logican, http://www.thelogician.net/6_reflect/6_Book_6/6f_chapter_14.htm (accessed December 30, 2012).
[417] Al Stefanelli, "A Voice of Reason in an Unreasonable World: Homophobia – The Fear Behind The Hatred," https://alstefanelli.wordpress.com/2010/02/28/homophobia-the-fear-behind-the-hatred/ (accessed March 16, 2013).
[418] Sion, "Logical and Spiritual Reflections."
[419] David Kupelian, WND Archives, http://www.wnd.com/author/dkupelian/ (accessed March 27, 2013).
[420] Book Description, The Marketing of Evil, http://www.amazon.com/dp/1581824599/?tag=googhydr-20&hvadid=9618339261&hvpos=1t1&hvexid=&hvnetw=

g&hvrand=12323796415594788578&hvpone=&hvptwo=&hvqmt=b&ref=pd_sl_5kqpdwi w41_b (accessed March 16, 2013).
[421] "Homosexuality Statistics," Conservapedia, http://www.conservapedia.com/Homosexuality_ Statistics (accessed February 12, 2013).
[422] "Causes of Homosexuality."
[423] Sion, "Logical and Spiritual Reflections."
[424] Ibid.
[425] "Homosexuality and Choice," Conservapedia, http://www.conservapedia.com/ Homosexuality_and_choice (accessed February 12, 2013).
[426] "Homosexuality and Choice."
[427] Ibid.
[428] Ibid.
[429] Ibid.
[430] "Sexual Orientation and Homosexuality," 1.
[431] McKnight, *Straight Science*, 77.
[432] Ibid.
[433] Peplau, "Human Sexuality," 38.
[434] Ibid., 37.
[435] "Sexual Orientation and Homosexuality," 4.
[436] OdysseyNetworks, "Interview: Why Rob Bell Supports Gay Marriage," YouTube, 02:48, http://www.huffingtonpost.com/greg-carey/rob-bell-comes-gay-marriage_b_2898394. html?utm_hp_ref=fb&src=sp&comm_ref=false (accessed March 28, 2013).
[437] Greg Carey, "Rob Bell Comes Out for Marriage Equality," http://www.huffingtonpost. com/mobileweb/greg-carey/rob-bell-comes-gaymarriage_b_2898394.html?utm_ hp_ref=fb&src=sp&comm_ref=false (accessed March 28, 2013).
[438] "Limbaugh: Gay Marriage Is 'Inevitable'," ABC News, http://abcnews.go.com/m/ blogEntry?id=18835812 (accessed March 29, 2013).
[439] Doug Mainwaring, "I'm gay, and I oppose gay marriage." http://www.lifesitenews.com /news/im-gay-and-i-oppose-gay-marriage (accessed March 28, 2013).
[440] Mainwaring, "I'm gay, and I oppose gay marriage."
[441] Adams, *Counselor's Manual*, 404.
[442] Mainwaring, "I'm gay, and I oppose gay marriage."
[443] Peplau, "Human Sexuality," 39.
[444] Peter Sprigg, "New Study on Homosexual Parents Tops All Previous Research," Family Research Council, http://www. frc.org/issuebrief/new-study-on-homosexual-parents-tops-all-previous-research (accessed March 16, 2013).
[445] "Family Violence in Canada: A Statistical Profile," Canadian Centre for Justice Statistics (Ontario, Canada: Minister of Industry, 2011), www.statcan.gc.ca/pub/85-224-x/85-224-x2010000-end.pdf (accessed January 5, 2013).
[446] "The Daily Canadian Community Health Survey," Canadian, http://www.statcan.gc.ca/daily-quotidien/040615/dq040615b-eng.htm (accessed March 16, 2013).
[447] "Every One Needs Vaccinations!" Immunization Action Coalition, http://www.immunize.org/catg.d/p4115.pdf (accessed March 14, 2013).
[448] Pamela Arsove, MD, FACEP, "Lymphogranuloma Venereum," http://emedicine. medscape.com/article /220869-overview (accessed March 12, 2013).
[449] Ulrike Boehmer, Deborah Bowen & Greta Bauer, "Overweight and Obesity in Sexual-Minority Women: Evidence From Population-Based Data," http://www.ncbi.nlm.nih.gov/ pmc/articles/PMC1874217/ (accessed March 16, 2013).

[450] R. Rosenblatt, "More Gay Men Using Meth, Study Finds," *Los Angeles Times*, April 11, 2007, 6.
[451] Susan D. Cochran and Vickie M. Mays, "Physical Health Complaints Among Lesbians, Gay Men and Bisexual and Homosexually Experienced Heterosexual Individuals: Results from the California Quality of Life Survey," *American Journal of Public Health*, 97/11 (2007): 11–12, http://ajph.aphapublications.org/doi/pdf/10.2105/AJPH.2006.087254 (accessed March 14, 2013).
[452] K. Welch, *Think Human Sexuality*, 129.
[453] Ibid.
[454] E. Welch, *Blame the Brain*, 163.
[455] Mark 12:31 (NIV).
[456] Isaiah 53:6 (NIV).
[457] Matthew 12:31 (MSG).
[458] Job 42:2 (NIV).
[459] Romans 10:13 (NLT).
[460] Proverbs 28:13 (NIV).
[461] James 5:16 (NIV).
[462] 1 Corinthians 1:18 (MSG).
[463] John 14:15 (NLT).
[464] Leviticus 18:22–23 (NIV).
[465] Mark 7:21–22 (NIV).
[466] Romans 1:20–27 (NIV).
[467] 1 Corinthians 6:9 (NIV).
[468] 1 Timothy 1:10 (NIV).
[469] E. Welch, *Blame the Brain*, 153.
[470] 1 Corinthians 7:2 (NIV).
[471] Wink, "Homosexuality and the Bible."
[472] Genesis 1:27 (NIV).
[473] Dean A. Byrd, Ph.D., Shirley E. Cos, DSW, Jeffrey W. Robinson, Ph.D., "The Innate-Immutable Argument Finds No Basis in Science," http://www.narth.com/docs/innate.html (accessed February 2, 2013).
[474] *The New Bible Dictionary*, Leicester, England: Inter-Varsity Press, 1003.
[475] Jude 1:7 (RSV).
[476] Genesis 19:13 (RSV).
[477] Genesis 19:5 (NLT).
[478] Geisler, *Christian Ethics*, 261.
[479] Ibid.
[480] Leviticus 18:24 (NIV).
[481] Ezekiel 16:49 (RSV).
[482] Geisler, *Christian Ethics*, 257.
[483] "Witness Freedom Ministries," http://www.witnessfortheworld.org/homont.html (accessed March 20, 2013).
[484] Ezekiel 16:50 (RSV).
[485] "Causes of Homosexuality Environment," http://www.conservapedia.com/Causes_of_Homosexuality#Nature_of_man_and_causes_of_homosexuality (accessed March 12, 2013).
[486] "Causes of Homosexuality Environment."
[487] Paul Benware, *Survey of the Old Testament*, (Chicago: Moody Press), 1993, 61.
[488] "Author George Bush," http://en.wikisource.org/wiki/Author:George_Bush_(1796–1859) (accessed March 26, 2013).

[489] George Bush, *Critical and Practical, on the Book of Leviticus* (Minneapolis, MI: Christian Publishing Company), 1979.
[490] "Witness Freedom Ministries."
[491] Ibid.
[492] Ibid.
[493] Leviticus 18:22 (NIV).
[494] Leviticus 20:13 (NASB).
[495] "Witness Freedom Ministries."
[496] Geisler, *Christian Ethics*, 262.
[497] Leviticus 20:13 (NIV).
[498] E. Welch, *Blame the Brain*, 159.
[499] Ibid.
[500] Ibid., 160.
[501] *The New Bible Dictionary*, 676.
[502] Judges 2:11–13 (NIV).
[503] "Witness Freedom Ministries."
[504] David & Pat Alexander, *The Lion Handbook to the Bible* (Icknield Way, England: Lion Publishing), 1973, 195.
[505] Benware, *Survey Old Testament*, 77.
[506] "Witness Freedom Ministries."
[507] Ibid.
[508] Walter Wink, http://en.wikipedia.org/wiki/Walter_Wink (accessed March 27, 2013).
[509] Ibid.
[510] 2 Samuel 1:26 (NIV).
[511] "What was the Relationship Between David an Jonathan?" http://www.gotquestions.org/ David-and-Jonathan.html (accessed January 20, 2013).
[512] Geisler, *Christian Ethics*, 265.
[513] Ibid.
[514] Ibid.
[515] Acts 13:22 (NIV).
[516] John L. Hill, *From Joshua to David* (Nashville: Convention Press), 1959, 106.
[517] 1 Kings 14:22–24 (NIV).
[518] "Witness Freedom Ministries."
[519] Benware, *Survey Old Testament*, 122.
[520] "Witness Freedom Ministries."
[521] Benware, *Survey Old Testament*, 122.
[522] New Bible Dictionary, 604.
[523] "Witness Freedom Ministries."
[524] Richard Pearce, et al., *1 Corinthians: Taking on the Tough Issues* (Littleton, CO: Serendipity House), 1988, 23.
[525] Paul N. Benware, "*Survey of the New Testament*" (Chicago, IL: Moody Publishing), 2003, 176.
[526] Benware, "*Survey of the New Testament,*" 176.
[527] 1 Corinthians 6:9–10 (NIV).
[528] Kelli Mahoney, "What the Bible Says About…Homosexuality." About.com Christian Teens, http://christianteens.about.com/od/whatthebiblesaysabout/f/homosexuality.htm (accessed October 2, 2012).
[529] Robin Scroggs, "Summary of 'The New Testament and Homosexuality," http://www.lionking.org /~ kovu/bible/section09.html (accessed March 12, 2013).
[530] E. Welch, *Blame the Brain,* 154.
[531] 1 Corinthians 6:11 (NIV).
[532] Geisler, *Christian Ethics,* 271.

[533] Wink, "Homosexuality and the Bible," 1.
[534] Revelation 21:27 (NIV).
[535] Robert H. Gundry, *A Survey of the New Testament* (Grand Rapids, MI: Zondervan), 1994, 383.
[536] Romans 1:26–27 (NIV).
[537] "Witness Freedom Ministries."
[538] Geisler, *Christian Ethics*, 259.
[539] "Article: John Boswell," http://en.wikipedia.org/wiki/John_Boswell (accessed March 25, 2013).
[540] Greg Koukl, "Paul, Romans and Homosexuality," Stand to Reason, http://www.str.org/site/News2?page =NewsArticle&id=6289 (accessed March 24, 2013).
[541] F.F. Bruce, *Paul Apostle of the Heart Set Free* (Grand Rapids, MI: Eerdmans Publishing Company), 1977, 16.
[542] John B. Polhill, *Paul and His Letters* (Nashville, Tennessee: Broadman and Holman Publishers), 1999, 5.
[543] Polhill, *Paul and His Letters*, 5.
[544] Galatians 5:19 (NIV).
[545] Ephesians 5:3–7 (NIV).
[546] Gundry, *Survey New Testament*, 401.
[547] Ibid., 394.
[548] Colossians 3:5–7 (NIV).
[549] Ibid.
[550] Michael Bott and Jonathan Sarfati, "What's Wrong With (Former) Bishop Spong?" UK Apologetics, http://www.ukapologetics.net/08/spongwrong2.htm (accessed March 25, 2013).
[551] John Shelby Spong, "In the Modernity Ward," http://www.touchstonemag.com/archives/ print.php?id=03-04-009-f (accessed March 13, 2013).
[552] "What's Wrong With Bishop Spong?"
[553] 2 Corinthians 12:7–10 (NIV).
[554] John Spong, "I was Given a Thorn in My Flesh: Paul and Homosexuality," Revelife, http://www. revelife.com/754851828/i-was-given-a-thorn-in-my-flesh-paul-and-homosexuality/ (accessed February 12, 2013).
[555] Ibid.
[556] Ron & Joanne Highley, "Come Let Us Reason Together Part 1," Living In Freedom Eternally, http://www.lifeministry.org/come-let-us-reason-together-part-1 (accessed March 1, 2013).
[557] Ibid.
[558] James 1:13 (NASB).
[559] Highley, "Come Let Us Reason Together Part 1."
[560] Church of St. John the Baptist, "Homosexuality," http://www.catholic.com/tracts/ homosexuality (accessed January 2, 2013).
[561] 1 John 1:9 (NIV).
[562] Geisler, *Christian Ethics*, 271.
[563] Chambers, Homosexuality 101, DVD.
[564] "Regnerus Study on Homosexual Parenting."
[565] "Talk: Homosexuality Statistics," http://www.conservapedia.com/Talk: Homosexuality Statistics (accessed March 21, 2013).
[566] E. Welch, *Blame the Brain*, 152.
[567] Chambers, Homosexuality 101, DVD.
[568] Titus 2:12 (NIV).
[569] E. Welch, *Blame the Brain*, 176.

[570] John 8:32 (NASB).
[571] E. Welch, *Blame the Brain*, 175.
[572] 1 John 1:8 (NIV).
[573] J. John, *Marriage Works: The Ultimate Guide to Marriage* (Colorado Spring, CO: Authentic Media, 2008), 251.
[574] Shalit, *A Return to Modesty*, 171.
[575] Song of Solomon 6:3 (NIV).
[576] Sweetman, *Marriage*, 109.
[577] Driscoll, *Real Marriage*, 108.
[578] Powers, *Marriage and Divorce*, 27.
[579] Ibid.
[580] Ibid., 7.
[581] Sweetman, *Marriage,* 110.
[582] Andrew Comiskey, "Tell the Truth," Desert Streams Ministries, http://desertstream.org/Groups/1000040181/Desert_Stream_Ministries/Looking_For_Help/Free_Resources/Free_Resources.aspx (accessed October 3, 2012).
[583] Sweetman, *Move,* 67.
[584] John 15:13 (NIV).
[585] "Hupatasso," BibleStudyTools.com, http://www.biblestudytools.com/lexicons/greek/kjv/hupotasso.html (accessed March 24, 2013).
[586] Ibid.
[587] Bell, *Sex God,* 109.
[588] Ibid., 147.
[589] Genesis 2:24 (NIV).
[590] Powers, *Marriage and Divorce,* 30.
[591] Driscoll, *Real Marriage,* 110.
[592] Proverbs 5:15–19 (NIV).
[593] Song of Solomon 6:2 (NIV).
[594] Ibid., 23.
[595] John 11:35 (NIV).
[596] John 13:23 (NASB).
[597] Peplau, "Human Sexuality," 37.
[598] Ibid.
[599] Shalit, *A Return to Modesty*, 171.
[600] Ibid., 94.
[601] Rosenau, *A Celebration of Sex*, 177.
[602] Shalit, *A Return to Modesty*, 116.
[603] Rosenau, *A Celebration of Sex,* 54.
[604] Ibid.
[605] Ibid., 35.
[606] "Risks of anal sex, other than STIs?" Go Ask Alice, http://goaskalice.columbia.edu/risks-anal-sex-other-stis (accessed March 27, 2013).
[607] Powers, *Marriage and Divorce*,15.
[608] Rosenau, *Celebration of Sex*, 38.
[609] Ibid., 50.
[610] Ibid., 37.
[611] Ibid., 42.
[612] Ibid., 185.
[613] Ibid., 185.
[614] Ibid., 50.
[615] Ibid., 18–19.

[616] Genesis 1:31 (NIV).
[617] Genesis 1:28 (NASB).
[618] Ibid.
[619] Genesis 2:15 (NASB).
[620] Psalm 139:14 (NIV).
[621] Rosenau, *A Celebration of Sex*, 52.
[622] Ibid., 48.
[623] Ibid.
[624] Ibid., 161.
[625] John, *Marriage Works*, 263.
[626] Ibid.
[627] 1 Corinthians 6:19 (NIV).
[628] Song of Solomon 8:12 (NIV).
[629] Rosenau, *A Celebration of Sex*, 86.
[630] Phillipians 4:8 (NKJV).
[631] John, *Marriage Works*, 256.
[632] Ibid. 262.
[633] Ibid. 22.
[634] E. Welch, *Blame the Brain*, 15.